FREE!

Presented to

My presence will go with you.

Exodus 33:14

FREE!

*True Release in Christ
in a Bangkok Jail*

RITA NIGHTINGALE

with David Porter

Marshall Pickering
An Imprint of HarperCollinsPublishers

Marshall Pickering is an imprint of
HarperCollins*Religious*
part of HarperCollins*Publishers*
77–85 Fulham Palace Road, London W6 8JB
www.christian-publishing.com

Freed for Life first published in Great Britain
in 1982 by Marshall Pickering
Copyright © 1982 Rita Nightingale and David Porter

Freed for Ever first published in Great Britain
in 1985 by Marshall Pickering
Copyright © 1985 Rita Nightingale and David Porter

This edition 2000

10 9 8 7 6 5 4 3 2 1

Rita Nightingale and David Porter assert the moral
right to be identified as the authors of this work

A catalogue record for this book is
available from the British Library

ISBN 0 551 03264 2

Printed and bound in Great Britain by
Caledonian International Book Manufacturing Ltd, Glasgow

Contents

FREED
FOR LIFE

*To Mum and Dad, and two very special sisters,
Ann and June, for their love, courage and devotion*

Contents

Foreword

'So, who is Rita Nightingale?' I remember asking my associate the first time he told me the story of the young British girl in a Thailand prison. Prayer groups seemed to be springing up all over the world for her.

'I mean, why all the fuss?' I persisted. Sure, it was a tragic case: young girl on a pleasure jaunt meets glamorous boyfriend and then is 'set up'; the police find bags of heroin in the false bottom of the suitcase her boyfriend gave her; and the Thai courts throw the book at her, twenty years caged in an Oriental prison. But I had heard of hundreds of other cases like hers. We receive mail almost every day from Americans caught in prisons around the world: no friends, no money, unable to speak the language.

Indeed as the facts emerged, we learned there was much unusual about Rita Nightingale's case. We received letters from two missionaries who had visited her, giving an exciting account of her dramatic conversion to Christ. Then some Christian lawyers in Australia wrote me with a full account of her case. Government officials in England, I soon discovered, were interested in her case; there was even discussion in the House of Commons. Newspapers were writing extensively about her. And everywhere I heard about people praying for her. I came to realize that God must be doing something very special through her life in that far-away jail.

My close friend, Fred Rhodes, who helped start Prison Fellowship with me tried to see Rita when he was in Bangkok attending some Baptist meetings. He arrived at the gates of the Lard Yao Prison, but after a long wait, the officials refused to let him inside. He brought back, however, an appalling description of the place; with its open sewers, heat, insects and stench.

Over the next months, several other Christian friends

tried to get inside the prison. Each one was rebuffed. Then Kathryn Grant, who for twenty years was a missionary in the Orient and now Vice President of our ministry for international affairs persisted – and in November of 1979, through some nearly miraculous circumstances, succeeded. Kathryn met alone with Rita, and then again with all of the other Western women.

It was Rita's spirit – her warmth and radiance – that so impressed Kathryn. Kathryn wrote to me at the time of her visit, 'Rita is beautiful, with soft brown wavy hair, lovely warm complexion, a very soft person, extremely refined, cautious, no coarseness. You would think if you met her that she was just a lovely young Christian girl going to church. And joyous. To feel that joy, you'd have to see what conditions they're living under. No American or Westerner can conceive of the living conditions. The heat! No screens . . . an incredible diet . . . yet over and over, Rita was saying, "You know, all of my bitterness is gone. I don't ask questions any more. I just say, 'Thank you, Lord, for what you've done.'"'

Kathryn's report went on to describe how Rita had promised the Lord that the minute she was set free, she would go back to start working in the prisons, bringing the hope of the Gospel to others.

It was obvious then that God was grooming and training this young British girl for something big and important. Yet, what could it be? She had nearly seventeen years remaining on her twenty year sentence. So we continued to pray for Rita as did the hundreds, perhaps thousands of Christians around the world who were part of the prayer chains. But our hopes dimmed as the months passed. Government officials who worked on her case held out little hope.

It was as if God had to show us that all of our efforts would be in vain, that the situation was humanly impossible, before he would release her from prison. Only when we came to the end of our own efforts would we be able to see the magnificent working of our sovereign God. It was divine intervention that ultimately set this young Lancashire girl free.

The story you are about to read is thrilling, gripping, and at times frightening. But it is more than the story of one woman's nightmarish ordeal in a far away continent. It is a story of how God reaches into the lives of ordinary people, sometimes using the most extraordinary means to raise up those he calls for his purpose. Ironically, it often happens that a prison cell is his testing ground. It was for Joseph, for Jeremiah, for Paul, Peter, and in modern times, for Dietrich Bonhoeffer and Alexander Solzhenitsyn. And now for Rita Nightingale.

The message of this book goes far beyond the thrilling adventures of this young British girl. There is in Rita's experience the most profound and prophetic challenge to our materialistic Western culture. Solzhenitsyn summed it up beautifully when he was writing from the Gulag, 'Bless you prison for having been in my life,' he wrote, for there it was lying on rotting prison straw that he learned that 'the meaning of earthly existence lies not, as we have grown used to thinking, in prospering, but in the development of the soul.'

God used prison to reverse the course of my life. I could not forget what I had seen, and what I had lived with; and so I began to go back and back, which was the beginning of the Prison Fellowship, a ministry now reaching out to inmates all around the globe. God put the same call on Rita Nightingale, and I am proud to have her as my co-worker and colleague in this ministry.

Be prepared as you read on. For the One who called this young girl to his service through the remarkable chain of events described in this book may put a call on your life as well.

Charles W. Colson.

The facts recorded in this book are true to the best of my knowledge, and the opinions expressed are honestly held

Rita Nightingale

Preface

In working with Rita on her story I have been helped by a large number of individuals and organisations. I am especially grateful to the Editor of the Lancashire Evening Telegraph, who made available to me the newspaper's unique archive of material concerning the case, and to David Allin, News Editor of the same newspaper, whose articles over three years played a major part in maintaining public awareness of Rita's plight. I have also been given access to family papers, letters and other documents by the Nightingale family.

Acknowledgement is gratefully made to Dr. Ann England, Mr. Peter Elsom, Mrs. Jane Winter, Mrs. Daphne Boddington, my wife Tricia, and a number of others who kindly read the manuscript. Technical help has been supplied by Mr. Ken Davies. I have made use of a large number of books, including Apa production's encyclopaedic Insight Guides, and have been given assistance by the Hong Kong Government offices and several London embassies. Any faults in the book cannot be laid at the door of any of the foregoing, nor can the help given by official agencies be interpreted as an endorsement by any government of the views expressed.

All names have been changed with the exception of family and close friends. In general, names in common use have been substituted. It is regretted if unintentional embarrassment is thereby caused to individuals happening to bear these names.

David Porter

1 Bangkok

*All foreign visitors entering Thailand must
be in possession of a passport . . . endorsed
and valid for Thailand. As a general rule,
all foreign nationals are required to apply
for and obtain visas from Thai Embassies
or Consulates abroad. Every kind of visa is
valid for 90 day period from the date of
issue. Customs regulations: prohibited items.
All kinds of narcotics – hemp, opium,
cocaine, morphine, heroin; obscene
literature, pictures or articles.*

(Thailand in brief, Public Relations
Department, Government of Thailand)

I ran a finger round my neck, easing the damp collar of
my blouse. Reaching for my handbag, I extracted my
powder-compact, opened it and peered at my reflection
in the tiny mirror. My nose was getting shiny again. I
squinted sideways and applied the powderpuff until I
was satisfied.

Holding the mirror further away, I inspected myself
and nodded complacently. I was looking good. My short
dark hair framed a face which, with its well-defined
cheekbones and almost slanted eyes, had sometimes been
mistaken for that of an Asian girl. I always took a lot of
trouble over my looks. My lipstick was just right, my

eyeshadow had that casual look which takes half an hour in front of a mirror to achieve.

I snapped the compact shut, slipped it back into my bag, and wriggled myself into a more comfortable position. The air-conditioned departure lounge was cooler than the remorseless Bangkok heat outside, but it was packed with people and the heat was becoming oppressive.

I'd packed warm clothes when leaving Hong Kong, ready for the chill of Paris in March; I smiled at the thought, as I glanced down at my expensive white silk suit and the smart stilettos I'd kicked off. Above and around the milling passengers, impersonal loudspeaker voices in Thai and English announced arrivals and departures. Soon the Paris flight would be called.

My baggage had been checked in, and I had nothing to do but kill time. I fanned myself lazily with a magazine. Nearby, a couple of Europeans were playing cards; watching them out of the corner of her eye was an incredibly beautiful Thai girl. I felt myself becoming drowsy.

Somebody was tapping my shoulder. I jerked myself awake. A Thai airport official, coolly immaculate in slacks and crisp white shirt, stood looking down at me.

'Miss Nightingale?' he asked quietly. 'I am from the Customs Department. Please come with me.'

'I beg your pardon? What . . .'

'You must come with me, please.'

His voice was neutral, his expression unreadable. I didn't know what he could possibly want, and I wasn't much bothered; I just hoped it wouldn't take too long to sort out. It was almost time for my flight. Irritated, I picked up my handbag and radio, and went with the official.

He escorted me to an office, where several Customs

staff looked up as I came in. Something about their manner gave me a sinking feeling inside; this was one of those official holdups, a piece of red tape that was going to take time to go through; they won't hold the Paris flight for me, I thought, and cursed my luck. Delayed in a random customs check a quarter of an hour before leaving. At least there wasn't anything that they could arrest me for, I thought cynically.

Even when the officials demanded my passport and plane tickets, I still thought it was a routine check. Everybody was speaking Thai; I couldn't understand what was happening. When I asked what was going on and why I was being detained, they wouldn't say directly. One of them gave me a strange look and asked, 'What do you know about heroin?' I laughed; I still thought they were going through the usual formulas. Then one of them reached for my passport and cancelled my departure visa. I stopped laughing. Whatever was going on was serious.

The Paris flight long departed, I was still in the Don Muang Airport Customs Offices. It was about half past ten at night. I was taken to another room where there were about ten customs officers and several policemen. There was also a young Chinese man sitting apart from the others, nervously twining and untwining his fingers. He was watching everything that was going on, his eyes as hard as flint. My bags were on a long trestle table. As I watched, the officials began to unpack them systematically, which brought the smile back to my face; I knew they were on a wild goose chase. They took each item out, shaking it or feeling it with probing fingers. I watched scornfully as the pile of garments and other possessions mounted up. As the last odds and ends were taken from the bags, examined, and placed on the pile, my smile broadened.

A moment later the smile was gone again. One of the

3

officials was still exploring the empty bag. He stood it on end and felt round inside, grunting with satisfaction as he withdrew a large flat leather-covered board. Discarding it, he delved deeper and began to pull out heavy plastic bags. The holdalls had been fitted with false bottoms.

I began to tremble. There hadn't been any false bottoms in them when I'd packed them in Hong Kong. Incredulously, I saw the packages of pinkish-brown stuff being pulled from my luggage. I'd never seen them before. The official showed them to his colleague: the other bag was examined. It had a false bottom too.

Some of the bystanders remarked 'Heroin!' in pleased voices, as if they had hoped for such a discovery. I felt sick. So that was what was in the packages. I'd smoked marijuana, but never had anything to do with hard drugs. I always thought it was a white powder, but this was more like brown sugar.

There was pandemonium. Several of the officials watching were clearly delighted at the discovery; it seemed that I was quite a catch. They joked and laughed among themselves. Somebody shouted at me in English, 'You like heroin? They shoot you – they give you thirty years! Ha ha!' People were coming in and out, staring and pointing. By now there were police officers in the room, watching the proceedings. They wore the normal uniform, slacks and short-sleeved military shirt given a touch of formality by the hard-peaked police cap and the efficient leather belt slung round the waist carrying hand-gun and ammunition. I'd passed such men scores of times in the last few days without giving them a second glance; now I avoided looking at their weapons. Some of the uniformed men were carrying machine guns.

The guns made a bizarre and frightening contrast to the carnival atmosphere of the room. I noticed that one of the officers, for no apparent reason, was wearing a

4

shirt decorated with **Mickey Mouse** cartoons. Nearby, somebody was making a video film of the whole thing; there were several photographers present. I tried to hide myself behind a cardigan when I saw the cameras pointed at me, but I couldn't avoid them all. For some reason, I don't know why, there were children in the room, laughing and giggling at me. The officials even turned the radio cassette player on, but they weren't satisfied when it proved to be working; they proceeded to pull the back off. To my horror I saw that one of the loud-speakers had been removed. In its place was more of the brown stuff.

I couldn't cry at first. I was completely numb. Then the numbness gave way to blazing anger, and I did cry, great gulping angry sobs. I wanted somebody to go out and get the guy who had set me up for all this. 'Simon . . . Simon . . .', I muttered, over and over. It must have been Simon. Of course, I saw it all now; they should look for Simon, I insisted. He was still at the hotel, so far as I knew. But I couldn't make anybody understand. I was taken to yet another room. A woman officer ordered me to remove my clothes. I was searched efficiently and without comment, the way an animal might be searched for parasites. The fright and degra-dation only intensified the feeling, taking root in me, that this was some sort of weird nightmare, that in a few moments I would wake up.

All told, this ordeal went on for another three hours.

Repeatedly, a document was placed before me, an official form on government paper filled out in the elaborate Thai script. I couldn't understand it. 'What is it?' I demanded.

'It's a formality, it's nothing; it says that these things were found in your possession when you were attempting

5

to leave the country. It's a formality. You must sign it.'
A pen was jabbed at the place where I was to sign.

I refused. I refused several times, vigorously. Eventually a police captain arrived. He was calm and reasonable. Even the sight of his uniform was reassuring; he was clearly a senior officer, he would take charge of this circus and sort everything out.

He sat down and looked at me thoughtfully. 'Now. Tell me exactly what has happened.'

'Can't we go somewhere quiet to talk?' I pleaded. I just wanted to fit the pieces together, to find out what was going on. He agreed, and took me to a bare, cell-like room, lit by a single harsh unshaded bulb. We sat down. He took a notebook and pencil from his shirt pocket and placed them on the desk in front of him.

'You must find Simon,' I said desperately. 'Simon will know what this is all about.'

The captain scribbled. 'Your boyfriend?'

'No, not my boyfriend – James is my boyfriend, James Wong, he's meeting me in Paris; that's where I'm supposed to be.' Inwardly, I shuddered, and wondered how long it would be before I got there. 'Simon – Simon Lo – he's the guy I travelled to Bangkok with,' I persisted. 'He had my bags in his room. It must have been him.'

He stared at me impassively and waited for me to continue. I stumbled on.

'We were staying at the Asia Hotel. I checked out from there today. He must still be there. I know he is.'

He smiled sceptically.

'He must be!' I said angrily. 'He was there when he said goodbye to me – he put me in a taxi there. Why don't you go and arrest him?'

The captain tapped his pencil on the desk and considered. Then he left the room, and I heard him talking to the customs officials in the corridor. When he returned, he nodded brusquely. 'You will come with us to the hotel.' It was an order, not a request. I was relieved and excited. I was going to get my own back on Simon. He wasn't going to get away with it, it was going to be all right; soon I would be on my way to Paris.

By now it was early morning. The captain, another policeman, and two policewomen escorted me. There was little conversation. We drove in two police cars to the Asia Hotel in the silence of the curfew: martial law was then operating in Thailand. Dawn was just breaking. The gilded temples and lush tropical trees lining the empty streets appeared through a drizzling mist. I paid little attention to them. The driver stared at the road ahead, occasionally exchanging a comment in Thai with one of his colleagues. I sat hunched up in the back of the car, a policewoman by my side, wanting it all to be over.

The hotel gates were locked. We waited grimly for somebody to come down and open them. One of the policewomen was detailed to wait with me in the reception area while the others went upstairs. After a few minutes the captain rang down to say I was to be taken upstairs. My heart pounded as we stood in the elevator.

The police officers were standing in the open doorway of Simon's room. He was in there, sitting on the bed in vest and pants, self-assured even in that stupid situation. He looked up as I arrived. 'There he is!' I cried. Simon looked at me slowly, with contemptuous, bleak eyes.

'Who are you?' he demanded.

I almost went berserk. I think it was then that I knew, with a hopeless certainty, that I was in really big trouble.

2 Australia

*'We went to Tarronga Zoo last week and
it was fabulous . . . the things I liked
best were the Koala bears and baby
kangaroos . . .'*

*'I've got in a bit of a rut here, it's all work
and watching telly or reading, I'm reading
between five and six books a week. I
haven't got much interest in anything, so it's
time I got out for a while . . .'*

*'After a while Carl and I became more than
friends. Nudge, nudge, wink-wink, say no
more!!!'*

*'Don't worry, Mum, if I get into any
trouble you'll hear about it . . .'*

From various letters home, 1976

Travel was in my blood. It was a fever I had had since
childhood. My father, Harry Nightingale, had travelled
the Far East as a regular soldier before the war and had
loved the people and places he had seen. He used to tell
me and my two sisters that the world was large and
exciting. He urged us to travel as soon as we were old
enough. 'The world's a bigger place than Blackburn,' he
said. I loved travel, and enjoyed being a stranger, some-

8

one from far away. When I thought of my old friends in England I pitied them. They were stuck back there, and I was in the exotic East, living the glamorous life I'd always dreamed of.

My home town, Blackburn, was an industrial town in the north of England set among windswept moors and the foothills of the Pennines. We were, and are, a close-knit family. We lived in an apartment above the Stokers Arms, the pub my parents ran. When I left school, I did a term's pre-nursing course at a local college, and then started work as a cadet nurse at Queen's Park Hospital, Blackburn. I hoped to become a State Registered Nurse, but I never completed my training.

It looked as though I was going to spend my life in Blackburn, close to my family, working in the town's hospital. My mother had to run the pub nearly single-handed; Dad was seriously ill upstairs. I and my sisters helped out when we could. Though there was lots to be done there was time for a social life as well. I met John, a tall lean blond boy from Stockport. We began to see each other regularly. I was fascinated by him. He had travelled, through Europe to Greece and on to Israel. He had the glamour I was looking for; he could tell stories of foreign countries. His friends were travellers; they mostly lived in the Lake District. It was a different set to that I'd known in Blackburn. None of them had much money, but that was part of the fascination.

We talked about our dreams of travelling, and our frustration at the cramped surroundings of Blackburn. Our friendship grew and developed into something more serious. I was seventeen; I thought I knew it all. I gave up my job and married John against everybody's advice. The wedding was overshadowed by the forebodings of relatives and the knowledge that Dad, who was too ill to attend, was dying. His funeral followed our wedding by

9

only a few weeks. Nine months later I left Blackburn with John. We were bound for Sydney, Australia. A new life, a new world.

I loved Australia. At first we lived in Sydney, where we soon lost our English pallor. We surfed and swam. We ate prawns and other delicious food. We spent our free time lazing on Bondi Beach, which I'd heard about in England and promised myself I'd see one day. John was unemployed, but I picked up enough work for us to scrape by. You could have said I was happy, but in reality I was confused and mixed-up. Only months after arriving in Sydney I was really miserable.

For a start, I was terribly homesick. I would never have left Blackburn if I hadn't married – I loved my family too much. Hardly a day went by without wistful thoughts of Mum and my sisters, aunties and uncles, and the .pub on the street corner in Blackburn town centre.

Also our marriage was going wrong. Daily, in a hundred little ways, John and I were drifting apart. We didn't talk about it to each other – we spent most of our time together arguing – but I didn't need telling that things weren't working out. I was resentful that I had to go out to work while John mostly stayed at home. Even our first anniversary was marked by a massive row. I was beginning to realise that my determination to stand on my own two feet and to see the world hadn't solved the frustration I'd felt in England. My new marriage, my new start, was falling apart already, and I knew it was more my fault than John's. What had started as a teenage love-affair fed on dreams of travel wasn't strong enough to survive our growing up. There didn't seem much I could do to alter matters, and to be honest, I didn't try very hard.

Perhaps a change of surroundings would help. We moved to Adelaide, and from there we decided to go north, hitch-hiking to Darwin through the outback. It was the sort of adventure we'd talked of back in England, when we'd planned and dreamed of the things we were going to do. The reality wasn't glamorous. We fought and hurt each other all the way north. When we finally arrived in Darwin and settled in a caravan park, I knew that it was the end. One day I wrote a note for John when I left for work. I said I didn't want him any more. He was still asleep. I left the note on the table and walked out of our flat and out of our marriage. It had lasted six months after our emigration.

John went back to England, and I was alone in Australia. My family urged me to come home too. I almost did, but in the end decided to stay on. Travelling had left me restless and unsatisfied. I wanted to settle down, get my life together, and have somebody care for me. I wanted love and affection.

I hadn't much time to feel lonely, however. I moved to the Darwin YWCA, got a job as a barmaid, and made scores of friends, throwing myself into a hectic social whirl. I told myself I was having a great time. Before long I was going out with Bernie, a curly-headed bronzed Lancashire man I'd met in the bar where I worked. He was attractive, kind, and had a wonderful sense of humour. We grew very close; soon we were lovers. One day we were laughing at something when he suddenly fell silent.

'What's up?' I demanded.

He looked at me speculatively. 'Ever thought of getting married again?'

I shrugged. 'Once bitten . . .!' I countered flippantly, and changed the subject.

He didn't raise the matter again, and I certainly didn't want to remind him.

After a few months I left the YWCA and moved in with him. I was able to convince myself I was happy, at least for most of the time. I began to feel things for him I'd never felt for John. Sometimes it seemed that I was happier then than I'd ever been before. But I had come to Australia with the idea that after two years I would go back home to visit my family, and even when I was living with Bernie this idea persisted. Bernie, who'd made the trip himself several years before, understood how I felt. In 1974, after being in Australia for just under two years, I left. Bernie was going to follow in a few months. By then, we'd begun to talk of marriage.

I planned to be in England for my twenty-first birthday. Shirley, an English friend in the lawyer's office where I was working, wanted to go home too. We decided we would travel to England overland. We flew from Darwin up to Bali, then travelled through Java and Sumatra and over to Penang in Malaysia. From Penang we went to Singapore and up the east coast to Thailand and Bangkok. There we seized the opportunity to take a cheap flight to Hong Kong, where we stayed six weeks intending to return to Bangkok and go on to Nepal.

One morning I was sitting at breakfast in our Hong Kong bedsit, opening some mail that had been waiting for me. I finished reading, groaned, and sat back in my chair. Shirley looked up.

'Problems?'

I indicated the letters. 'From my sisters. Trouble at home. Mum's been having some problems with the pub.'

Chinese music floated up through the open window from a transistor radio below, mingling with the traffic noises and the perpetual babble of conversation in the streets. Another hot Hong Kong day. Sightseeing, shopping, perhaps a trip out to the countryside. It was enticing.

'What do you want to do today?' asked Shirley. A

wave of homesickness swept over me. I made up my mind.

'I'm going home, Shirley. By plane. Tonight.'

I arrived in England the next day. At first I worked with my mother but I found it very difficult to settle down in the job. A pub is almost a twenty-four hour commitment, and after my travels I couldn't cope with the lunchtime, suppertime and evening work, day after day. I daydreamed a lot about Australia and South-East Asia, comparing the glamour of those places with the routine of the pub. In any case, it takes a lot of grace to live and work with somebody, and soon I was falling out with Mum. To add to my confusion, Bernie arrived in England and proposed. But he had been delayed by the cyclone which devastated Darwin that year, and it was twelve months since I'd seen him. In the interim I had become confused again. I couldn't work out what I wanted from life, and his visit wasn't a happy time for either of us. In the end he went back to Australia without me, and things got so tense between me and my mother that I decided I would have to stop working at home. I went back to Blackburn Hospital where I enrolled as an auxiliary nurse.

I stayed there for several months, working nights. But once again I found it impossible to submit to discipline and a regular and well-ordered life. The hospital seemed to be closing round me like a prison, trapping me. Gradually, I began to make plans to leave home again.

My family would have liked me to stay. Mum needed me, but more than that she had the fears and worries of any mother seeing her daughter going abroad. Years later she told a reporter: 'It would have been easy to say, "Don't travel – it will worry me to death." But you just can't do that to your kids, can you?' So she wished me

13

well and even lent me money to supplement the few hundred pounds I'd saved.

I travelled back with Bernie's sister, Pauline. We spent a few weeks in Singapore and then arrived in Darwin. Pauline and I stayed at Bernie's place, but I found it impossible to pick up the threads again. I needed time to sort out my feelings. I slept on my own. It wasn't sex I needed. I wanted to sort out my head about whether I loved this man enough to settle down for life.

Our relationship deteriorated. Once again, I found myself unable to change things; I saw the danger signs and was powerless to do anything about them. Twenty miles out of town, with no car, I was living in the house of a man I couldn't decide to marry and I didn't know what I wanted any more.

I moved to a government hostel, bought myself a motorbike, and made a number of friends. But I was oh, so unsettled. For me, Darwin was Bernie; and things were bad between us, and it was my fault, and everywhere I went in Darwin reminded me of him. I stuck it out for nearly a year, until finally I said to myself, 'What you need, Rita Nightingale, is a little break.'

I made my plans. I would take a few months off, and travel again. I would clear my head, think things through, and hopefully come to some decisions. And I would take the same route that I had travelled with Shirley, but this time I would go alone.

In Bali I met Carl, a funny, outrageous guy who was good to be with. We travelled together for a while, sharing my motorbike and his sleeping bag. At Bangkok, he left for England. He wanted me to go with him. He was a great companion, I'd had a wonderful time with him, but he was a distraction. I was travelling in order to sort myself out, to find out what I wanted from life, to think about Bernie, about home, about the future. I was unhappy and I knew that there was something missing, and I didn't know what it was. Certainly the last thing I was looking for was yet another heavy relationship to get involved in.

And so late in 1976 Carl and I said goodbye at Bangkok Airport. He went back to London, and I flew to Hong Kong.

3 Hong Kong

*It's girls that one goes to a place like the
Kokusai for, and the Kokusai has plenty of
them, all very attractive and all very
accommodating . . . A hostess can set you
back HK$15 for every 15 minutes you're
trying to make conversation with her. No
problem buying a hostess out, but that'll set
you back a lot more dollars.*

Tobin's guide to Hong Kong nightlife, by
Anthony L. Tobin

I arrived in Hong Kong a few days before Christmas
with Sue, a girl I'd met in Java. She'd been on the same
plane. I caught my breath as we walked to Nathan Road
from Kai Tak Airport. The excitement I'd felt when I
had last been to the Colony was back. High above us,
hanging from the buildings and festooned across the
street, were thousands of garishly coloured signs and
advertisements in bold Chinese calligraphy, festooning
the towering buildings in blue, scarlet and white. At
street level, the shops open to the pavement were packed
with tourists, deliberating over displays of everything in
the world that one might want to buy. Impatient crowds
pushed past as I drank in the spectacle; the roar of traffic
forcing its way down the street, people of all nationalities
thronging the pavements, Chinese music blared from
loudspeakers in shop doorways; and a magical, shim-

mering view of the harbour was just visible beyond it all at the end of the thoroughfare. A mixture of traffic fumes, cooking smells and the occasional whiff of fish from the harbour pervaded the air, and over everything a mist blurred the tops of buildings and the view of the harbour.

'This way!' I said to Sue, my voice raised against the noise. I'd met up with her on the plane from Bangkok. I already knew her – we'd met in Bali – and we'd decided to team up in Hong Kong for a while.

We made our way down Nathan Road, stopping to gaze at shop windows piled with jewellery, calculators, cameras and other luxuries, and even the voices of passers-by grumbling at us were an exotic mixture of languages. I loved it. It was what travel was all about, so far as I was concerned; and my own delight was doubled by witnessing that of Sue, who hadn't been to Hong Kong before.

At its harbour end, Nathan Road becomes the 'Golden Mile', where night-clubs, bars and hotels jostle the large shops. I indicated a side road, and we turned down a crowded alley. 'Chungking,' I announced, as we stopped in front of a shabby sprawling tenement block of enormous size. Sue looked up at it doubtfully. 'This is it?' she said. I laughed. 'This is Chungking Mansions.'

I'd stayed at Chungking when I was last in Hong Kong. It's a conglomeration of lodging houses, shops and cheap eating houses; the whole thing forms one of the larger blocks in Nathan Road. We wanted cheap accommodation, and Chungking was certainly cheap; you got what you paid for. I'd told Sue about it and she had been enthusiastic. Now we were there, she hovered uncertainly.

'The Hilton's quite near, if you'd prefer.' I teased, pointing back towards Nathan Road. Sue grinned.

'In for a penny . . .'

We entered the block. Around the courtyard we entered were different shops, and here and there elevators. A notice-board was placed at each elevator entrance. We scanned the scraps of paper and picked an apartment which looked reasonable.

A middle-aged Chinese in singlet and shorts, sitting on a balcony, announced himself as the landlord of the apartment. He seemed supremely uninterested in doing business, but eventually we managed to persuade him to rent it to us. 'You pay rent in advance,' he emphasised.

'That's fine,' we said. He extended a hand for the money.

I kept my hands in my pockets. 'We'd like to see the room first.'

He scowled. 'Why you want to see room? It's a room, that's what you want, isn't it? Maybe you don't want room.'

He turned his back and studied the courtyard below. It took us several minutes of further bargaining before he reluctantly took us to the apartment.

It was small and uncarpeted. Two single beds, a chest of drawers and a dilapidated wardrobe took up most of the available space. By Chungking standards, it was quite pleasant, and – a real luxury in Chungking – it possessed a window, from which there was an impressive view of the back of another wing of the Mansions. We looked at each other, smiled happily, and paid the attendant. Thrusting the cash into his pocket, he shuffled away down the corridor complaining bitterly under his breath.

We dumped our rucksacks, put away our belongings, and went out to explore.

'What first?' I said.

'Food!' cried Sue. 'I'm starving!'

We found a small Chinese restaurant, where we sampled the exotic delights of the menu; we were both hungry, and we ate until we could eat no more, and then sat and watched Hong Kong go by until we felt ready to move again.

It was mid-evening. The neon signs were lit in Nathan Road, thousands of them; a slight evening chill offset the sultry heat as the sky darkened into night. Sue wanted to explore on her own, and I had a number of things I wanted to do, so we agreed to split up. I stood in the street and planned my evening. Should I go down to the harbour, or wander round the shops in Nathan Road, which was becoming even brighter and more exciting as the neon signs illuminated and colourful Chinese lanterns appeared in the restaurant windows? It was all so exciting; the familiar thrill was very strong. It was good to be back. I decided first of all to see whether any of the people I'd known last time were still around. I'd been quite friendly with a girl called Robin, who worked at the Kokusai night club in Nathan Road near Chungking. I wanted to see her again. I set off for the Kokusai.

The entrance, like those of most of the better-class clubs, was a discreet doorway. I peered in. The reception lounge was deserted. Nobody was around; it was nine o'clock – still early for the club to be open. The turbanned door-keeper I remembered was nowhere to be seen. I went to the back entrance and pushed the door open. Framed colour photographs of the dancefloor, the hostesses and the band lined an expensively-carpeted staircase leading down to the Kokusai.

Downstairs, the empty club looked drab and unused. The lighting was harsh and revealing, and the mirrors which lined the walls reflected empty seats and tables. The bandstand was deserted. A barman was polishing glasses, slowly and with an air of boredom, behind a tiny bar. A smell of stale tobacco smoke hung in the air.

A Eurasian girl was sitting at a table reading a magazine. She looked up.

'Want something?'

'Is Robin here?' I asked.

She shook her head and turned a page. 'No – she doesn't work here any more. You know her?'

'Not really,' I said. 'I just got to know her a bit when I was last here.'

She closed her magazine. She seemed glad of a chat. 'Cathy took Robin's job. She's here. Do you know Cathy?'

'Cathy? I don't think . . .'

'Oh, she's great!' said the other girl. 'You'll like her. Come and say hello to Cathy.'

She seized my arm and took me through to the hostesses' dressing room, where I had sometimes called to meet Robin. It was as I remembered it. Two or three girls were sitting at the long row of mirrors, putting on makeup and doing their hair. Lipsticks and pots of face cream were strewn along the bench and expensive dresses were tossed casually over the backs of chairs.

A pretty dark-haired girl in a kimono was delving into a pile of clothes. 'Mary-Rose!' she shouted sulkily as we entered. 'Where's my slip? You've dumped all your things on top of mine . . .'

She stopped short as she saw us.

'Hi! Who are you?'

'She's looking for Robin, Cathy.'

Cathy inspected me. 'Robin's left here. Move some things and grab a seat while I get myself sorted out. Just flown in?'

I liked Cathy immediately. We got into conversation and I told her about my travels and my previous visit to Hong Kong. She introduced me to the other girls. One of them reached out a hand and touched my face. 'You look so fresh!' she said. It was true. I was wearing no

20

make-up, and I'd been travelling in the sunshine for several weeks. These girls worked for months on end without seeing much daylight.

After a while Cathy asked, 'How long are you going to be in Hong Kong? Do you want a job?'

It wasn't something I'd given much thought to. 'What sort of job?'

'Here; you could be a hostess.'

'What's a hostess do?'

'You entertain people – sit with them when they come in the club . . . dance with them, let them buy you drinks, maybe other things, you know? That's up to you. It's a good job. You'd enjoy it.'

'No,' I said. 'I don't want to be a hostess.'

Cathy hesitated and dropped her voice, looking at me shrewdly. 'You needn't tell anybody, but I'm leaving here soon. I haven't told them yet. You could have my job. I'm a receptionist here.'

I knew what receptionists did through knowing Robin. It was a glamorous life. You greeted people when they came in, looked after them, assigned them a hostess, and only kept them company further than that if you wanted to.

It didn't take me long to decide. 'Yes,' I said. 'I wouldn't mind.'

By midnight each night the Kokusai was transformed. There were red roses on each table, and lamps with crimson shades which made intimate alcoves of light where visitors sat with their friends or with a club hostess. The small dance-floor was usually full of couples dancing to the Filipino band.

The job was marvellous. I couldn't believe my luck. It wasn't like work at all. I'd always enjoyed having a good time, I liked parties and dancing, and I'd missed them on my travels. For the first few nights I simply enjoyed being there, smiling happily at people and making them welcome. Then one night Cathy said to me, 'Come on, I want you to meet someone; he's a really nice guy.' He was a good-looking German. He beamed at me.

'Rita. That is a nice name. So. You would like to dance?'

I was more than happy to dance with him, sit with him at his table and generally look after him. It was like any evening spent with a pleasant companion. After an hour or two I suddenly thought, 'Well, I guess this is supposed to be what I'm paid for!' I always found it difficult to think of visitors as 'work', and I certainly enjoyed being paid to have a nice time. In fact the only visitors I didn't get on with were known and disliked by all of us – the hard drinkers, loud talkers and clumsy gropers; most of the girls flatly refused to sit with them. So did I after a few experiences, including the occasion when one of them pawed me furtively on the dance-floor. I managed to throw him off balance, and he ended up sprawled among the band.

The Kokusai wasn't like some Hong Kong nightclubs which are notorious pick-up places, where the girls are prostitutes in all but name. Some of the girls from the Kokusai were using the club as a base for prostitution, but not all. Officially, the club's policy was clear: any such arrangements made between a visitor and a hostess were nothing to do with the club. Girls could be entertained away from the premises by arrangement with the management, but the fee charged was on the basis that the girl was going merely as an escort. I found myself attending some very grand balls and banquets myself, escorting wealthy visitors who needed a companion.

Quite a few of the visitors to the Kokusai made it obvious that they were interested in rather more than dancing and conversation. I was invited back to hotel rooms many times, and became skilled in fobbing such suggestions off. I had no moral objections; I'd slept with several boyfriends in the past. But I hated the idea of being bought, of having my availability taken for granted. Sex was something for relationships, not for one-night stands. In any case, most of the men were much older than me, and I didn't fancy them anyway. Some of the girls, who slept with any customer willing to pay for it, thought I was arrogant or at best stupid. One evening one of the girls beckoned me to a quiet corner. She nodded in the direction of one of the customers.

'That guy – see him?' She giggled. 'He wants to take you out.'

I looked across at him. He was a well-dressed, middle-aged man. I recognised him. He saw me looking and smiled confidently back. I stared at him coldly; he winked and waved a hand. 'Oh, he does, does he?' I retorted. 'Well, I'm not going.'

'But . . . he's a movie star!'

'I don't care what he is,' I snapped. 'I know what he wants and he's not getting it. I'm not going.'

That night, in the dressing room, one of the Chinese girls stormed in. She threw her things onto the floor and marched up to me. 'Who do you think you are?' she demanded, furiously. 'You think you're better than the rest of us? You think you've got something special?'

I was fumbling for a reply when another Chinese girl defended me in a torrent of scathing Chinese, and the first girl retreated, glaring at me and swearing fluently. Later, my protector advised me, 'Don't be pushed around, Rita; don't ever let them push you. I've worked here for fifteen years, and I've never slept with anybody

23

for money. So don't let them tell you you've got to. You haven't.'

Cathy became a good friend and was very kind to me. On my first day, when I told her I had no nice clothes to wear in the club, she lent me one of her own beautiful dresses. Later, she asked me where I was staying. When I told her, she wrinkled her nose expressively.

'We've got space in our apartment,' she said thoughtfully. She and her husband lived in an attractive block not far from the Kokusai. 'You could come and bring Sue.'

We leaped at the chance to have our own rooms, with television and the use of a kitchen. We were only at Chungking for a few days, and left without regrets.

Sue worked at the Kokusai too for a while, but her tall frame and boisterous American humour didn't adapt well; she soon left, and found a job at a Wild West saloon where she was a great success.

Cathy left the Kokusai, as she had intended, a short time after I arrived. She also left the apartment, and her husband. She went to live with her lover, in his hotel. Sue and I stayed on in the apartment, and so did Cathy's husband. One night, we were sitting chatting in my room, when he suddenly leaned over and grasped my hands.

'Sleep with me tonight, Rita,' he pleaded. 'I need to hold somebody again.'

'Oh, get away!' I scoffed. 'Go down to Wanchai and find yourself a woman!'

He let go my hands, a hurt expression in his eyes, and left the room; he never referred to the matter again.

The weeks I'd intended to stay in Hong Kong lengthened into months. I was glad to be earning, and it was a good life, the sort of life I'd always dreamed of. But when I was on my own, I sometimes found myself depressed and discontented, though I couldn't put my finger on the reason. It was strange, I thought: how could anybody be having this good a time, and not be happy?

4 James

Dear Mum,

Well, what a mess I've got myself into.
Make no mistake it's very serious. I shall
start from the very beginning . . .

Letter home, 19 April 1977

Two men appeared at the Kokusai at the time of the
Chinese New Year. They stood chatting with one of the
receptionists. I recognised one of them; he was a regular,
the star of many kung-fu films. I'd spent whole after-
noons watching matinee films, in Chinese with English
subtitles, and I adored them. He had starred in several
of my favourites. I'd got used to seeing him at the
Kokusai.

I didn't recognise his companion, but I liked what I
saw. 'Wow!' I said to myself. 'He is some guy!' He
certainly was. James Wong was taller than most Chinese
men, twenty-seven, very good-looking and very, very
smooth. He was beautifully dressed, too: white suit, silk
shirt. I couldn't take my eyes off him, and when he
asked me to go over and sit with him I went like a shot.

We chatted. He was charming. I found it easy to relate
to him as a person, not just as a visitor who had to be
entertained as part of the job. Time passed very quickly.

He looked at his watch. 'I have to go on somewhere

else. Would you like to go for something to eat after you finish work?'

'Yes, sure,' I said (as if I wouldn't!). 'But I don't finish here until three o'clock . . .'

'Doesn't matter,' he said easily. 'I'll be back at three to collect you.'

As I left the Kokusai he called to me from a brand new BMW sports car. He smiled as he held open the door. 'What sort of food do you eat?'

'Oh, whatever you like,' I said, sinking back into the luxury of the upholstered seat. He took me to a Chinese restaurant, not one that catered for the tourists, but a genuine Chinese establishment. I'd been to such places, but only with Chinese companions, as they didn't have English-speaking waiters. They certainly had the best food.

The meal was wonderful, and James was attentive and talkative.

'What do you do for a living?' I asked, as the waiters brought yet another interesting delicacy to the table.

'Oh – cars, mostly.' He speared a fragment of meat with a chopstick. 'I own a showroom – BMW's. I'm in exports and imports.'

'Sounds very interesting.' I probed further. 'You said "mostly" – what else do you do?'

'I follow motor racing,' he replied. 'I go to the big meetings whenever I can manage it. Sometimes in Europe.'

I liked the fact that he enjoyed travel. Most of the men I had got to know in Hong Kong rarely travelled beyond it, and I didn't often find someone who understood my own wanderlust. We talked about my journey to Hong Kong, and he prompted me with occasional questions, the sort you can only ask if you know the places yourself. He said very little about himself, but was interested in my family, my home in England, and

27

my plans after Hong Kong. By the time the meal was over, he had learned quite a lot about me.

He drove me back to my apartment. He asked for my telephone number, and when I gave it to him, asked if he could see me the next night. I agreed.

I let myself in, flopped onto the bed and kicked my shoes off. Sue popped her head round the door. 'Good time, was it?'

I gazed at her. 'Sue,' I announced raptly, 'I think I'm going to like James.'

We were soon meeting regularly. I'd met many men in Hong Kong, but James was different. He had all the glamour I wanted – he was rich, foreign, and had a hint of mystery about him. I felt safe with him. I didn't consider money to be very important in my life, but having tasted the pleasures of wealth I found I enjoyed them. He was considerate and generous; he often gave me presents, and he always had enough money to go where we wanted and do what we wanted. From the first, I thought he was very sweet. He sometimes seemed surprisingly young for his age, though at other times he looked old and hard. At the beginning of our relationship I found myself wanting to mother him, and that was always a part of my feelings for him. But he was affectionate, too; he would kiss me without warning, when I was least expecting it. I loved his shyness. He was reserved in public, but when we were alone we would cuddle in each others' arms for hours. I even enjoyed his fits of jealousy – he once forbade me to go out with another man who'd taken me to lunch, and was adamant about it.

He was always interested in my family, and often asked after my mother – sometimes he would give me money, and say 'Why don't you ring your Mum?' My family were very important to me, and it was something else I could share with James. And on top of all his good qualities, he was stunningly good-looking! Gradually I was falling in love. Sooner or later, I knew, we would end up in bed. I didn't mind; I wanted to. Perhaps, I told myself, this was really it, what I had been looking for.

We spent hours driving round Hong Kong at night. James adored fast cars, was a very fast driver and was also a very good one. He'd collect me from the club at three o'clock and we'd go off, anywhere. Though Hong Kong City has the distinction of being the most densely populated city on earth, the countryside in the north of the Colony is sparsely populated. At three in the morning the country roads are virtually empty, and Hong Kong has some very fast roads. I think we were as close to each other then as we ever were, just sharing each other's company, hurtling through Hong Kong in the sleepy hours before dawn.

In my job I'd become skilful at persuading men to talk about themselves, but James preserved his air of mystery. I knew he had been living in Amsterdam, but when I asked him where he was living in Hong Kong, he didn't answer directly. 'Oh . . . nearby. I'm waiting to get my own place now I'm back from Europe. I'm living with my aunt and uncle. They're old-style Chinese – I couldn't take a girl back there. And there isn't much point in giving you the phone number. They don't speak English.'

He rarely went into the Kokusai, though he was usually waiting for me when I left work. I never needed to telephone him anyway; he was always there, and I spent most of my free time with him. Sometimes he would suddenly announce that he had to go to Taiwan or somewhere else for a few days, but he always rang me as soon as he got back, and he brought beautiful presents.

29

One day quite early in our relationship I got a message from James asking me to meet him at a restaurant we'd been to occasionally – a bistro where a Filipino played guitar. James greeted me at the door. 'I want you to meet a friend of mine,' he said, and took me over to meet Simon Lo.

A youngish man in his thirties rose politely to shake hands. I tried not to stare at the enormous scar running from his forehead to his jawline. Whatever had caused it must have just missed his left eye. Despite the scar (maybe because of it) he was very good looking, and he had a broad smile.

James ordered our meal. After a few pleasantries he smiled apologetically at me. 'Excuse me,' he said, and began a lengthy conversation with Simon in Chinese. It was quite usual for this to happen when we were with James's Chinese friends, and there was nothing out of the ordinary in it. One of James's good points so far as I was concerned was the fact that he always apologised to me courteously before starting a foreign conversation – most other Chinese men I knew tended simply to turn their backs on me and get on with it.

Simon seemed to be around quite often, and there were frequent long Chinese conversations, during which I enjoyed my meal or gazed round whatever glamorous nightspot we happened to be in. James was always especially attentive to me afterwards. Once, half-exasperated, I teased him. 'Do you have to bring him with you every time? Is he your bodyguard, or something?' We both laughed.

We spent one of my days off in Macau, the old Portuguese territory near Hong Kong. Macau city moves at a slower pace than Hong Kong, and it was a relief to get away from the ceaseless bustle and wander round the ancient buildings and monuments, painlessly absorbing centuries of Portuguese history.

We ended up in one of the city's numerous casinos. James was an expert gambler, and rich enough to indulge his taste. We wedged ourselves into a crowd of people standing round the gaming table, and I screamed with delight as James began a winning streak.

'You're bringing me luck,' he grinned. He shoved a pile of chips into my hands. 'Here. Now you try for a while.'

He had to show me how to bet, but I was soon flipping the chips onto the table like an expert, biting my fingernails as the wheel rattled round. I jumped up and down and clasped James's arm as the croupier pushed a stack of chips over to me. Some of the others players laughed and applauded. James smiled.

'See? You are lucky. Now . . . we'll try our luck at blackjack.'

The evening was wonderful. I lost count of whether we were winning or losing. James told me that the chips he had given me had been hundred-dollar chips. It was staggering; I'd been throwing them down like confetti. Eventually, we left the casino and made our way back to the ferry. At Hong Kong, we drove to the Peninsular Hotel at the end of Nathan Road. Anybody living in Hong Kong knows about the Peninsular Hotel. It's one of the oldest in the Colony, dating from the days when it was the hotel rail passengers used while awaiting the train to Europe. It's still an exclusive and very expensive place, and I'd often seen the fleet of Rolls Royces provided for guests' use. The evening was turning into a fairytale. 'Fantastic!' I exclaimed, when James announced calmly, 'We'll stay here tonight.' He'd booked an enormous suite, with all the trimmings. I couldn't believe it was happening.

We became lovers that night. It was wonderful, and

it was inevitable. Part of me still wanted to hold back. I'd had a string of relationships which had left me unsatisfied; what could make me think James could give me what I wanted? I was suddenly aware of all the differences between us.

'Don't be silly: don't get too involved here,' one part of me was saying. But another part of me argued back. 'Well, you're having a good time, he's nice to you, he doesn't push you into anything; so why pull out now?' So we became closer and closer.

We'd been seeing each other for about three months when he came to me with some news.

'I'm going to Europe on business, Rita.'

I was disappointed. 'Oh, James, do you have to?'

''Fraid so. I can't change my plans. It's really important.'

'When will you be back?'

He didn't answer the question, but asked me one instead. 'Don't you have some holiday due to you?'

My eyes sparkled as I began to see what he was leading up to. 'Yes – a fortnight.'

'Well, I've a plan that will mean you can see your mother and family for a while.'

I gasped. 'James! How –'

'Simple. You come with me as far as Paris, then we split up. I look after my business deals, and you go on to England and see your Mum. I'll pay all your expenses to Blackburn and back.'

I was still badly bitten by the travel bug, and I was missing my mother very much. I knew it wasn't the right time to go back to England for good – but here was James offering me an all-expenses paid trip to Blackburn, with the return ticket in my pocket as an effective reply to any pressure that might be put on me to stay. I agreed joyfully. I did want to see Mum again.

We planned the trip. James had far-reaching plans

beyond my return from Blackburn. I'd evaded conversations previously about where our relationship was heading; now James was very direct.

'When we get back we'll get an apartment together. Wouldn't you like that?'

I wasn't sure.

'Well, then; we'll get married if you'd rather do that. What do you think?'

It was all happening too quickly for me. I guess I was scared. I told him I didn't think I was ready for marriage; 'But an apartment is a nice idea. We could do that.' It didn't commit me, it kept my options open, and I enjoyed his company anyway.

If anybody had told me twelve months before that within a year I would be a hostess in a glamorous nightclub in Hong Kong, rubbing shoulders with the rich and famous, I wouldn't have believed them. Yet here I was, with a rich boyfriend, a nice place to live, friendly workmates, and a lifestyle which included fast cars, expensive restaurants, yachts and film stars, calmly discussing a joyride halfway across the Western world. It was what I'd always wanted; it was what my travelling had been for.

And yet . . . and yet. Despite everything, I was miserable. A young girl in a foreign city can find herself desperately lonely, even when surrounded by people; and though loneliness was only part of my depression, it was a focus I could concentrate on. I needed James. He was attentive, and he seemed genuinely to care for me as a person. However I rationalised it, he was someone to cling to. And I did.

Even my love for James couldn't dispel my unhappiness completely. I dreaded going home, and being on my own. I knew there was something desperately wrong, and I didn't know what it was. I used to get home sometimes, put one of my favourite Rod Stewart records on the record player, fling myself on to my bed, and cry and cry. I used to rage at myself: 'Well, what do you want? Is it marriage you're after?' I would demand. 'Do you want to go back to Australia, marry the good man you left behind – is that what you want? No, you just came from there, you couldn't settle down. Do you want to live at home? Are you missing your Mum? You know very well that you tried that for twelve months and it just drove you both crazy – you ended up even falling out with her. You couldn't settle down there either . . . So what do you want? You've got what you've always set your heart on. You've got this glamorous life, this amazing boyfriend. You've got everything you ever wanted . . . haven't you?'

I had no answers to my own questions. I didn't know what I wanted. I didn't even know the right questions to ask.

5 Arrest

*I haven't been able to write much before
now . . . it's an odd feeling wanting to
wake up from a nightmare and eventually
realising it's no dream.*

Letter to Mum, 19 April 1977

I looked forward to my trip to Europe with great excitement. I thought about writing to Mum to say I was
coming, but decided against it – it would be so good to
surprise her, simply to knock on her door and see her
face when she saw me standing there. I couldn't resist
giving her just a hint on the telephone. We'd planned
for her to come to Hong Kong later in the year, and
while calling her one day I casually mentioned that she
might possibly see me before then. She hadn't the fain-
test idea what I was talking about.

I kept on working. James wouldn't commit himself to
a date for our departure, so I carried on as usual, working
at the Kokusai and seeing him at night. Finally one night
I left the club and saw him standing by his car holding
two tickets. It was settled; we would leave on March 17.

'Make sure you are packed and ready in the morning
– I'll pick you up at your apartment,' he said.

March 17, I suddenly realised, was St. Patrick's Day
– the day on which, several years before, I had first left
England for Australia.

I began to worry about luggage. I'd come a long way since arriving in Hong Kong with my ancient rucksack, but that rucksack was still the only luggage I possessed. I didn't fancy cramming my things into it for a trip to Europe. When I mentioned this, James presented me with three expensive holdalls of his own, in hand-stitched soft leather. He pointed out that I would need warm clothes if I was going to England in March. He took out his wallet and handed over 200 dollars for a new wardrobe. He shrugged aside my thanks. I had a great time spending the money.

I got everything packed and sat in my apartment on the morning of the great day. When the doorbell chimed I rushed to let James in. One look at his face told me immediately that something had gone wrong.

'What's happened?'

'I really am sorry, Rita. Something's come up. I will have to stay here for the next few days on business. I can't possibly come with you today.'

I stared at him, dismayed. 'Well, I'm not going if you're not. Let's forget it.'

He shook his head. 'That's not possible. The tickets are paid for, and it's too late to cancel.'

'You can afford to lose the money.'

'That's not the point. It's stupid for you not to go. You've been looking forward to it.'

'How could I possibly go now?'

James outlined his alternative plan. 'Look, Rita. You can fly via Bangkok. You leave here today, get to Bangkok tomorrow, stop over there, and fly on to Europe. We meet up in Paris. So we only have to alter the first bit of the plan.'

'Is it worth the trouble?' I didn't like this change of programme.

'Worth it? Of course it is. You get an extra holiday in

Bangkok. Arrive in Paris with a nice tan. I'll pay the extra, don't worry.'

I hesitated. I didn't want to appear ungrateful, but I didn't want to go on my own, after looking forward to going away with James. I tried to explain this to him. He produced his trump card. By a coincidence, Simon Lo was travelling to Bangkok that day. He would fly on the same flight as me, book in at the same hotel and handle all the bills. 'You'll have no problems,' James assured me, 'Simon will look after you.'

The change of plan left me a little uneasy. Odd ideas flitted through my mind. Was James getting bored with me? Was this some complicated method of ditching me? I decided that couldn't be right. It was too complicated a way of going about it. In the end I agreed to the new suggestion, though I wasn't too happy about Simon suddenly appearing in the plan. On the other hand, James's travel arrangements were often haphazard, and he would change his plans at the last minute. The last thing in my mind was the possibility that this change of plan might have any sinister purpose.

Was I so stupid to think that I could have a holiday with a young, rich, handsome boyfriend – for nothing? I didn't think so for one minute. Scores of men had asked me to go on similar trips at the Kokusai, but I'd always said no because I'd never cared for the men. James was different. He was my lover, he wasn't just any boring old middle-aged charmer who'd walked into the Kokusai.

Simon met me at Kai Tak Airport for the Bangkok flight. I hadn't often been on my own with him. He was pleasant enough, but rather distant. He handed me a new radio cassette player. 'From James – a present for your mother.'

We said little on the flight; Simon buried his head in a newspaper, and I had my own thoughts.

It was lovely to be back in Bangkok. We checked into the Asia Hotel, taking separate rooms, and had dinner together that evening. Simon was punctilious and courteous, but conversation was intermittent. I hardly saw him after that first evening. I had some shopping to do the next day; James had given me some spending money. I spent some of the day lazing by the hotel pool and the rest of it sightseeing.

Under the present monarch, King Bhumibol Adulyadej, Thailand's Westernisation has advanced dramatically, but it's still a land of contrasts. I wandered round modern department stores and ancient temples, down streets where western dress and traditional Thai silks appeared side by side. The heat was welcome after Hong Kong, which had been quite cool when we left. Down by the river, tourists thronged the tree-lined boulevards. I bought my lunch from a street trader's stall, and ate it in a shady corner of a public square where businessmen sat among saffron-robed monks.

The Paris flight was scheduled for 11 pm the next day. I had to check out of my room by noon. Simon, who was staying on, suggested that I leave my things in his room, and helped me to move them. He suggested I take advantage of the Asia Hotel's beauty salon, and I booked an appointment for 4 o'clock. I whiled away the time sightseeing and shopping, then went back to Simon's room to get some money from my luggage.

Simon didn't answer my knock immediately. When he appeared, he held the door closed behind him. He sounded embarrassed. I assumed that he had found himself a woman. I explained what I wanted, and he went back into the room, closing the door, and reappeared with a bundle of money – 500 baht, which I wasn't going to refuse. So I didn't go into his room, and I hadn't seen my luggage since noon.

The beauty salon was fantastic. Simon, I discovered, had paid in advance, probably to be rid of me for the afternoon. I had a steam bath, massage, facial, manicure, pedicure and shampoo and set – all for the equivalent of ten English pounds. At 7 o'clock he collected me. We had dinner together and drinks afterwards in the hotel bar. Then I went to his room to use his shower. My luggage was there, waiting for me. I took a few odds and ends out for the journey. Most of the clothes in the bags were winter ones, and it was about 90 degrees in Bangkok.

At about 9.30, Simon came down to the foyer with me and called a taxi to take me to the airport. When the taxi arrived, he kissed me on the cheek. It was the closest we'd been for the whole trip. He smiled at me coolly. 'Take good care of yourself!' He waved, and went back into the hotel.

Soon I was at the airport.

Then the nightmare began.

6 Detained

I think I'm going to need more than a good lawyer . . .

Letter to Aunt Margaret and Tom, 10
June 1977

'Who are you?'

The icy words reverberated in my head. I stared in disbelief.

Simon turned away from me with a sneer and reached for his trousers. I leaped at him, my fists whirling, sobbing and shouting. The police seized me. The captain pointed to the door. 'Take her outside to wait.'

I argued hysterically with the police-woman, in the front seat of the police car. They brought Simon down after a few minutes and bundled him into the back seat with a policeman. He looked dishevelled, as if he had thrown his clothes onto his body. As we drove off I subsided into exhausted silence. Simon sat calmly behind me, saying nothing. I didn't look out of the window and had no idea where we were going.

The cars pulled up in the courtyard of a large brick building, several stories high. It was still dark. The police-woman helped me out, and we went inside. It was some sort of police station. She exchanged a few words with the police captain and took me upstairs. On the bare landing she took a key from her pocket and opened the door of a cell. I shrank back in horror. The cell was dark and dirty, and several large cockroaches scuttled across the floor. I've always been terrified of cockroaches, even small ones. These were large, glossy brutes, like ones I'd seen – and avoided – in Australia.

'I can't go in there. I can't go in,' I pleaded with the police-woman. She shook her head and smiled sympathetically.

'You'll feel better in the morning,' she said. She pushed me gently forward, and locked the door firmly behind me.

I was standing in a small room, one wall of which was a floor-to-ceiling grille of bars with the door in it. Most of the space was occupied by a raised wooden platform which I took to be my bed. Through a doorless doorway I could see the back of the cell, where a trough and water pipe were visible. A tin dipper lay in a puddle of water in the trough. Nearby was the toilet; two wooden footrests, with a hole in the floor between them. Somebody had provided a piece of dirty hardboard to cover the doorway and secure some privacy. It was only waist-high, and had slipped over on the sloppy floor.

The dipper-shower and the simple toilet weren't new to me. I'd seen them in Bali; they're very common in the Far East. But it was very different seeing them in the spacious, airy rooms of Bali hostels and friends' houses. There they had been fun, part of the exotic pleasures of travel, a symbol of the passion most Far Eastern people have for cleanliness. In the dark cell they just looked squalid, and had been left none too clean by previous inhabitants.

I wandered round and round the little cell, my mind in confusion. The police-woman reappeared with a bundle of my clothes. 'We must keep your bags for now,' she explained. I accepted the bundle gratefully. Picking out a few pullovers and skirts, I constructed a makeshift bed on the wooden pallet and lay down. It was harder than any bed I'd slept on for a long time. Outside the cell door, an electric light had been left on. I pulled the clothes over my head and tried to sleep. Time passed, but I lost track of it.

A movement outside made me look up. A skinny, very short man in vest and pants was looking in at me. I was suddenly aware of a raging thirst. Seeing him, I croaked 'Drink! Drink!'

He grinned and extended cupped hands. 'Money!'

I'd changed my money at the airport, and only had French francs. I offered him a banknote. He waved his hand dismissively. He pointed at my bracelet. 'Nice. I take it, give you water.'

I turned my face to the wall and wept in frustration. I didn't understand the way things operated in prison, and this trading for water seemed barbaric and cruel. I screamed at my tormenter: 'Dog! Dog!' He only chuckled. When I looked round again he had disappeared.

More time passed. There was a jangle of keys. I sat up. The police captain was opening the cell door; he came in, locking it behind him. He looked as if he had had a good sleep.

My clothes were sticking to me in the heat, and my face was hot and sticky. He looked at me sympathetically. 'Are you thirsty?'

I nodded. 'A man came – he wouldn't take my money – he wouldn't give me water . . .'

'Ah! The cat-man. He feeds the cats, you see. It is to keep the vermin down.'

I shuddered. The captain called to somebody outside the cell, and there was a clatter of feet down the stairs. 'He is getting you a coke,' he explained.

'But I haven't any baht . . .'

'Don't worry, it doesn't matter.'

The coke arrived in the usual polythene bag, tied at one end with a straw sticking out – warm but very welcome. I drank it gratefully. There was food as well – some kind of rice dish. I couldn't face it. It was days before I managed to bring myself to eat again.

The captain was a frequent visitor to my cell.

'How long are you going to keep me here?' I demanded.

The captain waved a hand genially. 'Oh . . . maybe six days, maybe thirty . . .' Without waiting for a reply he began to ask me questions.

'What do you know about Alan Soon?'

I had never heard the name, and said so. But he kept returning to the same question.

'How did you meet Alan Soon? When did you arrange to fly with him?'

'I don't know anybody called Alan Soon . . .'

'What was your rendezvous plan with him?'

'I don't know what you're talking about . . . Who is this Alan Soon guy, anyway?'

Eventually the captain told me. 'Soon was flying with you. He was in the Customs Hall when you were arrested. Come, Miss Nightingale, you must have seen him.'

I suddenly remembered the flint-eyed Chinese man who had been watching while my bags were searched.

'Tell me the whole story, one more time,' said the captain, flipping the pages of his notebook.

I told my story repeatedly, hoping desperately that I was telling it the same each time, because my head got so confused about the chain of events. I became very despondent. The captain comforted me.

'Don't worry – those other two, Soon and Lo; we know they're involved in drugs, they're well-known to the police. We've been watching them for a long time. But you're not being held on a drugs charge. We're holding you under Article 21. That's breach of the peace. Your lawyer will explain everything.'

'My lawyer?'

'Of course! You will have a lawyer. Your Embassy will arrange it.'

'I must let James know. He's meeting me in Paris.'

The captain gave me an odd look. 'The British Embassy will arrange all that.'

As he was leaving I said, 'How long will I be in here? When will you let me out?'

He paused at the door. 'We have to hold you here for thirty days. It is the law. You'll be all right. You'll see.' He scratched his nose. 'How much money do you have?'

I didn't want to seem rich and therefore a possible drug-smuggler, so I said that I had a few dollars in Australia. Later I met people who had bribed their way out of trouble, and wondered what would have happened if I had tried to do so then. The captain merely nodded, said 'Don't worry,' and went downstairs.

I was fingerprinted several times, and photographed holding a placard with an identity number and an inscription in Thai. Dozens of people, officials, other detainees and others, came to the cell to look at me. Once I woke up and saw a guard watching me. He was leaning against the wall outside, looking unbearably cool and relaxed in his official uniform of khaki drill trousers and shirt. I scowled at him.

'What d'you think you're gawping at?' I demanded.

He offered a pack of cigarettes. 'Would you like one?'

'No I wouldn't.'

He lit a cigarette and inhaled thoughtfully. 'You know, I'm really very sorry about what's happened. I'm really very sorry indeed . . .'

He was trying to cheer me up, but I was in no mood to be consoled. After a while he went away.

44

I wondered when I would hear from the Embassy and when a lawyer would arrive. I began to fret about my mother. What would she say when they heard about all this? I imagined her opening an official letter and reading a formal announcement that her daughter had been detained in connection with heroin smuggling. What would her reaction be? Would she know who to contact, what to do? I brooded over the grief that this was going to cause my family, and I couldn't bear the thought. I even imagined her deserted by her friends and neighbours because of the disgrace that I had brought upon Blackburn. I didn't know then that the people of Blackburn would support Mum the way that they did. I thought I would be condemned, and that Mum would suffer.

In fact she learned the story in the worst possible way. On the day following my arrest, an item appeared in the newspapers. A Reuter's correspondent in Bangkok had cabled the story to England, and my sister Ann saw it in that night's Lancashire Evening Telegraph. Mum had just that brief paragraph to go on until more detailed news arrived from the Embassy. It was weeks before I could bring myself to write. If I was going to be out after thirty days, I thought, it would be better not to write for a month than have Mum get a letter from me on police notepaper.

I was taken to an office for yet another interview. This time it was my lawyer. He was a Thai gentleman, with a round, pleasant face. Despite the heat, he wore a dark suit and tie, and carried a small briefcase which he placed carefully on the desk. He shook hands soberly.

'My name is Sorochai,' he announced. 'My firm is Tilleke and Gibbins. It is a very old-established law company in Bangkok. The British Embassy has asked us to help you.' He took a neatly folded handkerchief from his pocket and carefully mopped his brow. 'I am very sorry that you are in trouble.'

Opening his briefcase, he transferred a bundle of papers onto the desk. 'I must ask you what happened. Please tell me the whole story.'

He listened patiently, his hands placed together, pursing his lips and nodding. Occasionally he asked me to repeat a part of the story. 'I see . . . I see . . .' he murmured. 'Go on.'

I finished. Mr. Sorochai was sitting back in his chair, looking at the ceiling, deep in thought. I could hear people shouting in the courtyard outside. He slowly lowered his gaze until he was looking at me. He sighed. 'Well?' I demanded rudely. Mr. Sorochai raised his eyebrows. My voice tightened.

'What's going to happen? When can I leave?'

He looked at me appraisingly. 'I think this is a very difficult case,' he said flatly.

'But it wasn't my heroin . . . I knew nothing about it; they must release me!'

'This is difficult,' he repeated. He gathered his papers together and placed them carefully into his briefcase. Standing up, he extended his hand. 'I will be back very soon,' he promised. 'There is much to do. Papers must be obtained, questions must be asked. The courts here do not move quickly. It is for your protection.'

At the door he bowed gravely as I was led back to my cell. 'I am sorry. This is not an easy case. Be patient.'

Next day I was taken to another large room in the building. It was like a small courtroom. On one side were a number of benches, and on the other a long table. Behind the table a number of people were seated. An English woman was, I found later, the British Consul. Two or three official-looking people sat in the centre, flanked by military officers in full braid and insignia. I sat on one of the benches. A policewoman sat next to me.

Two more police officers arrived, escorting two men. When I saw who they were, my heart raced. They were Simon Lo and Alan Soon.

I was being prodded to stand up. The man who appeared to be in charge was an Englishman.

'You are Rita Nightingale?' His voice was level, his manner efficient and as crisp as his uniform. I nodded. The policewoman nudged me. 'Yes,' I said faintly.

'I am an Interpol officer. Do you understand what Interpol is?'

'Yes.'

'Your home is in Australia? Your nationality is British? On what date did you leave Australia?'

The questions followed each other like machine-gun fire. I answered mechanically. I was questioned about my job in Hong Kong, about the trip to Paris, and about James. They wanted dates, times, all sorts of details. I told them all I could remember. Before long I was permitted to sit down. It was the turn of Lo and Soon to be questioned. Their interrogation seemed to be the real reason for the interview. They refused to answer questions, looking straight ahead. The Englishman tried to make them respond, then the other officials interrogated them in various Asian dialects. They remained silent and tight-lipped. The meeting ended abruptly. The officials left the room and we were taken away. Neither Lo nor Soon acknowledged me in any way.

No word came from James. I was worried that my arrest had caused problems for him. He was planning to meet me in Paris, and I wasn't going to be there – he would be frantic with worry. I'd given James's name, and the address of the hotel we were to meet at, to the police at the airport.

A niggling fear began to grow at the back of my mind. People asked me questions about James, but when I asked them if any word had come from him, they were non-committal. Other prisoners in the police station said I was a fool to have been involved with him. I began to remember the questions about him that the Interpol team had asked.

Worry for James was soon replaced by anger. Whatever had gone wrong with the arrangements, he could at least have got in touch with me. I decided I was going to have some strong things to say to James Wong when I got back to Hong Kong.

I lapsed into a sullen bitterness. I was furious that nobody was prepared to see that the whole thing was a misunderstanding. Instead, I was going to have to hang around in a cell for a month while the thing got sorted out. James was having a good time in Paris and I was stuck in Bangkok. I didn't even know the procedure for getting released. I hoped that somebody would come and explain to me how the Thai legal system worked, but nobody did. I pieced together what I could, from odd comments people made, but I was confused about it all.

The captain who was responsible for me was very friendly. After the first flurry of interviews was over and things had begun to settle down into a dull routine, he sent for me. I was taken upstairs to the large general office, a large room with a pair of ancient filing cabinets and a number of desks. The captain looked up and smiled as I came in.

'Rita . . . you look pale, you need some fresh air!' He waved me over to his desk, which was near an open window. Papers lifted and rustled in a gentle breeze. I sat down. Two enormous fans in the ceiling creaked rhythmically overhead. I looked outside. In the courtyard was one of the foodstalls that are found everywhere in Bangkok. A bored teenage stallkeeper lounged in its shadow. People were talking to each other in shaded corners; uniformed officials were going about their business; I could hear the cheerful noises of traffic. It all looked beautifully normal. I swallowed, suddenly aware of a lump in my throat. The captain rubbed his hands together noisily.

'Hah! You have not been eating,' he scolded me. 'You must eat, you know. Pretty girl like you must not starve! You're not on a diet, I hope?'

I smiled wanly and shook my head.

'Right!' he said enthusiastically. 'What do you want to eat?'

'I don't know what there is.'

'Well, do you like fried rice? Noodles? Noodles are very nice.'

I decided I was quite hungry. He sent one of the office boys to get the food, and I watched the boy appear below me in the courtyard and consult with the stallkeeper. As he walked back carefully carrying a bowl of food I envied him the simple freedom to go where he wanted.

I perched on the captain's desk eating noodles and drinking Coca-Cola. We talked and talked, about anything and everything; travel, films we'd seen, things in the news. I responded to him because he had sat down and listened to my version of what had happened, but I liked him anyway; he was good-humoured and sympathetic. It was only when I raised the matter of my release that he became vague and evasive.

When the captain sent for somebody to take me back to my cell, I was calmer and almost cheerful. During my detention at the police station he sent for me several times and allowed me to sit at his desk.

The return of Mr. Sorochai brought hardly any encouragement; there was no definite news. He came several times, bringing a gift of food or drink with him, and – after I begged for something to read – a supply of magazines. He dressed immaculately; though he always looked hot in his suit, he declined invitations to take his jacket off. He was friendly and usually had time to chat – he mentioned once that his wife was expecting their first baby, and we told each other about our families.

He didn't smile very often. I wanted him to, and tried to break his reserve with jokes, but he maintained a sombre expression. I wanted him to smile because it would have made matters seem less ominous. Though he never scowled, and was gentle and courteous, his refusal to make light of my problems made me increasingly worried, and his repeated assurances that much work was being done on my case made me no less alarmed. He was definite about one thing. There was to be no overnight miracle. I was going to have to spend the full thirty days in the police station.

'And then?' I persisted.

But Mr. Sorochai would not be drawn on that.

When I walked out of that cell back into the outside world, I vowed, it was going to be with head held high and eyes bright. One thing was for sure; I wasn't going to vegetate. I looked for things with which to occupy myself.

I persuaded the guards to give me cleaning materials, and started to clean the cell. I had a rag which I used to scrub the floor. This helped to lay the dust, and then I started on the crevices in the wood and the grimy bars of the cell.

As my frustration increased my temper grew shorter. I snapped at everybody and complained bitterly at everything. I was a far from well-behaved prisoner. Once I was doing something which involved the use of a small pair of manicure scissors. A sudden exclamation outside the cell made me look up. A guard was pointing at the scissors and holding out his hand for them. Thinking he wanted to trim his fingernails I passed them out to him, whereupon he immediately put them into his pocket.

'Why did you do that?' I demanded fiercely.

'Not allowed!' stated the guard matter-of-factly. 'Weapon. Sharp!'

I lost my temper and shouted at him, swearing like a trooper. 'What do you mean, you stupid idiot?' I howled. I pointed to a row of bottles standing in the cell, which had held sauce and cold drinks. I waved one of them at him. 'What do you think this is? Isn't this a weapon?'

I stood there shaking, holding the bottle. I wanted to smash it on the bars to prove my point. The guard looked at me as if I were mad, laughed, and walked away.

The Foreign Office in London issued a sombre statement to the effect that court action might well turn out to be a lengthy business. For the present, they intended to watch carefully and keep a low profile. 'She is legally represented, but there is nothing new. We have advised her relatives this could take some time. We don't know how long.'

I was never quite sure what precisely was happening about my case, as life at the police station ground slowly on. None of the officials were unkind to me. In fact the general attitude shown to me was one of off-handedness, of submitting to tedious routines. Various Embassy staff were sympathetic and concerned, but were not able to give me any more information or say how things would turn out. I was grateful to the Vice-Consul – amazingly, he was a Blackburn man – who, as he left the interview room with his colleagues, turned back to me, smiled encouragingly, and said 'Keep your chin up, lass!'

Food was being sent to me in my cell. Even at first, when, unable to face the idea of food, I made no arrangements to buy any, meals appeared, and good ones at that. At first I assumed it was the normal police station food, but later I gathered that standard prisoner's food was very plain and simple. When a Thai girl was put in the cell with me later, we shared all sorts of delicacies brought in by her family, including, once, a bottle of brandy. Obviously this wasn't prison fare; and I began to wonder again what the system was and where my own luxurious food was coming from.

Sitting in the captain's office one day, I was looking down at the foodstall. I suddenly asked him, 'The food that comes to my cell. Is that provided by the government?'

The captain grinned broadly. 'The government? No! They provide good food, but not like what you are eating. That's from your friend downstairs.'

'What do you mean?'

'You know – your friend, Simon Lo. He's in a cell downstairs. He buys the food for you.'

'He's not my friend! I won't eat it!' I screamed, and for a few days I did refuse it, though later I accepted it again, thinking I may as well use Simon seeing that he had used me. When eventually I left the police station Simon and Alan Soon were still being held – I know, because I was asked 'Do you want to say goodbye to your friends?'

'They're not my friends!' I shouted again. A week afterwards, they were deported from Thailand.

One Thursday, when I had been in detention for twenty-six days, Mr. Sorochai arrived with news.

'Next week the thirty days are up. You will be going to court.' He arranged where he would meet me at the courthouse and various other details.

Next morning I woke up in confusion. Somebody was shaking my shoulders.

'Huh? What – what time is it?'

The policewoman released my shoulders. 'It's six o'-clock. You must get up. This morning you go to court.'

'Today? That's crazy! I'm not supposed to go till next week!'

She was unperturbed. 'Please dress. You must be ready quickly. And pack your belongings. You must bring them with you.'

As I pulled on my things I argued frantically. 'Look, are you sure you've got it right?' I groped for my jeans and slid into them. 'My lawyer doesn't know. How can I go to court if my lawyer isn't here? Why am I going, anyway? What's going to happen?' I began to throw clothes and other possessions into my bags. 'I want my lawyer. Please, will somebody call Mr. Sorochai?'

I was driven in a Landrover through the city, demanding. 'What's happening? Why are we going today? Where's my lawyer? Why hasn't my lawyer been told?'

'You won't need your lawyer,' the officials replied.

7 Lard Yao

*I know you are strong Mum, and believe
me, I am going to be the same. It is no
good for me now to look back and say, I
should have had more sense or I should
have had an idea. I cannot go back, only
forward . . . Don't be upset too much
Mum, I have done the crying for both of us.*

Letter to Mum, 19 April 1977

The courthouse was a large building of grubby stone
with an imposing flight of steps. At the back was a
courtyard. A senior officer told me to sit there, and then
he disappeared into the building. People thronged the
yard, and the usual food booths were everywhere. In the
distance I could hear traffic noises, people laughing and
shouting to each other outside the courtyard. I suddenly
realised that I was alone and unguarded. I could have
got up and walked away. Numbly, I contemplated how
it might possibly work. I knew a well-known hotel in
Bangkok where I had stayed, where friends of mine had
been able to get fake passports and documents – there
was a Frenchman there who had the whole thing organised. And after that? Well, I had friends all over the East
. . .

But I was too confused and frightened to get up and
walk away. And I was still thinking, 'It can't be all that
serious. I'm not involved, after all. It wasn't my heroin.

I must be all right. After all, I'm only being held under Article 21.'

I was frightened, though. Sitting in the courtyard I asked each passer-by, 'Do you speak English?' Eventually somebody sent a Thai woman lawyer over to me – Jennifer, who spoke excellent English. I explained that my lawyer didn't know I'd come to court.

'Oh, that will be all right. I'll give him a telephone call.' He had given me his telephone number: I told it to Jennifer.

'They shot a guy this morning, you know.'

I looked at her incredulously.

'Yes, he was a Chinese guy on drug charges. The American drug enforcement officers are over here at the moment.' She grinned. 'Don't worry. I'll see your lawyer is told you are here.'

My officer returned, and motioned me to pick up my bags. Now in greater fear than ever, I was led into a huge courtroom. Some Thai prisoners were already there, seated on the floor. The men were in leg-irons, and there were a few women prisoners. Many of them were handcuffed together. The guard brought a chair for me; I was the only prisoner to be given one. As I sat down, he leaned towards me and murmured, 'You know, I feel so sorry for you.'

The black-gowned judges entered. One began to read names from a long list – I assumed that they were names, because people were standing up and sitting down as the list was read. The proceedings were in Thai. Suddenly the guard poked me in the ribs. I had missed my name. I stood up. A moment later he tugged my arm and I sat down again.

'What's going on?' I whispered.

'Oh – prison,' he said. 'You're going to prison.'

I burst into tears. 'Where is my lawyer?' I wept. 'I

want to see him, I want my lawyer.' The guard repeated, 'I feel sorry for you, I feel sorry for you.'

At the back of the court my bags were unceremoniously emptied into a large cardboard box, which was handed to me. I was taken to a cell in the courthouse. It was about twenty-five feet across. At least eighty Thai women were in there. The noise was indescribable. Some were eating, others were holding shouted conversations above the general uproar. A guard began to examine the contents of my box systematically, presumably looking for dangerous weapons. She removed a razor, a pair of tweezers, some aspirins and other items, and put them on one side. As the lovely clothes I had bought for Paris were taken from the box one by one, the women fell upon them with cries of delight. Horrified, I watched the clothes pass from hand to hand and disappear from view. The guard appeared oblivious.

I didn't know where I was; I was in a trance. I thought I was in prison already. I'd no idea what the inside of a prison would be like, but this was bad enough to fulfil my worst expectations. I stood helpless at the edge of the cell, looking at the mass of women. Gradually I realised that some of them were gesturing to me. When I didn't respond they pulled me by the sleeves, across the room. I picked my way past seated and prone figures. I was being dragged to the far wall, where through a six-foot gap scores of people outside were gesticulating to the prisoners, shouting to them above the din, trying to establish contact. As I neared the gap I saw a familiar Thai face. It was Mr. Sorochai.

'What's happening?' I shouted desperately. 'I can't stand it, I don't know what's happening – you've got to get me out of here!'

He smiled, a rare thing for him. 'Don't worry,' he called. 'We are applying for bail. Just wait a little longer.'

In the press of people he was flustered and hot, but he beamed confidently. 'Don't worry!'

'You must get me out now,' I insisted. 'I'll go mad – I can't stay here, I can't!'

As I was pushed back by the crowd, into the clamorous room, he called after me, 'Don't worry – it will be all right, you'll see . . .'

All my possessions found their way back to me, after the other occupants of the cell had satisfied their curiosity. The Thai people are insatiably inquisitive about anything European. I was confused and resentful, and snatched my things back angrily as they came within reach.

I heard the other prisoners talking about me. '*Farang . . . aayuu towrai? . . . geh . . .*' ('A foreigner . . . how old? . . . a young one . . .') A Thai girl was offering me food, speaking English, but I refused. I sat and brooded. It was still like a bad dream. Half an hour later my name was called. I was taken to a police office in the building. As I was brought in a dapper figure rose to his feet. 'Don't worry,' said Mr. Sorochai. He sat down heavily. 'We are applying for bail.'

I stared at him blankly. He leaned forward. 'We are applying for bail, Rita. You understand what that means?'

'When do I get out?' I demanded dully.

'Soon, Rita, very soon.'

'Today?'

'No, no; it's Friday today; no way to get the application processed until Monday. But first thing on Monday we will –'

'What will they do with me until Monday?'

Mr. Sorochai faltered. 'Oh, they'll take you out to the prison.'

'What's it like?'

He brightened. 'It's better than here.'

I was taken back to the corner cell, and I sat there until six or seven in the evening, resolutely refusing food and drink offered me by different Thai girls. The heat was unbelievable. Normal Bangkok heat is bad enough, but the number of people in the cell made the temperature almost unbearable.

When it was time for the prison bus to leave, everybody began crowding towards the door. I decided I wasn't going to try to be among the first out – I had my cardboard box full of belongings, and I didn't want to get caught in the scrimmage that was developing. One of the Thai girls, seeing me hanging back, took my arm. 'Come! You have to be at the front!' I shook my head: 'No, no!' I became quite nasty about it, but I was terrified and apprehensive. So I staggered after the crowd, carrying in my cardboard box the contents of James's three holdalls.

The most dilapidated van imaginable stood outside. It would seat about twenty-five in comfort. I saw now why everyone wanted to be first out. Everybody, young, old and pregnant, rushed to clamber on. I managed to find a place somewhere. As the van lurched off, I clutched my box and began to cry again.

'Don't cry.'

It was the Thai girl who had spoken to me earlier. 'It's not so bad out in the Monkey House, you'll see. Maybe there'll be something to eat when we get there. It'll be all right. Don't cry.'

Eventually the hot cramped journey came to an end, as the van drew up at the Lard Yao Women's Prison.

We stopped in front of an enormous pair of iron gates. It was almost dark. Somebody was opening the gates. We drove through, and they slammed shut behind us.

Everyone clambered out. A battery of bright lights blazed overhead, dazzling after the gloom of the van. I felt hot and headachy. We were in a small enclosure, bounded on two sides by walls, on the third by the gateway we had just driven through, and on the fourth by another iron gate facing it. The enclosure rapidly became chaotic as the prisoners spilled out, chattering and in some cases crying.

We were being marshalled into the semblance of a queue. On one side of the enclosure a desk had been set up. Two or three women in uniform began to organise us brusquely and efficiently.

'Everybody must surrender any cash or valuables in their possession.' The announcement was made in Thai and English. Slowly, the disorderly file of people began to move past the desk, handing over money and personal treasures. I was in no mood to be co-operative. As my turn approached I watched the Thai girl ahead of me handing over a single ring. She began to cry as it disappeared, labelled, from view. I stepped up to the desk feeling very angry. The woman behind the desk pointed to my watch and some items of jewellery I was wearing.

'I'm not giving you these,' I said emphatically. The officer was inflexible.

'*Mii* (Yes), you give it. But we pass it to your Embassy for safe keeping.' My protests fell on deaf ears. Eventually I submitted, seething.

Our valuables deposited, we were herded out of the enclosure through a small door which was part of the big iron gates. We found ourselves on a pebbled path. I clutched the cardboard box which held my possessions and looked around. In the twilight, I could see trees surrounding a large compound, in which were several two-storey wooden buildings. In the nearest of these I was searched again.

'Remove your bra and pants. You can put your other clothes back on.' I was searched efficiently and very thoroughly. To add to the trauma, a stream of Thai prisoners wandered through while I was being searched, consumed with curiosity about whether a European woman was different to themselves.

These admission procedures only emphasised my situation. I was in other people's hands now; no longer the girlfriend of a charming and wealthy playboy, on my way to spend a few all-expenses-paid weeks in England – but a prisoner, to be searched, ordered around and told what I could and could not do. It was unbearable; I had revelled in money and freedom. As the dreamlike trance fell away and I began to take notice of where I was and what was happening, I was gripped by an icy fear. I had no idea what I had been sent there for; I didn't know whether I would be kept there for a long or short time; nobody had told me.

The officials began to search my possessions. As I watched helplessly, a woman appeared, a plump bespectacled lady in nightdress and flipflop sandals. 'I'm Hannah,' she said, calmly and reassuringly. She began expertly to translate what the officials were saying. 'You can't have that – that will have to go to the Embassy – yes, you can have that – and that – no, those will have to wait . . .' One of the officers held up my contact lens case. In fluent Thai, Hannah explained what contact lenses were. When she had sorted things out with the officers she took me across the grounds to another wooden building, where the prison kitchen was. 'I'll get you a cup of tea,' she said.

Hannah put the kettle on, and we sat down facing each other across a scrubbed wooden tabletop. The kitchen was a fair size, plain and unwelcoming, but the kettle boiling on the stove was a cheerful sound. I wasn't feeling very cheerful. Apart from anything else I was having difficulty keeping my eyes open.

'I'm Rita.' I thought I might as well take command of the conversation.

60

Hannah nodded. 'I know. We heard about your case when you were arrested,' she explained.

I took another look at her. 'Are you a guard or something?'

Hannah laughed: a short, loud guffaw. 'Fat chance! I live here. I'm a prisoner. Like you. Been here three and a half years.'

I was stunned. My thirty days in the police cell had seemed like a life sentence.

Hannah got up to make the tea. When she sat down she resumed: 'We figured you must have bribed your way out of it – most people get sent here after twelve days or so. Well – so here you are now. Heroin. You were the one with the heroin at the airport.'

'Yes,' I admitted.

'That's bad.'

'Oh,' I said, nettled, 'it's not as bad as it looks. You see, they're not holding me on a drugs charge.'

Hannah gave me an odd look. She spooned sugar into her tea. 'And what exactly are they holding you on, then? They don't send people out here for nothing.'

'Article 21. That's breach of the peace. My lawyer's going to get me out on bail on Monday.'

Her body shook with an enormous gale of laughter. 'You silly little cow!' she roared. 'Article 21? That's a Martial Law Order – everything from treason to traffic offences! They can do anything to you under that order, *anything*, do you realise? "Not as bad it looks . . ."!'

I paled. *It's happened*, I panicked. *I'm here for ever. I'm going to be shot. Oh God, what's going on?*

'But I'm innocent!' The words came tumbling out frantically. 'I didn't do it, it wasn't my heroin – I didn't know about it, you see it was –'

'Don't give us any of that stuff,' said Hannah, not unkindly. 'We don't want any of that. You're in prison now with the rest of us. We're all innocent in here, you ask any of us.' She got up from her chair. 'I'll show you where the wash-house is.'

She produced soap and a towel. 'You can borrow these.' We went to the wash-house. Hannah indicated a long low trough, like a stone horse-trough. A pipe above one end trickled water. I couldn't see any taps. 'There's no water in the trough,' I said. She picked up a bucket.

'You fill this from the pipe, and you wash like this –' she mimed pouring the water over herself.

It was only slightly less adequate than the dipper-shower in the police station. I was hot and sweaty after the journey and was longing for a wash. Gratefully, I peeled off my sticky clothes. Clad only in my pants, I reached for the bucket. A snort from Hannah made me turn round. She was staring at me in vexation. 'No, no!' she said. 'That's not how you do it. You mustn't go naked. The Thais don't like it.'

I didn't know about the extreme modesty of the Thai people, or that nudity is something that they avoid. I just got angry, ignored Hannah, and had my wash. 'Stupid animals!' I muttered vindictively as I scrubbed myself. 'There's no understanding them. We're all females together, after all.' Hannah watched me glacially.

After my wash I felt a bit better, and Hannah didn't mention the nudity question again. She took me back to the kitchen and made another pot of tea.

'I'll see about getting you a decent place to sleep,' she remarked as the tea brewed. 'Some of them are worse than others.'

I had no doubt that Hannah would be able to fix it; she seemed that type.

We finished our tea. I rubbed my eyes and yawned. 'Come on,' said Hannah sympathetically. 'I'll take you to where you'll be sleeping.'

I collected my cardboard box and followed her across the grass to another of the two storey wooden buildings.

A few guards were the only people to be seen. We climbed up the steps to an open-sided landing, from which various doors led off. Hannah opened one of them. 'That's the room prisoners usually go in when they come straight from court.'

It was terrible. It looked as though there were about a hundred women in the dormitory, sprawled on the floor, sitting talking, sleeping or arguing. The heat was overpowering: though it was a large room, it was crowded. It smelt of too many hot people too close together. Hannah laughed. 'Don't worry, I've found you a better place.' She took me to another room. It was smaller; there were less than thirty women in it, all Asian. They looked up in curiosity as I came in. Behind me, Hannah said 'Good night,' and closed the door. I clutched my box like a shield, and looked around.

A fat woman of about fifty got to her feet. She looked more Chinese than Thai. She was wearing baggy Chinese trousers and a blouse which struggled to contain her huge bosom. She was pointing at me. I stood uncertainly at the door. She gave a wide, gappy smile and said something in Thai. When I didn't reply, she advanced towards me, gesticulating.

'*Mama-san*!' She pointed to herself. The word is a useful Chinese expression meaning anything from a brothel Madame to the woman who supervises the girls in a night-club. I knew the word well. I gathered she was the person in charge.

'Where's my spot?' I demanded harshly. The floor looked full of mats and blankets spread out for bedding. Each place was occupied. The Mama-san beckoned one of the Thai girls. 'Spot?' she queried. The girl spoke rapidly in Thai. The Mama-san's frown cleared. 'Spot!' she announced. 'There!' She pointed to the far end of the room. 'There – for you, there.'

I looked at the three floorboards which were my bed. Next to them a really filthy woman was sleeping. Lice crawled on her clothes and her skin. Shuddering, I laid a few things on the floor for bedding and lowered myself gingerly down. The filthy woman stirred in her sleep. I turned the other way. A Thai girl in her twenties smiled at me and said a few words in her own language. I ignored her and stared at the ceiling, remembering the antiquated but effective fans that had hung in the police captain's office. Only a naked light bulb hung from this ceiling.

There was no way I could sleep. Angles of my body ached against the floor, and the other women touched me inquisitively from time to time. After a few minutes I felt a stinging pinprick in my thigh; it was my first mosquito-bite. Horrified, I saw things crawling out of the gaps between the floorboards. I pulled a sweater from my box and wrapped it round my scalp. It only made the heat more difficult to endure.

The light was not turned off that night. It wasn't turned off any night, and for the whole time I was in Lard Yao, I longed for the luxury of a dark bedroom. That first night I had no defences against the heat, the light, the mosquitoes or the lice. Others in the room talked and moved around noisily late into the night; my body ached; I thought I would never be able to close my eyes, but tiredness won. Soon I was dozing fitfully, and by morning had fallen asleep.

8 Betrayed

*The crackdown on drug smugglers in
Thailand has come in conjunction with an
attempt . . . to re-educate the hill tribesmen
in the notorious 'Golden Triangle' of
Burma, Thailand, and Laos . . . the Thai
spokesman said 'Now that the supply of
opium and other drugs from the Triangle is
drying up, smugglers have been running
drugs into Thailand from other parts of the
world.'*

Lancashire Evening Telegraph, 31 May
1977

I woke early, stiff but partly rested, despite the numerous bites that covered my arms and legs. A few of the
others were awake. One or two smiled at me; the rest
just stared, openly curious. The Mama-san was awake.
She grinned broadly when she saw me, and said something to her neighbour, who turned to me when she had
finished: 'She says you are not to be angry about where
you sleep. Very full of people now. When other girls go
out, there is more room for you.' The Mama-san nodded
furiously. She took a small tin from her clothing and
noisily inhaled a pinch of black snuff. Then she sighed
heavily and relapsed into her thoughts.

I sat on the floor and examined the room. It was very
spartan, with wooden walls and floor. At the end at

which I was sleeping, there was a roughly-screened cement trough and a Thai-style toilet. The occupants of the room slept surrounded by piles of clothes and various belongings.

Half an hour passed. Then there was the sound of doors being unlocked. Everybody rushed out. One of the Thai girls said to me, 'You must take your things with you. Door not open after we go. What you need, you take.' I hurriedly gathered everything together in my box. I was one of the last to leave; a guard stood ready to lock the door again when we had gone. I had no idea what I was supposed to do next, so I decided to go to see Hannah again.

In the daylight I was able to see the prison properly. It was about the size of a large football field. The block of offices in which we had arrived in the van the previous night was a two-storey building, with the main gate in the centre. There were, I found out from Hannah, various offices and interview rooms there, and the Warden's office. The compound itself was surrounded by a wall topped by an electric fence; it was about thirty feet high in all. Houses outside the walls later proved to be guards' houses. The prison buildings themselves were grouped in a rectangle, separated by grassed areas and cultivated patches. Round the perimeter of the prison was an open sewer. Vegetables were growing nearby.

I found Hannah working in the kitchen. She nodded a greeting and waved me to a chair.

'What do I do?' I asked helplessly.

'Have you had a wash?' asked Hannah. I shook my head.

'You can use my things again. Can you find your way? Anyway, follow the crowd.'

By the time I got to the wash-house the queue of people had diminished. Standing at the entrance of the last in the line of toilet cubicles was a prisoner who was obviously in some sort of command; she was staring grimly at us, arms folded. When a prisoner tried to take an extra bucket of water, the stern-faced girl barked an order, and the attempt was abandoned. Nobody seemed to be taking very much notice of her. The Thai prisoners were more interested in me, giggled and pointing. One or two of them tried to start a conversation with me; I grunted non-committedly in reply. I was more discreet in my washing this time, reasoning that I may as well get through the weekend without too much aggravation if I could.

When I returned, Hannah made some coffee. While she was doing this, the heavy reverberations of a struck gong sounded in another building. 'What on earth is that?' I asked.

'Breakfast time,' she said. I looked out. From all sides, women were converging on the refectory. As the queue formed, the chant of Buddhist devotions began – a rising and falling rhythmic incantation. Still chanting, the queue shuffled forward into the room. Nothing would have induced me to go in.

'Not hungry?' enquired Hannah sardonically.

I shuddered. 'I can't take it . . . all those people . . . how long does the chanting go on for?'

'Oh, they quit after a while,' she said. 'Here . . .' she placed bread, butter and jam before me. 'Not prison rations, I'm afraid. You'll have to fend for yourself if you want to eat like this all the time. Of course, there's the prison food . . .' She gestured towards the refectory, where breakfast was now well advanced and animated conversation had replaced the chanting.

'What do they give you?'

'Oh, rice . . . vegetables . . . fish . . . it's wholesome enough. Just not so interesting. Dull, in fact.'

'Tell me what all these buildings are.'

Hannah reached for pencil and paper. I munched

67

bread and jam as she sketched. 'I'll draw you a map
. . . right. Now, here's the gate where you came in last
night. Over here we've got Building No.1. That's where
the long-stay people are. Women with over ten years.
Downstairs is the factory.'

'Factory?'

'Sewing workshop . . . we call them factories. Building No.2 is where the "on trial" people go, and a few
lucky ones who should be in Building No.1. That's
where you are. Downstairs is the laundry and the library
– you'll find a few English books there. People leave
them when they go out. Oh, and there's the beauty
salon.'

'What?'

'Oh, yes. Mind you, it's not cheap, and you can't
depend on it. The results are unpredictable. You can use
it if you've got the money. Just don't rely on things
turning out how you want them . . . Now here, is Building 3, where the light sentences go. Six months to a year,
that sort of thing. Another factory underneath . . . and
if they can't find space for you anywhere else, you go in
Building No.4. Not a good idea. The nursery's
underneath.'

Later when I visited the nursery I saw what she meant.
It was in the heat of the afternoon. Mothers were changing their babies, lines of cloth-wrap nappies were hanging up to dry, still more were waiting to be dealt with,
and there was a din of crying. The noise and smell were
awful. Thai people are clean by nature, but you can't fill
a room with so many babies and expect it to smell nice.

Hannah added two more rectangles to her map: the
hospital building and another sewing factory. She added
a pond beside the hospital. 'And that's it,' she finished.
'Lard Yao Women's Prison. Welcome.'

Something was bothering me. 'Hannah – you said I
was on trial. You mean some kind of probation?'

She laughed grimly, removed her spectacles, and rubbed the bridge of her nose. It was a habit with her I'd already noticed. 'They sure didn't tell you much, did they? You're on trial. That means your case is being heard before the courts. You'll go to goodness knows how many preliminary hearings and one day they'll tell you how many years you got. Then you're not on trial any more. Then, you're sentenced. Now, you're on trial and you live in Building No.2. OK?'

I gripped the edge of the table. I could feel the blood rushing to my face. 'But I'm going out on bail next Monday . . . Mr. Sorochai . . .'

Hannah shook her head in frustration. 'Look, honey, face facts. There's no way you're going out of this place on Monday. They're not going to give you bail. That was one hell of a lot of heroin you were carrying. Three and a half kilos! There's kids in here that had fifty grammes of the stuff. Their lawyers can't get them out on bail. Who's going to pull strings for you?'

My heart was pounding. 'I'm English, I'm a foreigner,' I stammered. 'They can't do that to me.'

'I'm German-American,' said Hannah. 'They did it to me.' She laughed. 'I wasn't carrying any stuff, either.'

Monday came and went and, just as Hannah had said, no word came from Mr. Sorochai. I realised that it was going to be some time before things got sorted out. I remembered what Mr. Sorochai had told me about the slow judicial procedure in Thailand. Things looked very bad.

I worked the events of the past weeks over and over in my mind. As days turned into weeks, I pieced the story together. There was still no word from James. I asked Hannah what she thought, and she was characteristically blunt.

'You're a naive young fool,' she said crisply.

'But it was Simon, **not James** . . .'

'And James had never met Simon, I suppose?' asked Hannah sarcastically. 'Don't be a silly goose, Rita. Face facts.'

After a number of such conversations I began to realise that, however much it hurt, the truth was that James had been involved in the heroin planting. I couldn't believe it at first, but gradually my thoughts began to alternate between stark disbelief and a cold certainty which, try as I might, I couldn't argue away. The comments of lawyers and Embassy officials visiting me provided missing pieces of the jigsaw. As the story sank in, I was forced to believe it.

James and Simon had set me up well and truly. During that long lazy afternoon at the hotel, while I was blissfully luxuriating, Simon had fixed the false bottoms into my holdalls and packed them with heroin. The young Chinese prisoner, Alan Soon, had been Simon's spy, flying on the same plane and keeping an eye on me to make sure that things were going as planned. His role was that of 'escort'; I was the unwitting 'courier'.

In fact, it seemed, things had gone wrong from the start. Word had apparently been sent from the Hong Kong police informing the Thai authorities that we were going to Bangkok and would be attempting to leave on the Air France flight AF-193. I never found out what led the Hong Kong authorities to send the message in the first place, though it was rumoured that somebody had tipped them off.

The police had been waiting for us at Don Muang Airport; they searched Soon's suitcase before I went through the baggage check, but found nothing. He was taken into custody at the same time as I was, which explained why he was in the room when my bags were opened.

70

Simon Lo and Alan Soon were deported from Thailand after their arrest and detention, as 'undesirable aliens'. It was said that they had bribed their way out of trouble. I believed it. I would have believed anything of those two. Well before it was all officially confirmed by my lawyers, I knew that all three men had used me without any thought about what would happen if I was caught. It was only the freak tip-off which had involved them in the arrest at all. It was I who had been the mug, carefully chosen by James and cynically shepherded by Simon, the one who was to carry the heroin, and, if necessary, carry the can.

Strangely, my first anger was directed against myself. How could I have been so stupid? I was the one who knew about men, who could pick out the gropers and the charmers and deal with them expertly. I was the smart one, the traveller; how could I have fallen for such an easy trick?

Then my anger at myself passed, to be replaced by a bruising hurt. Was it possible, I asked myself incredulously, that James had been so loving and considerate, knowing all the time that he was going to use me like this? The answer had to be yes. *But I loved him*! I cried, thinking it through in the long hot nights. Memories of other nights spent together, of embraces in the hills and good times in restaurants and clubs, flashed across my mind, and try as I might I couldn't erase the memory of James's handsome, heartless smile. It was the one time in my life I have really understood the way a murderer must feel. I would have killed him. But he was back in Hong Kong, at the Kokusai, at all the places we'd been together, and I was locked in Lard Yao.

It helped to be angry; it was a vent for my feelings. But there were times when the anger was spent, and all that was left was a desolate, empty misery. I'd loved James. We were going to live together. I'd built what

71

hopes I had for the future round him. Now it was all finished. Now there was nothing except my family, and they were half a world away.

9 Jailers

In the daytime it's not too bad, as there are
four other foreigners here . . . After I'm
locked in at five pm, I'm just with Thai
women, and not being able to speak and
share their jokes, is a bit lonely, and it's
very rare that anyone speaks even a few
words of English. So you see why I'm
trying to learn the language, I'm not doing
too bad, but I'm far from a conversation
yet.

Letter to Auntie Margaret and Tom, 10
July 1977

I was gradually beginning to find out what was going on.
I received visits from the British Embassy, lawyers, and
various officials. It emerged that I would be dealt with
under standard Thai legal procedure, which involved
regular visits to the courts to comply with the 'holding
procedure' – I had to sign documents each time which
held me for a further period. My trial would consist of
several appearances; at the preliminary hearing, the
police would give their evidence. I would be allowed an
interpreter, and I would be required to plead guilty or
not guilty.

The preliminary hearing was set for 6th June. If I got
bail, at least I wouldn't have to sit it out in prison.

Oh God, I screamed silently, *why are you doing this to me?*

I was sitting on the grass, watching the other prisoners. It was just after the evening meal.

A few yards away a tall Thai girl, light-skinned and attractive, was squatting. She was working at a piece of embroidery, her hands drawing long delicate threads from a complicated design. She frowned as she worked, and occasionally drew on a cigarette which she was sharing with another prisoner. Her name was Muur; Hannah had pointed her out to me. Muur's work ended up in the prison shop, where it was sought after for its fine quality. I had only said hello to her when I was briefly introduced. She spoke good English, but we hadn't much to talk about. Muur was in for twenty-five years. She had killed her husband with a table-knife.

Near her was Waneeda. Waneeda was short and stocky. Her arms and hands were covered in crude, home-made tattoos. She wasn't doing anything; she was sitting smoking, looking into space with a vacant expression. Hannah had pointed her out to me as well. Waneeda was a heroin addict. She had been in Lard Yao thirty times. She was twenty-eight.

There were many murderers and many addicts in Lard Yao. After a few weeks I didn't think twice about it, except for the frequent outbursts of violence and tension. In any case, I didn't want anything to do with my fellow-prisoners. I despised the Thai people; not only the judges and police who had put me in Lard Yao and the guards who were now running my life, but also the ordinary people in the prison with me, whose different way of life and priorities made them targets of my scorn and anger. I wrote letters full of bitterness. I was critical of everybody who tried to help me. I scorned my lawyers, the British government and its representatives, the Thai authorities and just about everybody else. I raged at them all: in letters home, in public at anybody who was within earshot; and also I raged at God.

I knew about God. I'd been to Sunday School regularly from the age of four up to eleven or twelve. My sisters and I went to a little chapel every Sunday afternoon near our home. Our parents didn't go, but we were regular attenders on Sundays and at the Girls' Club meetings during the week. One summer I even went on a Sunday School camping holiday. When I came back I'd made a 'commitment to Christ', as they called it. I wasn't very clear about it all – I didn't understand all the talk about being 'saved' – but I was curious, and stayed behind after one of the evening talks to learn more. Despite my uncertainty about the details, I felt that something very important and worthwhile had happened. In addition to that, I was confirmed. This came about because a friend of mine went to the local Anglican church. When she began to talk about 'being confirmed' and going to 'confirmation classes', I thought, 'That sounds interesting – I'll do that too.'

Yes, I knew about God. I was a law-abiding English girl, who tried to be a good daughter and not hurt anybody on purpose. I always considered myself a Christian. I continued to do so even after the Sunday School and church-going faded away – which they did, as I entered my teens. I believed in God: he was basically good and kind, and preferred people to be good and kind as well. I believed in God as creator of the universe, too; I couldn't go along with the theory that human existence was merely the result of an accident. The complexity of our own bodies denied that. I had a great admiration for Jesus Christ, too. I didn't know very much about Christianity.

A faith like this was scarcely enough to support me in prison, and as I began to realise the full seriousness of what had happened, the last shreds of my habit-formed

Christianity fell away. All that was left was a fierce anger against God. If he existed – if he was good and kind – why had he allowed me to get into this mess? I hadn't done anything wrong; it wasn't my heroin in the bags. Why wasn't Simon in prison instead of me? Where was James at this moment? Why had God allowed him to use me as he had?

It's not fair! I shouted at God. *Why me? What have I ever done to deserve this? And what about James and Simon? Why have you let them get away with it?*

Outwardly I put on a brave face, writing to my mother that 'the bastards won't get me down, no matter how hard they try.' Inwardly, I raged away.

Look at all these people! I stormed. *What chance have they had? Stuck in here . . . If this is the way you run the world, I'm not interested. I don't want to know.*

To onlookers I must have seemed to be adapting fairly well to the prison routine; I kept myself clean and tidy, and I fitted into prison life quickly. I expected to be leaving soon, and I intended to keep myself in shape.

The worst thing was that there was no freedom of action. If you were supposed to be at a particular place at a particular time, there at that time you had to be. Out-of-doors it was pleasant enough – often, sitting on the grass with the sun shining I thought how unbearable it would have been to have been in prison in the middle of a city, miles away from growing things. But it was a prison regime, with tedium and rules. The problem with the rule books was not that they were rigidly enforced – quite the opposite. A rule could be rigidly enforced in one situation, and then ignored in an apparently identical one. Sometimes you were allowed to leave your room at night for a while; other nights it was impossible – 'against the rules'. You weren't allowed to have eyebrow tweezers with square edges; they were a potential weapon. You were allowed, on the other hand, to accumulate as many glass bottles as you liked.

I attempted to argue with the guards at first.

'Of course I can have this box of chocolates. It was sent in by the Embassy. It's got my name on it.'

'Not allowed,' was the stolid response.

'But I was allowed to have the box that came in last week for me. If it's allowed one week, why isn't it allowed this week?'

'Not allowed, not allowed.'

In the end I accepted that when they gazed at me with that blank incomprehension there was no use trying to argue further.

The guards were always around. They varied from quite pleasant women to vicious disciplinarians. Some of them were feared. One, known as 'The Motorcycle', always wore blue sunglasses, whatever the weather. When the Motorcycle was around you watched your step. She carried a swagger stick, and used it.

'Nightingale to report to the interview block!'

The loudspeaker crackled imperatively. I had quickly become used to its continuous music interrupted by official orders. Thai people have a constant background of music in their lives; prison was no exception. I made my way to the gatehouse block, taking care not to walk too quickly. No point in seeming over-keen.

An elderly man was sitting in the bare office. As the guard opened the door, he rose to his feet with elaborate courtesy. The guard took up her position impassively by the door. The man shook hands gravely.

'Albert Lyman,' he said. His voice was a loud Southern drawl. 'Honoured to make your acquaintance, Ma'am.'

I blinked. He wore a lightweight suit without a tie. He was almost bald, and slightly stooped. He gestured elegantly towards the other chair. He seemed to have appeared from another century.

'Who are you?' I demanded.

He pointed a finger at himself. 'I am the senior partner, Ma'am, of Tilleke and Gibbins. Mr. Sorochai is my colleague.' He tipped his open briefcase onto the table between us. A sheaf of papers fell out. Peering at them with watery eyes, Mr. Lyman selected one and scrutinised it. 'I have taken a great interest in your case. A very great interest.'

'When are you going to get me out?' My voice was harsh and tense. Mr. Lyman looked up in surprise.

'When? Why, as soon as possible.'

'When's possible? Why can't I get bail?'

Mr. Lyman caressed his lapels. 'My dear, it's difficult, a case like this. You must understand, there are many things involved. There sure are. Why, there are papers to sign, the police have to present their case . . . it all takes time.'

'Do you know what it's like in here?' The words tumbled out. 'Do you think I want to be here one minute longer than I have to be?' The guard stood tranquilly at the door. I didn't know how good her English was and I didn't care. 'There are thirty of us in that dormitory. I want to get out. Now.'

Mr. Lyman sat back, his expression one of hurt surprise. 'But we will get you out,' he said. He rose to his feet. 'We'll get you free, li'l honey!' he declaimed. 'We'll get you outta here!'

He gathered his papers together. 'You'll have a visit from Mr. Puttri. He'll be representing you in court.'

'Puttri? Who's he?'

'Mr. Puttri Kovanonda. He is my colleague, and he is Thai. Consequently he is legally allowed to speak for you in court.'

'I thought you were my lawyer.' It was becoming impossibly confusing.

'Only Thai nationals are allowed to speak in court.' He brightened. 'But I'll be working on your case and preparing your defence. Yes Ma'am, we'll get you out, don't you worry about that. You'll be free soon. You'll be seeing a lot of me, li'l honey.'

He grasped my hand and shook it warmly. Then he was gone. The guard stepped forward. We walked back into the compound.

My mind was a turmoil. I wasn't going to get bail, I wasn't going to be released immediately; I was going to have to go to court, and Albert Lyman wasn't even going to be allowed to speak on my behalf. *Oh God*, I thought, *why are you doing this to me?*

By now I was writing home and receiving letters from my family. I filled pages with accounts of Albert Lyman, 'an old American fool who is definitely gone senile.' He later became one of my dearest friends. He was head of the leading law firm in Bangkok and was widely respected as a lawyer. His only fault was that he misread my anger and tried to enthuse me out of depression. He tackled my case with a fiery crusading zeal, took an intensely personal interest in it, and veered between black despair and buoyant optimism as the court reports alternated between good and bad news. I knew none of this then, suffered him in frustrated silence, and struck up a better relationship with his assistant Leonie who sometimes came to prison with the lawyers.

My life settled into a dreary pattern. The day began with the unlocking of the dormitory doors at six, and until five in the evening the dormitories were prohibited. Everything we might need during the day had to be taken out with us in the morning. Still in pyjamas, I had

79

to take washbag, towel, and clothes with me. Every prisoner carried a similar bundle. That was one of the things that most got me down. A common grumble among the prisoners was that some had more things than others and were taking up too much space. But how much do you need to live? You had to carry any special food like a tin of meat or packet of noodles. The Thai prisoners, who didn't drink coffee, didn't collect the morning ration of hot water and so were less laden. But everyone needed a bucket, or preferably two, for washing.

It was a gnawing grumble of prison life. Often, picking up my bundle of possessions yet again, I longed for somewhere to put it all. 'If I had one little locker, just one, that I could leave things in!' But there were no lockers. When important visitors came and the prison was tidied up for their benefit, everything had to be concealed. Finding places was a perennial headache. In the end it was easier to pay another prisoner to find somewhere.

So, hot and sweaty and clutching our bundles, we were let out at six. The favoured prisoners, who helped the guards and did various prison tasks, were let out first, which was considered a great privilege. When they had washed, the rest of us had our turn. There was a pitched battle as we struggled to fill our buckets from the pipe, but there was no alternative; it was impossible to do without the morning bath, the nights were so hot. Afterwards, those who had paid the night before for hot water for coffee and ice for the drinking water went to collect it.

At about seven the loudspeakers began relaying Thai classical music and opera. This normal aspect of life in Thailand added to the general clamour of the prison. When one day there was a power failure the loudspeakers were beautifully silent (and that night, with the light off in the dormitory, I had the best sleep I'd had for weeks).

Like other foreign prisoners, I never joined in the rush for the refectory as the gong struck to announce breakfast. There were two sittings for each meal, and over two hundred prisoners in each. I usually ate in the kitchen. Breakfast was bread and jam or something like that which I'd bought. As I ate I heard the droning of the chanted devotions, followed shortly by an uproar of conversation. The staple diet provided by the prison was red rice, vegetable stew and meat or fish. The meals weren't too bad nutritionally, and many of the prisoners grew fat on the rice, but to my prejudiced eye the food looked unappetising. Also it was boring. The Thai prisoners supplemented their diet with food brought in by visitors, and I bought all my own food. I was able to eat fairly well. I had about 2,000 francs on me when I was arrested (about 200 US dollars), and that was put in my 'prison account' when I arrived. The Embassy staff changed it to baht for me, and I was then able to use the prison bank which issued a coupon currency valid at the prison shop.

This was a building in three parts. In one section you could buy toiletries, writing materials, and miscellaneous things like condensed milk. There was also a sort of delicatessen, which sold such things as bananas cooked in rice and wrapped in banana leaves and also unusual fruit like mangoes when in season. In a third part cooked food was on sale, and it was there that I learned my first sentences of Thai. Each evening the menu for the next day was posted up and it was written in Thai. You had to give in your plate accompanied with your order and collect it next day. Each morning I found out how well I had translated the list the night before. I bought myself the occasional peculiar meal, but there were always plenty of people who would help to dispose of food which I didn't fancy.

Breakfast over, it was time to go to work. As an 'on trial' prisoner, I wasn't required to work in the prison workshops. I worked with Hannah in the kitchen, making biscuits and cakes for the prison shop. It was a good place to work. There were plenty of titbits. I paid a weekly sum to Hannah, and in return had my meals provided. Also, she was able to get various delicacies sent in from outside. I didn't have to use the shop to buy food at all.

I got on quite well with Hannah. I'd never met anybody like her before. Characteristically pessimistic, she did not expect much of prison life and as a result was fairly comfortable. She chafed constantly at the rules and regulations. She had been married in prison, to the man she'd lived with before her arrest; they weren't even allowed to kiss at the ceremony. Her husband was serving an identical sentence in the men's prison over the road. She was allowed to send him meals but visits between them were out of the question. She had been very wealthy, but now her only regular income was an ex-serviceman's pension which her husband received.

I think she quite liked me, because I wasn't a drug addict. I'm no great intellectual, but some of the girls who came in were so hung up on drugs that they were incapable of stringing any sort of conversation together. For my part, I found that Hannah's dour pessimism matched my own mood of bitterness. She tended to expect the worst out of life, and I responded to this.

Working in the kitchen, besides being a good source of food, solved one of the worst problems of my new life. It gave me somewhere to go during the day. That was another dreadful thing about being a prisoner. If you weren't working, there was nothing to do but sit round the place. The duties were straightforward. Each day there were tasks to be done for each day's cooking. On a good day they were finished at about half past three. Prison lunch was at noon, but we usually grabbed ours when we could. Midday was chaotic at Lard Yao because the prisoners had to get what they wanted at the shop before two o'clock (or that day's issue of coupons became invalid), and then the lunch gong sounded. As there were over 1,000 prisoners the chaos can be imagined. Hannah and I stayed well out of it.

When work was over, it was necessary to find somebody who would stand in the queue for you for the evening bath. Usually somebody would do this for payment. You could usually find somebody to do any prison chore for a small sum. By evening the water was less plentiful in the pipe, and it was essential to secure a place in the queue. This was a sociable time of day, after the evening meal, when everybody was in their nightwear and bathed. For Hannah and me it was particularly good because we didn't have to queue at the shop for food. People chatted, sat on the grass, watched the numerous children playing, and generally relaxed until the gong sounded for bedtime.

Just before five o'clock the Thai prisoners had their evening devotions, which meant more chanting; and before re-entering the dormitory the prisoners had to sing the Thai national anthem. I kept my mouth firmly shut.

Because I was 'on trial', I had no more duties after five. Those who had were called out to do things like cleaning the sewers or receiving new prisoners. That was what Hannah was doing when she greeted me on my first night. On weekdays there was great excitement at six when the court van arrived, and those not locked in their rooms brought back news for the rest of us.

'Hey! There's another *farang* (foreigner) come in!'

A babble of interest: 'What's she like? How old?'

'Well, she's pretty, this one . . .'

A guard was on duty in each building to let people back in after their work, and by half-past nine everybody was finally locked in.

The day was over. Those who were able to, slept. The rest chattered or paced restlessly to and fro. Smoking was forbidden, but nobody heeded it, though fire was a constant fear. Nobody cared to contemplate what would happen to the prisoners locked in the wooden buildings if a fire began. Getting a light for a cigarette was difficult. I had a petrol lighter, for which I stole petrol from the prison lawnmower. The usual method was to get a light from an adjoining dormitory by passing your unlit cigarette through a hole in the wall – the lighted one was never passed through to you, and by the time you got your own back it had been half smoked already.

The more tender-hearted guards often came up to the dormitories for a chat. It wasn't unusual to find them pouring out their troubles to you. Even though I was preoccupied with my own troubles and bitterness, I found myself feeling sympathy for them as they complained of hard work, low pay and hostility. But I conscientiously refused to allow this to distract me from my anger. I wasn't their friend and counsellor. They were still prison guards, part of the system I had sworn to resist. 'The bastards won't get me down,' I had written to my mother. And I was determined they wouldn't.

10 Maria

Dear Ann,

*Wow! Are you well thought of here! Your
recipe for booze caused so much excitement,
we were all (foreigners) dashing around
madly stealing this and that. Whatever it
comes out like I assure it'll be drunk.*

Letter, early summer 1977

Three beds away two girls were embracing under a blanket, oblivious of the crowded dormitory. I hardly noticed
them. I'd been in Lard Yao over a month now, and had
got over my first shock at finding that lesbianism, as in
any female prison, was common. I had more important
things on my mind than them. I was writing a letter to
my Mum.

My biro flew across the paper. There was a lot to tell
her. Balancing the pad on my knee, I scrawled furiously.

'. . . The Consul came yesterday – what a performance, the Warden had us up most of the night cleaning,
and yours truly was thoroughly briefed . . . she's probably gone away thinking the place is a garden of Eden.
I must admit the parts she saw, the garden and kitchen,
do look nice; but the point is I'm not worried about
conditions here, I just want a fair trial and to get out
. . .'

I sighed, and put my biro down. It was always difficult

writing to Mum. I wanted to reassure her I was all right, that she needn't worry; but also I wanted to tell her the facts, because I knew other people in England saw my letters.

I looked around. It was about seven o'clock. Francoise, a French girl I'd got to know a little, was combing her curly hair. I envied her for her looks. She was extremely pretty, with beautiful olive skin.

She saw me looking and smiled. 'Tell them all about this terrible place, Rita.' Her eyes widened in mock horror. 'Don't miss anything out'.

I grinned. 'Not enough paper,' I retorted. Francoise returned to her combing. Unlike many who came to Lard Yao, she was very sensitive and never pried into my background or why I was there. I picked up the biro again', grateful that Francoise had not asked who I was writing to. I didn't want to talk about it.

I decided to finish the letter cheerfully; I'd sent enough depressing ones recently. 'I've had a medical check-up. I had to go to the men's prison for it. What a treat, to see males again! The guard was like a hawk, but I managed to get a few words with an English guy, who'd waited all morning to see me, he heard through the grapevine that the English girl was coming over . . . my blood pressure's a bit low, but that's nothing. I had a chest X-ray and gave blood samples and had my teeth checked . . . everything OK I'm sure. So don't worry, I'm as fit as a fiddle – at least I will be when I walk out of this place . . .'

I put the letter down and stretched out on my bed, flinging my arm over my eyes to shade them from the light. They were moist. *Come on, girl*, I scolded myself. *You don't have to let everybody know you're upset.* I wiped my eyes with my forearm. As I opened them again Francoise glanced sympathetically at me.

Keys rattled. Standing at the door was a guard and a tall woman in her mid-forties. I remembered some of the girls saying earlier, when the prison van came, that there was a new foreign prisoner. The foreign prisoners were put in the better dormitories, where we were regarded by the Thai prisoners with a mixture of curiosity, fear, and envy.

The Mama-san was dabbing herself from a little bottle of green liquid, her favourite remedy for aches and pains. She stuffed the bottle into her pocket and shuffled to her feet. She greeted the newcomer, who stared at her blankly. The Mama-san tried a few words of English. The tall woman remained silent. She didn't respond to Thai or Chinese either. Francoise got up and gently took from the woman the box of possessions she was carrying.

'*Parlez-vous Francaise, Madame?*'

The woman's hunted expression cleared slightly. She nodded and spoke in an accent even I could recognise as execrable. '*Oui. Mais non l'Anglaise.*'

'*Comment vous appelez-vous?*'

'*Maria. Espagnole.*' As Francoise placed the box on the floor, Maria from Spain sat down heavily and stared at us all.

She looked sad and out of place in the dormitory. We were all in our night clothes. She was wearing a floral print dress and high-heeled shoes. She was very neat, her short thick black hair well styled. She was amply built, but carried herself well, with a regal air.

Francoise tried to draw her into conversation, but the only response was either silence or floods of Spanish. She was given a place next to mine on the floor. I was still in the place given me when I arrived – farthest away from the toilet. Maria looked incredulously at the bare boards. I gave her a blanket. Francoise tried to give some simple information about when we had to get up and so on, but didn't have much success.

As I dropped off to sleep that night Maria was still lying with her eyes open, shifting restlessly. I tried to catch her eye and comfort her, but her gaze was fixed on something in her hand. It was a rosary. Her lips were moving silently as she passed the beads between her fingers. I shrugged and went to sleep. I had enough problems of my own.

'*Sodom y Gomorrah! Sodom y Gomorrah!*'

I sat up, panicking. Maria was wailing, her head buried in her hands. '*Sodom y Gomorrah! Sodom y Gomorrah!*' she howled, over and over again. The other girls woke up and complained bitterly. Francoise came over, but Maria would only speak Spanish.

Eventually we persuaded her to tell us what the matter was. Stuttering incoherently, she pointed a trembling finger across the room. Following her horrified gaze, I saw that the two girls were still in bed together. They were grinning, their arms round each other. Clearly Maria had only just realised what was happening. I laughed. 'Just go to sleep and let 'em get on with it,' I advised her drowsily. 'It goes on all the time here . . .'

Though I got over my initial shock at the lesbianism in the prison, I never became used to it. I was often pestered by the more domineering girls. I didn't get involved because I wasn't interested. I couldn't believe how quickly – often in a matter of days – normal heterosexuals, finding themselves in an all-women prison, would strike up these relationships. Also I was so angry with everybody that I wanted no relationships beyond superficial ones.

Another unpleasant aspect of prison life was the number of prisoners who had serious drug problems. Most were inside for drug offences, and there were always several undergoing involuntary withdrawal. You couldn't get heroin into our prison.

One night after the van had been, a guard beckoned me from the door of the dormitory. 'There's a French girl arrived, she will have to sleep in here.'

'I don't speak French.' I was unwilling to lose even a few feet of floor space in that crammed room.

'Doesn't matter.' The guard was already bringing her in.

When I saw her, I thought: this one's going to have a bad time. One glance showed her to be a heavy heroin user. She was shivering. She didn't say a word to me, and my greeting was met with a resentful silence. I looked at Maria pleadingly: she could speak French. Maria sat rigidly aloof and avoided my eyes.

I found some bedding for her and generally offered help. She hunched into herself, stared round with blank, tired eyes, and lay down.

There is a stench that comes from heroin users who are on withdrawal. It's like a wild animal's, as characteristic as the smell of death on a corpse. Anyone whose bed was near the new girl's moved as far away as she could. But the weird smell soon spread across the dormitory, hanging over us like a fog. Clean and neat herself, Maria couldn't stand it. She muttered fretfully in barely audible Spanish and retreated to a safe distance, watching the girl balefully.

For a few minutes she lay rigid on the floor. Then she began thrashing around, kicking those within reach and waving her arms. A hollow ragged scream escaped her throat, cutting through the prison clamour, so that suddenly the guards reappeared. 'Do something!' they ordered, as if by greeting the girl I had become solely responsible for her. 'What can I do?' I shouted back. 'I can't speak French!'

She howled and thrashed for the next three nights, until we were exhausted and furious. In the daytime she was uncontrollable, but at least she wasn't in the enclosed dormitory. Having had some nursing training I felt I should be helping her, but I didn't know what to do. Her sickness wasn't like flu or bronchitis. Eventually we had to ask the guards to put her in with other prisoners who had been through the same experience. Maybe they could help her.

So she was transferred. Her new room-mates gave her cold water drenchings and sat by her for hours, thumping her rhythmically on the back with their fists. Apparently, it was an effective treatment.

After she and a few others had come to our dormitory, and we had lived through nights full of their screaming, vomiting, diarrhoea, and that inescapable stench, we begged Hannah to persuade the guards to put them in the large dormitory instead. We told ourselves that it was for their good, that they would be better looked after there, and full of gratitude to Hannah we went back to our relatively peaceful evenings.

So far as I know, nobody died in Lard Yao from drug withdrawal. I often saw girls who were going through it. They couldn't control their legs, and looked as if they were on a bicycle. They couldn't believe that the authorities were not prepared to help them with drugs – not even an aspirin.

After a month or two such sights faded into the background, unnoticed and unimportant compared with the endless prison routine and the slow workings of the legal processes.

The Foreign Office had already warned that the case would be prolonged and complicated. The Thai government is under tremendous international pressure to take a hard line against drug smugglers because of its key position in the infamous 'Golden Triangle': to smash the drug traffic at Thailand is an essential step in destroying the Triangle itself, by which drugs are carried from their countries of origin to Europe, America and beyond. It was not likely that my case would be pushed through quickly. The eyes of the world were on Thailand, and my plight was already attracting international interest.

If I thought about the problems of the Thai government at all, my anger made me dismiss them out of hand. The dominating thought in my mind was that I had been set up by three crooks, and I couldn't understand why I was in prison and they were not. I vented my rage on every Thai I met. Towards the Thai prisoners I preserved an aloof coolness; towards the prison authorities I maintained a defiant rebelliousness and contempt; and when I wrote letters home, I poured scorn on the Thai courts, their judicial system, and their lawyers. I called them fools and animals. I pounced on their faults and ridiculed them. I broke prison regulations. And once, when the prison censor passed a letter in which I had been outspokenly and blasphemously critical of the Thais, my contempt knew no bounds.

There were so many odd aspects to the story that I gave up trying to get the whole picture clear in my mind. There was a video film, for example, which had apparently been made of my interrogation, which recorded my reactions to the discovery of the heroin. The film was described by a journalist, David Allin of the Lancashire Evening Telegraph, who was shown it privately when he travelled to Bangkok on behalf of the paper. The film, he told his readers, revealed my reaction of total shock and disbelief when the heroin was discovered, and was for him a convincing proof of my innocence. But when it was finally produced as evidence at my trial, that section had been inexplicably erased; the only image left on it was of me sitting in a chair, my head in my hands, the very picture of guilt. It was never discovered who had wiped the evidence from the film, or why.

Mr. Lyman was confident he could get me freed. Having heard the other girls talk about their cases, I thought differently. I was sure mine was hopeless.

'I might as well plead guilty and be done with it,' I told him drearily.

He shook a long finger at me like a schoolmaster. 'Now why do you want to say a darn stupid thing like that?'

'The girls say that if I plead guilty I automatically get my sentence halved.'

'Sentence?' he bellowed. 'Sentence? You ain't getting a sentence. We'll get you free, li'l honey, if it takes twenty years!'

I wasn't impressed. Hannah had told me that I could expect thirty years if I were convicted. Half of thirty was five years less in Lard Yao than Mr. Lyman appeared ready to accept. I turned on him angrily.

'Have you ever won a heroin case?'

'Ah. Well, I believe . . . Humm.'

'Have you ever won just *one* single heroin case in court?'

He looked downcast. 'Well, no, as a matter of fact, it's true we haven't.' He banged the table. 'But yours is different! I do truly believe that we have a great case! And I won't hear talk of you pleading guilty, no sir!'

6th June drew closer, the date of the preliminary hearing.

The first letters from Mum and my sisters after my arrest had made one thing clear. Whatever happened, they believed in my innocence and were going to stick by me. I told them what I could in letters, and they rang the British Embassy and other government sources in Bangkok several times to find out more, until I begged them not to waste their money. It could aggravate relationships between me and the authorities, and in any case, we already had all the information that could be extracted. We would just have to wait.

In Blackburn, events gathered momentum. My arrest and imprisonment had been given national coverage in the British press, and our local newspaper, the Lancashire Evening Telegraph, began a campaign for my release, with David Allin's feature articles. The Daily Mail ran several articles about me. The British press were generally sympathetic. Even if I were guilty, it was argued, I should be brought back to serve my sentence in an English prison.

My mother was well loved in Blackburn, and the Evening Telegraph articles aroused great public sympathy. Letters, almost all sympathetic, poured into the newspaper's offices. The Rt. Hon Barbara Castle, our MP, gave the case her close attention, though like the Foreign Office she refrained from public discussion until the case went to court. In May it was announced that she had asked Dr. David Owen, the Foreign Secretary, to find out what conditions were like in the prison. He did so, and reported that I was being visited regularly by the British Consulate.

I saw none of the press coverage and only picked up a little of what was going on from letters and visitors. It was probably just as well that I did not see David Allin's story of May 31, with its headline: 'Jail girl *could* be shot, say Thai Embassy.' Article 21 was wide-ranging in its powers.

In Lard Yao prison I gratefully absorbed the home news in the letters. Mum told me what she was planting in the garden and said that I must get back home in time to see the daffodils in bloom. My sisters told me all the ordinary everyday things that were happening. Eagerly

I read about driving lessons, discos, and jobs. Ann's husband John sent a recipe for home-brewed alcohol which turned me into an overnight social success and made Hannah so alarmed that she poured it all away before it reached a drinkable state. I had a letter from Carl; he had stowed away on a Jumbo Jet and gone back to Australia. I enquired about the possibility of doing some studying while in prison. I even began to learn some Thai. It was best to be on the safe side. After all, I might be in prison for some time.

11 Court

But I believe in fate and destiny, and even
our June in her letter said everything is done
for a purpose, which is true, but not easy to
face in real life. What's hurting more than
anything, I will accept anything I get,
because it was my mistake. But you and the
family, what is it doing to you?

Letter to Mum, early summer 1977

The circle of girls and women were swaying in time to
a rhythmic chant. As I approached, I recognised the
Thai numerals. They were counting.

'*Sii*! (Four!)' – a tremor of excitement passed through
the crowd.

'*Ha*! (Five!)' – the circle pressed closer.

'*Hok*! (Six!)' – intrigued, I pushed into the group to
see what was going on.

A prisoner was standing against the steps leading up
to the hut. She was gripping the rail. Her knuckles were
white and her face screwed up with pain. Her thin sarong
was hoisted to her waist. A guard was standing behind
her, a stick raised to strike. The girl's bare buttocks and
thighs were bruising from the blows that had already
been struck. As the stick fell again, the crowd of prisoners watching took up the count again. One or two
began clapping their hands in a slow rhythm, urging the
guard on. Sickened, I turned away.

Beatings were common in Lard Yao. This one, I found later, was punishment for a fight. Dang was young and attractive, and was passionately devoted to a waif-like girl from the hill country who was also in Lard Yao. They were inseparable, and very demonstrative physically. The fight had started when Malee, Dang's girlfriend, had shown an interest in another woman. The guard had found them fighting and was punishing Dang, who had a reputation as a trouble-maker.

Dang was an intense person, and was often in fights. She had arrived in Lard Yao as the result of another relationship that had turned sour. She had had a girlfriend who had been seen in the company of an American soldier, Dang's boyfriend, in Bangkok; they went into a hotel together. When they came out, Dang was waiting for them. She threw petrol all over the girl, and then tossed a lighted match. The girl was burnt to death.

Dang, when her temper wasn't aroused, was a peaceable girl, and was one of the quieter occupants of our dormitory.

By the time 6th June arrived, I had made up my mind that I was going to plead not guilty.

I had weighed the matter carefully. On the one hand, I knew that a guilty plea would mean an almost automatic reduction of my sentence. The sentence for heroin exportation was thirty years; a halved sentence with remission for good conduct would come to about ten years. My fellow prisoners told me I would be crazy to plead any other way. 'You can't beat the system,' I was told. 'You're guilty unless you can prove otherwise in this country. How are you going to explain three and a half kilos? Who's going to believe you? Plead guilty and cut your losses.' As I saw other girls pleading guilty and returning from court with dramatically reduced sentences I could see sense in what they said. After all, I reasoned bitterly, who cared what the stupid Thais thought? It made no difference what those fools of lawyers thought of my guilt or innocence. Once out of Thailand, I vowed, I was never going to set foot in the place again, and the sooner I was out the better.

On the other hand, I was innocent. It hadn't been my heroin, it hadn't been my scheme to try to smuggle the stuff through customs. To plead guilty wasn't just to say to the authorities 'Yes, I'm an international drug smuggler, I tried to smuggle all that heroin out of Thailand, I've been very wicked, please be merciful' – though that was bad enough. A guilty plea was in effect to say to James and Simon and Alan Soon, 'OK: I'll take the rap; you go free, I'll stay in prison.' And that I wasn't going to do. It would be endorsed on my passport; I'd never be allowed into any country again. And what would it do to my family? They believed in my innocence; how would they feel if I pleaded guilty?

'You're a fool,' said Hannah.

'Well, what would you do?' I demanded. 'Go on, tell me.'

'I'd plead guilty like a sensible woman.' We were in the kitchen, making Chelsea buns for sale in the prison shop. Hannah attacked the dough viciously with a wooden spoon. 'Look, Rita, you haven't thought it through. You get fifteen years, and what happens? You're in your thirties when you get out. Earlier if you behave yourself. That's still time to make a life. Still young and pretty. Still time to find yourself a man who'll want you.' She gave the dough a final, unnecessary, thrust. 'You get thirty years and what do you look like when you get out? Think about it.'

I didn't need to. I'd thought about it, on and off, since my arrival. 'I'm pleading not guilty, Hannah.'

'But why? Tell me, why?'

I thought for a moment. 'For the sake of my family . . . Because I know I'm innocent . . . And because if I plead not guilty, there's a tiny chance I'll win my case and walk out of that court back to freedom.' As I said the words I realised how idealistic they sounded.

Hannah banged her floury hands together. White clouds flew. She shook her head in bewilderment. 'You've been reading too many fairy stories, Rita.'

The days passed and merged into a blur. Suddenly it was only a few days to the preliminary hearing. I was told there was someone to see me. It was the normal visiting period, and there was the usual crush of people. Suddenly I saw someone waving at me frantically. It was Shirley, who had been my companion when I'd first visited Hong Kong.

'I don't *believe* it! Shirley!' I shouted joyfully. 'What on earth are you doing here?'

'I just arrived in Bangkok!' explained Shirley. 'I've got permission to visit you every day!'

Seeing Shirley again made me deliriously happy. When she returned to Bangkok that day she telephoned my mother and gave her a glowing account of how well I was looking, which cheered Mum up a lot. She also went round various official departments foraging for information about my case. It was the second good report Mum had had of me recently – the Embassy official from Blackburn, who visited me at the police cell and also several times in prison, had visited Blackburn and while there had gone to see Mum. I wrote to her and told her how happy I was that Shirley was in Bangkok.

Correspondence with Mum, apart from being a precious link, often revealed interesting developments. Though I sometimes found it difficult to discover what was going on, the Embassy was very good at keeping Mum informed. Often the first time I heard about things was when she mentioned them in letters.

That was how I heard that attempts were being made to postpone the 6th June hearing to 16th June.

'What's the idea?' I asked Mr. Lyman.

'Perfectly routine,' he insisted. 'We may need to get some more evidence. We have somebody in Hong Kong right now looking for Simon Lo. We may be able to force him to attend your hearing. So we're applying for a postponement.'

'How many more times will it be postponed?' I said. 'How long is this thing going to go on for?'

'It's just a matter of time. It all takes time,' Mr. Lyman assured me. 'Lo and Alan Soon have criminal records for drugs in Hong Kong. If we could find the pair of them it could make all the difference. Your Foreign Office in London is very anxious we should make every effort.'

'How long?'

'Well,' he said carefully, 'If all goes well, I don't see why you shouldn't be through with all this legal business by Christmas.'

I would have been in prison nine months by then. The shock of this news was almost physical.

For Mum I put a brave face on things. 'I'm all ready to face the court tomorrow,' I wrote to her on 5th June, 'Nice cotton dress, clean hair, Shirley beside me, so best foot forward and head held high . . .'

Next day, the hearing was postponed to 12th July, and I had to settle down to wait again.

Matters moved forward. Back home, Mrs. Barbara Castle visited Mum and explained the steps that were being taken on my behalf by the British government. On 27th June I had another medical check, which proved satisfactory. I also had a further visit from Mr. Lyman. He was in high spirits.

'Remember I asked you to write to your family and tell them that character references from friends and relations would help your case?'

I nodded. I had written the letter some weeks previously. I'd thought the idea was a pretty stupid one but had fallen in with it. I shrugged my shoulders disparagingly. 'So what?'

Mr. Lyman smiled broadly. 'Well, will you look at these!' He dumped a pile of papers on my desk. 'Character references! Here's a stack of people believe in you, Rita, and they've written letters to prove it.'

Numbly, I leafed through the letters. They were from friends in Blackburn and elsewhere; from people who knew me through my family; some from previous employers. Representatives of organisations in Blackburn had written. An ex-Mayor of the town had contributed a letter.

I could only take in bits of what was written. '. . . Cannot conceive that she would knowingly be involved . . . a girl of excellent character . . . nothing to suggest she would knowingly harm or hurt anyone . . .'

Then I saw my sister Ann's signature.

I looked up at Mr. Lyman. My eyes were blurring. He was still enthusing.

'Every one of 'em states that from knowledge of you, li'l honey, over the years, it's not possible you could have been involved in smuggling drugs. Here, look at this from the doctor. He says –'

I walked unsteadily to a chair and sat down. He put down the papers, cleared his throat and began to sort them into a pile, somewhat embarrassed. I regained my composure.

'Well, Mr. Lyman . . .' I managed a smile. 'I'll definitely be pleading not guilty. Can't let these people down, can I?'

'Attagirl!' said Mr. Lyman.

I was still bitter and angry. My lack of knowledge of the language and my ignorance of Thai legal procedure reinforced my willingness to see all things Thai in the worst possible light.

The Thais are a people whose culture is centuries old. Thai Buddhism, the national religion, is part of the oldest branch of that religion. The Buddhist ideals of moderation and virtue in all things underlie architecture, literature, painting, music and everyday life. The present King and Queen, though their dynasty long since relinquished divine status, play a leading role in the religious life of the country. Despite the widespread influence of Buddhism there is religious tolerance, and under King Bhumibol Adulayev the country has gracefully Westernised itself in many ways.

I had seen little of this in my travels, because I had spent only a short time in Thailand. On the other hand, I was well aware of the less attractive side of Thai society; I had seen the red light district to which foreigners flocked, and I had heard there was an enormous trade in child prostitutes. My mind returned to these things as I brooded over the events of the past months. In other circumstances I would probably have conceded that my experience of the country was only partial; but I was anxious to believe the worst. I was living, too, in a prison, among thieves, murderers and other criminals. I suppose I saw as little of the beauty of Thai classical culture there as the average English criminal in Wormwood Scrubs sees of Shakespearian theatre . . .

I made it my business to be seen to be rejecting Thai customs and practices. I seized upon every fault and failing, and took them as proof that these people were just as I had said they were. There were beatings in the prison; I called the guards barbarians. Their food didn't appeal to me; I called it disgusting. Thai prisoners fought among themselves; I called them animals. I acquired a reputation as a trouble-maker, and it wasn't only because of the interest that was being shown in my case by the foreign press.

I made hardly any attempt to come to terms with cultural differences. There were frequent incidents in the dormitory. One night when I had only been there a few days, I woke up wanting to go to the toilet. We slept in two long lines the length of the room. Still a new girl, I was sleeping in the worst part of the room, farthest from the toilet. I got up and made my way down the centre of the room to the loo, picking my way down the line of feet where the two rows met.

There were a few girls still awake. I had already grown accustomed to sleeping despite the constant light, the muttered conversations and the occasional fight. As soon as I started to walk, everybody flew into a rage. I backed against the wall.

'What have I done? What's the matter?' I couldn't make sense out of the shouts and gestures, but I was sure I was going to be physically attacked. One of the Thai girls who spoke some English tried to explain. 'No! No!' she said, pointing downwards. 'In Thailand is no good. Feet! Feet!'

Apparently I had committed some serious social crime. I shouted back at them.

'How do you expect anybody to walk across the room, then? You can't tell me that in a room this size . . .' I wouldn't back down. It's hard to preserve your dignity when everybody can see you in the toilet, but I walked proudly back to my bed muttering 'Stupid Thais . . . how can they expect civilised people to understand them?'

The whole thing, when Hannah explained it to me next morning, turned out to be quite simple. In Thailand the feet are considered to be an inferior part of the body, and even to point your foot at somebody is considered insulting; you can easily offend somebody just by crossing your legs. Now I could understand why in the courtroom a guard had made me uncross mine.

I ran into trouble again when I decided to do something about my laundry. Where pretty lingerie was concerned, the natural curiosity of some Thai prisoners developed into theft. If you hung up a nice petticoat or bra to dry, you were quite likely never to see it again, or to see it in some other girl's possession. After a couple of such incidents I decided enough was enough; I hung my things on the wall of the dormitory over my head. Again, I was unknowingly insulting my fellow-prisoners. My clothes were hanging above the level of the sleeping girls' heads.

I found it difficult to understand why some Westerners devoted time and energy to building relationships with the Thai prisoners. I was scornful of two in particular. Jack and Gladys Martin were American Southern Baptist missionaries who came inside the prison for an hour once a month, to meet the Thai girls and any other prisoners who wanted to see them. I used to go to their meetings occasionally, just to get out of the routine, but I thought the Martins were crazy.

'Those people look really happy!' I said mockingly to Hannah after being at one of the meetings. 'You know what that woman said? She said that if she were a prisoner in here it would be all the same to her, because God was in charge and he would still be with her!'

We both laughed, and wondered what sort of a lunatic could say a stupid thing like that.

The character references from home softened my bitterness to some extent, and Shirley's visit made me almost mellow for a time. She was a visitor out of my old life. She brought a generous gift of money with her from Bernie in Australia; that was another link with the old, free world.

Also, despite my bitterness, I was beginning to build some relationships in the prison. I had got to know Francoise superficially; I knew Hannah quite well; the foreign prisoners got on quite amiably with each other, and I was even on reasonable speaking terms with some of the Thai prisoners, especially those in the dormitory. And I loved children, of which there were a great many in Lard Yao. Some women had brought their children into prison with them, others were pregnant when they arrived, so there were scores of children of various ages.

One in particular, a pale-faced two-year-old, attached himself to me and followed me everywhere. He had been born in Lard Yao. When he was five months old, his mother was released. She left him in prison when she went out. He seemed fairly happy, calling about forty prisoners 'mother'. They all fed and cuddled him, and he spent each night with whoever he had last been with that day. I often played with him, and we got on well. In one way having somebody to care for made me more contented, but it also increased my bitterness against the Thais. Perhaps the mother had believed the child would have a better life in Lard Yao than outside; perhaps she knew he would be better cared for or loved better than she could manage. I didn't care. I chose to see it as callous rejection. 'What animals,' I said savagely, 'would do that to their own flesh and blood?'

It was another excuse to be angry.

An Englishman pushed his way over to me as I stood waiting for my name to be called. 'Rita – I'm a journalist. Can we talk?'

It was 12th July, and I was back in the courthouse. Mr. Lyman was with me, and his Thai colleague Mr. Puttri who would represent me in court. The interview was short; I couldn't concentrate. When the journalist left he pushed an envelope in my hand. 'Press cuttings,' he said. 'Bring you up to date.'

'I'll read them later,' I replied, knowing I'd burst into tears if I looked at them there and then.

Mr. Lyman chatted to distract me. 'You'll be before Judge Udom Tuchinda,' he remarked. 'He's a good judge. Ought to be – he studied law in England. His wife's English, too.'

Mr. Puttri agreed, and they discussed the judge. I let the conversation flow over me.

Inside the courtroom the heat was stifling. A single fan suspended from the ceiling did little more than agitate the air. Although the proceedings were once again conducted in Thai, I was allowed an interpreter this time, so I could understand what was going on.

The judge sat beneath an imposing portrait of King Bhumibol. Before the hearing began he beckoned me and my lawyers to stand before him. He looked at me gravely.

'You intend to plead not guilty. I have to warn you that if you plead not guilty, and are then found guilty by this court, you will have incurred the full penalty.' His English was impeccable. He stared at me before continuing. 'A plea of guilty brings a comparatively light sentence,' he concluded.

My body tensed. *The case is being prejudged before the evidence has been given. I haven't got a chance*, was the only interpretation I was capable of putting on the judge's words.

Mr. Lyman became extremely angry. 'This is just the beginning!' he cried. 'We can appeal – take the case to the Supreme Court – even apply for a royal pardon!'

I was dazed and confused. The trial hadn't started and they were talking as if I'd been sentenced. Royal pardon? It was common knowledge in Lard Yao that the King had never pardoned anyone who was convicted in a heroin case.

We returned to our wooden bench. The hearing got under way. Five people gave evidence for the prosecution: three customs officers, a forensic officer, and somebody from the staff of the Asia Hotel. The British Consul, hot and uncomfortable, took careful notes. Mr. Lyman sat by my side in barely-controlled exasperation.

There was little to dispute in what was said. It was stated that heroin had been found in my possession. The results of chemical analysis were given. An account of my movements on 19th March was given. The judge sat in deep concentration, writing everything carefully down.

I was depressed and uncertain afterwards. The next hearing was to be on 19th August, when the police would state their case. There lay ahead several more hearings four or five weeks apart. While that was happening I would have to stay in Lard Yao. Knowing that I would have to decide quickly whether I was going to retain my plea of not guilty, I decided after agonies of indecision that I would not change my plea.

Infuriatingly, Mr. Lyman positively glowed with optimism as I became more and more pessimistic. My mother telephoned him that night. 'It's looking good for her,' he said. I couldn't see what possible grounds he had for saying that.

I wrote to Mum myself next day, but the letter was so depressed and black-spirited that I decided to write another, more cheerful one afterwards. Before I had begun the second letter I had some amazing news. Mum was coming to Thailand to see me.

12 Mum

*I could get forty years . . . what peace I
can find with a forty year sentence only God
knows . . .*

Letter to Mum, 17 September 1977

'She's coming here, Leonie – to Bangkok; I can't believe
it!'

Leonie, Mr. Lyman's assistant, was visiting me to sort
out some legal problems. Mum's letter had arrived a few
days before.

'We were going to have a holiday together next year
in Australia – I suggested we could use the money instead
for her to come here –'

'Seems sensible,' said Leonie.

'Yes, but the amazing thing is that we won't have to
use that money. The Lancashire Evening Telegraph –
that's our newspaper in Blackburn – want to fly Mum
here with David Allin.'

'The journalist?' I'd shown Leonie some of David's
articles that Mum had sent.

'Yes. All expenses paid, there and back.'

I wrote to Mum saying how thrilled I was: 'I'll be waiting
at the prison gates!' I wrote a rather different letter to
my sister Ann.

'I know it's going to be very emotional for us both
. . . At the moment all I feel like doing is breaking down

and sobbing my heart out on her shoulder. Oh to go back to my childhood and tell her to make everything better . . . I just want to go home . . .'

Though physically I wasn't in bad shape, and was adapting to prison life, I was beginning to feel mentally drained after the tension of the past months. The boredom was still a terrible problem. I asked Mum to bring me some European magazines to read; anything to pass the time more quickly. A very kind letter from Barbara Castle encouraged me. I had spent a whole day laboriously composing a letter to her, and I had (rather diplomatically, I thought) poured out all my grievances. Her reply held out no earth-shattering hopes, but it was a compassionate and positive letter, and it cheered me up. With Mum coming to see me as well, things looked a little more cheerful.

She left Blackburn on her 8,000 mile round trip on 13th August. 'I am going to Bangkok,' she told reporters, 'on a wing and a prayer.' The Mayoress of Blackburn wrote to her assuring her of 'the love, prayers and hope' of everybody in the town. Mum had a gruelling programme, with visits to the Embassy and other places in Bangkok, as well as visiting me in prison and going with me to court on the 19th.

Feeling desperately anxious to see her again, I began to make preparations for her arrival. I baked some special biscuits for her and got my nicest clothes ready. I didn't put on any make-up the day she was due to arrive, because I knew I'd cry all over it.

We were to meet in the 'lawyers' room'. This was considered a privilege. Ordinary, unofficial visitors waited in a large crowd before being admitted into a sort of enclosure near the main gate. The side of the enclosure had been made into a tall barrier. Facing it, about seven feet away, was another barrier, an enormous grille. This was the wall of the prison room into which those of us with visitors were sent. Visitors had to shout across the gap, competing with all the others clamouring to be heard. Visitors were usually allowed ten minutes or so.

For official visitors, lawyers, Embassy staff, and also those visiting prisoners who had any kind of influence, the 'lawyers' room' was available. This was a bare room with a grille bisecting a table in the centre. The visitor sat on one side, the prisoner on the other, and conversation was through the bars.

The two guards who accompanied me to the lawyers' room when my name was called were intent on everything being done in a law-abiding fashion. I was marched briskly to the door of the room.

Mum was sitting behind the grille. She looked tired and frail. Somehow she seemed very little, as if she had been shrunk by the inhospitable room. Leonie was with her.

I pushed the guards aside. They tried to stop me, but I was already running round the grille. I flung my arms round Mum, and we both wept and wept. Dimly I was aware of the guards protesting behind us, trying to separate us, and Leonie explaining the situation in Thai: 'It's her mother, do you understand? It's her mother . . .'

Eventually we stood back and looked at each other. Mum found some tissues in her bag. I wiped my eyes and produced a watery smile. I went round to the side of the partition I was supposed to be, and we held hands through the wire grille.

We talked of anything and everything. People back home, family, friends, my case – it wasn't important. Just being together was what mattered. The hour we had been allowed seemed like minutes. Finally we had to part.

'Rita tells me you have permission to visit each week-day, Mrs. Nightingale,' said Leonie. Mum nodded.

'Leonie,' I said urgently, 'make sure they understand – if Mum's here with a paper from the Embassy she's allowed to see me here, not in the visitors' enclosure. You must make sure they know. You must.'

'I'll make sure they get the point,' promised Leonie.

It was heartbreaking to say goodbye that first visit. But I left the room knowing I would see her next day. Next day, however, things began to go wrong. I waited all afternoon for my name to be called, until just before evening I was summoned – not to the lawyers' room but to the visitors' enclosure. I stormed in protest.

'You can't! She's my mother! She's come all the way from England, and I'm not going to shout at her across seven feet of empty space! She's entitled to see me in the lawyers' room.'

My arguments were useless. In the end, it was across the seven-foot gap that we met for the second time. There were no other visitors there. It wasn't a normal visiting time. The guards watched us as we talked the best we could. I longed to reach across the gap and take her hands in mine. I was almost glad that we were only allowed fifteen minutes.

That night I went to see the Warden. I had not made a good impression on her, both because of my attitude to Lard Yao and because of the press coverage my case was getting. Nevertheless she listened to what I had to say. I lost control of my emotions and poured out all my misery and frustration. 'And the guards won't even let me touch her. She's entitled to see me in the lawyers' room.'

She regarded me severely. She was about forty, and dressed expensively. Her clothes were of the finest quality material, her shirts silk. On her finger she wore a ring with an enormous diamond. As she talked, she fiddled with the stone perpetually.

'It is not possible to use the lawyers' room.'

There was no arguing with her implacable authority. Inside, I crumpled up.

'I can, however, understand how you feel.' She paused, her fingers manipulating the big diamond. 'I think it would be in order for you to sit between the barriers. Then you could be close to your mother. It will not be necessary for her to shout then.'

Next day, carrying a cup of iced coffee for Mum, I entered the gap. They'd given her a chair to sit on, and she was sitting there looking forlorn in the empty enclosure. When she saw me she brightened. We talked again. Each day for the rest of the week we met like that until the day came for her to leave.

I wish I could say that I cheered Mum up, that I lightened the burden of her sorrow by being happy, positive and contented. But I didn't. Instead I poured out my own sadness, and, try as I might, I couldn't hold back the floods of tears. Merely seeing her unlocked something in me. I'd been writing to her every week, sharing my hopes and fears, but now she was actually here I wasn't allowed to embrace her and this made my imprisonment seem more than I could bear. When she was back in England she decided not to come to Bangkok again. She couldn't erase that first stark picture engraved on her mind, of me in the interview room, tear-streaked, watched by guards, fretful and angry. It seemed to her that nothing could change it. She couldn't stand the thought of seeing my misery. Instead she waited faithfully for the day when I would be released.

The day we said goodbye I gave her a cake I'd baked on which were the words 'I love you, Mum.' She took it from me; our hands were trembling. She walked slowly away. At the door she turned and looked back, waved, and was gone. I ached for her. I wondered whether I would ever see her again.

Mum's visit inspired me; she was the visible goal of my efforts to be released. I even allowed myself a certain amount of optimism. But as September approached I began to sink back into gloom. I allowed myself to become withdrawn, obsessed with my troubles. A flow of visitors found me sullen and uncommunicative. Lawyers, officials, and Embassy staff were all greeted with silence or rudeness. I wasn't much more agreeable when others came to visit.

One day my name was called on the loudspeaker. 'Visitor for Nightingale!'

I made my way to the visiting compound and scanned the faces of those waiting. I didn't recognise anybody I knew. Two women, pressing against the barrier to see better, were looking at me excitedly. One was a pleasant-looking woman in her early forties; the other, an elderly white-haired lady.

'There she is!' exclaimed the younger of the two, and waved at me. 'Hi! I'm Lucille Lunceford, and this is Margaret Cole.'

'Hello,' I replied, as civilly as I could manage. I wasn't feeling very sociable that day.

'We saw your photograph in the newspaper this morning.'

I scowled. I'm like an animal in a cage, I thought.

They held up a paper bag. 'We brought you some fruit,' smiled the old lady. 'We'll send it in for you. I hope you like pineapple.'

Feeding time at the zoo, I thought bitterly. I succeeded in smiling. 'Thank you,' I called. It was difficult to converse. Other prisoners and visitors were talking on either side.

'We read about your case,' said Lucille Lunceford sympathetically.

'I was used as a drug-runner,' I stated flatly. 'But you know that. It's in all the papers.'

There was a pause. On my right, a visitor was arguing heatedly in Thai with one of the prisoners. I grasped the bars and tried to think of something to say.

'Why have you come to see me? It's a long way out of town.' I hoped that didn't sound quite as insolent to them as it sounded to me. I was trying to be polite, to make conversation for a few minutes until I could decently leave. 'What brings you out here?'

'We were praying together, and the Lord told us to come and see you.' The way Margaret Cole said it, it was the most normal thing in the world.

Oh no; the Godsquad. Visions, even, I groaned to myself. *What are these nutcases talking about?*

'Oh – thank you, that's kind,' I stammered. Silently, I was raging at them. *Don't you know what's happening to me in this place? Don't you know what's happened in my life? Christians are on another planet. Fine in church, but in the real world . . .!*

Margaret Cole was speaking. 'We came because God told us to. That means he cares about you, Rita.'

At least she talked about God in a normal voice. She hardly sounded religious at all. The way she talked, he was a real person. Unfortunately, I knew better. A few months in Lard Yao prison and you knew whether there was a God or not. *Don't give me any of that stuff about God loving me*, I warned silently.

Aloud, I made a lame response. 'Yes, I'm sure you're right.' Margaret Cole looked at me perceptively and changed the subject.

Soon their time was up. 'The cheek of it! Coming to a place like this and telling me God cares for me! They won't be back in a hurry,' I said to Hannah later. 'They've done their good turn for the day.'

'You shouldn't get so screwed up,' Hannah remarked philosophically. 'I like pineapples, even if you don't.'

Mr. Puttri brought news of a sort. 'I have heard that Wong and Lo and Soon have been arrested,' he said. I sat up.

'Why, that's wonderful!' I said.

'But I have heard also that they are still at liberty. Some say one thing and others another. It is hard to know.'

'Perhaps it's true. If it isn't, they might be arrested before long.'

'You must not place too much hope on that,' said Mr. Puttri. He shook his head mournfully. 'If they are arrested to go to trial in Hong Kong – which is only a possibility; and if, in that trial a sworn affidavit is produced – which is again only possible; then there is still no guarantee that such an affidavit would help you in any way.'

'But it must do!' I protested. 'An affidavit would make all the difference.'

'In such a case as yours it would make very little difference,' said Mr. Puttri sadly.

I was furious. I had been counting on some sort of written reinforcement of my story coming from Hong Kong. 'Anywhere else in the world an affidavit would have got me released!' I stormed. 'But not in crazy Bangkok, oh no – the judge won't even read it here!'

Mr. Puttri bowed stiffly and left me to my rage.

It was becoming evident that Mr. Lyman's estimate of a verdict on my case by December at the earliest was accurate. The preparation of my defence was taking time. Crucial evidence in my support was being sought, the British government was making enquiries, questions were being asked in Parliament. David Allin raised the matter in the press of the unexplained erasure of the Custom Department's film. He also did some research on his own account about Simon Lo. Odd things happened that I didn't hear about. While he was in Bangkok with Mum, he had been approached by someone straight out of a cheap thriller – a man touting for a rival law firm, pouring scorn on Tilleke and Gibbins and trying to bribe David to influence me into changing my lawyers. A big case like mine was presumably a profitable thing to be involved in.

I was not the only one whose case was making slow progress. There was something odd about Maria's. She'd been to court once or twice when she first arrived, just as I had. But for a long time she hadn't been called to attend. Things seemed to have ground to a standstill. Nobody spoke Spanish at Tilleke and Gibbins, who were representing Maria as well. Often when I was being interviewed by somebody from the firm Maria would be sent through too, because they were her lawyers; but she became very frustrated. 'No understand! No understand!' A woman who visited her from the Spanish Embassy spoke to her only in Spanish, so I didn't get much of a picture of what was going on.

Then the visits from the lawyers stopped, and the Embassy didn't contact her any more. Eventually we heard that an announcement had been made on the radio about Maria. She wouldn't be going to court any more, ever. She had already had sentence passed on her under martial law. She had been sentenced to life imprisonment.

'You've got to tell her, Hannah.'

A group of us were discussing the situation. Hannah agreed. 'Looks like nobody else is going to.'

We watched the conversation from a distance. Hannah

115

was speaking forcefully, emphasising her points with sweeping gestures; Maria was listening with a frown of concentration, straining forward as if by listening very hard she could make the words easier to understand. She had a polite smile on her face. Obviously she wasn't taking any of it in.

Later we made a concerted effort to explain matters to her. Picking our words from the scraps of Thai and French we had in common, we strung phrases together into statements which sounded bald and peculiar. How do you tell a woman of that age, who thinks she's going to get a short sentence or even be released, that she's been sentenced to life imprisonment – which in Thailand is 100 years? Maria sat listening, her fingers working away at her rosary. 'Life,' we repeated. 'They've given you life, Maria.'

Either she didn't understand or she wouldn't take us seriously. 'No, no . . .' she protested good-humouredly. 'You're crazy, crazy.'

But as the weeks went by and it became clear she wasn't going to court like the rest of us, it seemed that the reports had been true. She had been given life.

'This is Chris,' said Hannah.

'Hi everybody.' Chris was a striking blonde, tall and thin and Dutch.

A new foreigner arriving in prison was an event. 'What happened?' I asked. Chris grinned. 'Caught at the airport. Well and truly. Had the stuff taped to my body.'

The method was a well-known one. If you weren't body-searched at customs you could walk through carrying anything you wanted, usually in plastic bags stuck to your midriff with surgical tape. If you did get searched you were done for. There was no way out. The rewards were considerable, the risks worth taking, I was told by the several girls in Lard Yao who had tried the gamble and failed.

Chris put her things down. 'Wow!' she said, thumping the floor. 'Some bed!' She looked around. 'Won't get lonely, anyway . . . What's your name?'

'Rita.'

'Oh – I read about you in the newspaper. Heroin, wasn't it?'

'That's right.'

Chris smiled. 'Mine was supposed to be heroin. I was sure burned. I was supposed to be taking this heroin through, you know? So when I got caught I told them what it was and they were really heavy. Said I'd get a long sentence, all that sort of thing.'

I grimaced. I knew the sort of thing.

'Well, they analysed it, and you know what? It wasn't heroin at all. It was morphine. I'd been taken for a ride. I couldn't believe it. The guy who sold me the stuff really ripped me off.' She smiled, reminiscing. 'Worked out well for me, though. They tell me morphine carries a much lighter sentence than heroin. It's an ill wind.'

Though Chris appeared to be extraordinarily stupid as a drug dealer, she was very clever in most other ways. She learned Thai incredibly quickly, found her way around the prison in no time at all, and endeared herself to the Warden and guards because she was a workaholic, often working an eighteen-hour day.

At first I didn't see much of her, and in any case was not in a mood to make friends. She began to work in the kitchen with me, and despite myself I found myself liking her. She protected me against the more masculine girls. When any of them made advances to me, which happened from time to time, I only had to threaten to call Chris and they would back away.

'Chris, you don't have to stick up for me all the time, you know,' I said more than once.

117

'That's OK, Rita; you're my mate,' Chris would reply with her easy-going smile.

Even Chris's arrival failed to shift my black depression. I kept myself to myself most of the time, and refused to be a model prisoner. I refused to give the guards the correct courtesy greeting. I insisted on speaking English to them and would pretend not to understand even when I could make out what they were saying. I was a loner, and when the official holidays brought days of classical dancing and games I sulked in the dormitory. I questioned the guards' rulings and generally made trouble wherever I could. They often threatened terrible things that would happen when I was finally sentenced and the world press lost interest – 'You wait till you're sentenced, and then . . .'

I continued to write angry letters home, interrupted by occasional moments of cheerfulness when some sequence of events encouraged me. Hanging over me the whole time was the prospect of a sentence which could not be less than five years and which was beginning to look like thirty, forty or fifty. I calculated the odds against a not guilty verdict to be astronomical.

I chafed at the Thai system of evidence, which seemed to me to give the accused no chance. On those rare occasions when I conceded that my lawyers were in fact very good and the judge a distinguished member of the Thai bench, I fixed on the fact that my lawyers' impossible task was to convince the court that three and a half kilos of heroin – worth nearly three-quarters of a million English pounds – had come into my possession without my knowledge or co-operation. As one of the customs officials had remarked to me: 'That is an awful lot of heroin.'

A fifty year sentence seemed, likewise, an awful lot of time.

13 Plots

I will never plead guilty, and I now think
I've been a fool to keep getting that idea in
my head . . . Mr. Lyman is really going all
out to win this case.

Letter to Mum, 21 September 1977

'I'm going to write to my Mum.'

'And what d'you intend to say to her?' demanded Mr.
Lyman.

'I'm going to tell her the truth. She's only fooling
herself with false hopes. She'll be shattered when I'm
sentenced. She ought to know the facts. I'm going to
give them to her.'

'And what are the facts, might I ask?' A dangerous
gleam had appeared in Mr. Lyman's eye.

'I'm going to get given a big sentence.' He groaned
and began to speak. I carried on. 'And when they give
it to me, I'm not going to appeal.'

Mr. Lyman banged the floor with his stick. 'Not make
an appeal to the High Court? Why on earth not?'

'Because it will take a year to process the appeal.
Because I don't believe there's any chance of a sentence
being quashed anyway. Because if I'm going to get out
of this place, Mr. Lyman, it won't be through these
endless court appearances. It will be because England
and Thailand sort the thing out between themselves.'

'And how do you think they'll do that?'

'They can pull strings. They can work behind the scenes. I'm going to create such a stink in the press that they'll sit up all night to get me out faster.'

'It might not be that easy,' Mr. Lyman said. His eyes were sad. Leonie, who had not spoken, reached through the grille for my hand.

'Please, Rita,' she pleaded, 'Think about it. You won't lose by appealing. You don't even know that you'll be sentenced . . .'

I laughed, a short, humourless, wobbly sound. 'No, I don't. But I will be. You know it's true. God himself couldn't get me out of here now.' I laughed again. 'Especially God.'

My next court appearance on 26th September was, Mr. Lyman reckoned, the last before I would be called for sentencing. I slid into a cynical despondency, mistrusting everybody from God downwards. I hated my lawyers; I now believed I should have pleaded guilty in the first place and that they had persuaded me against doing so. But since I had pleaded not guilty I was going to stick to it, and I reacted angrily to Mr. Lyman's and Leonie's suggestions that I should now think about changing my plea.

'There's still time – just,' said Mr. Lyman. 'You can plead for leniency.'

'That's for cowards,' I snapped. 'It's my life, not yours, and I'll do what I want.'

Patiently, Mr. Lyman explained the situation, ticking off each point on his fingers. 'There's hardly any chance of finding any evidence about Lo and his friends. We've got the testimony from the bell-boy at the Asia Hotel. It's not going to be of much use.' (This had been a blow. We had placed great hopes on the statement of the bell-boy, who had since my arrest entered the Buddhist monkhood. Our hopes were sharpened by the difficulty

120

of extracting the statement. But he had said nothing to point to Simon and James.) 'All the press hoo-hah isn't making the Thai authorities look any too kindly on you. Your Mrs. Castle in England has made 'em wary too, simply by asking questions she's perfectly entitled to ask. You have to understand that the Thais are very awkwardly placed. After all, the West has told them long enough not to be lenient on drug smugglers. They're under a bit of a spotlight.'

It was a week after the two women had been to visit me. I heard different prisoners being summoned to the visitors enclosure and wondered idly whether I would have any visitors that day apart from officials and lawyers. It had been such a wonderful surprise when Shirley had come. I could do with more surprises like that.

It was Thursday, my day for visitors. They were allowed into the prison by rota, days being allocated according to the crime committed by the person they had come to see. Food brought in from outside was usually shared. Smart prisoners chose their friends so that one was a murderer, another a thief, and so on. That way there was a constant supply of titbits through the week.

After Mr. Lyman and Leonie had left, I heard my name being called. A visitor! I went over to the enclosure. There, pressed against the barrier by the usual crowd of people, were Margaret Cole and Lucille Lunceford.

'Hi!' said Lucille. 'How are you today?'

My heart sank. 'All right,' I volunteered. She held up a bag of food. 'We're sending this in to you,' she said. I felt a bit better. I could always make use of food. I'd better be nice to these people. Anyway, they were only allowed ten minutes.

'What's life like in the outside world?' I asked.

Margaret's face lit up. 'Well, now, God is really doing wonderful things. You should see the children I'm working with. They are refugees from Vietnam. We've seen so much blessing.'

It was as before; she was talking about God in a perfectly matter-of-fact way. As she and Lucille talked on, I became curious. Margaret Cole was an old lady with white hair – but she was doing a job which a younger person might have found strenuous. Lucille too seemed to lead a hectic life as a teacher.

'Why are you doing this?' I asked Margaret. 'Why do you work in that transit camp? Why have the two of you come to see me again?'

'Because God told us to. And because we want to,' they replied.

'You don't need to,' I said violently. 'God hasn't bothered with me so far. He didn't stop me being arrested. He didn't step in when I was left to carry the can for the guys who set me up.'

I paused, embarrassed. After all, they were only being kind. 'Sorry,' I said quietly. 'You just don't understand how it is in here. God hasn't done anything for me. If there is a God, he's left me in this place to get on with things. He doesn't come in here.'

'But he has, Rita,' Margaret said softly, barely audible above the raised voices of the other visitors. 'He told us to come here.'

Tears started to my eyes. 'It's easy for you,' I replied. 'You're free.'

I began to feel extremely lonely. I dwelt on the fact that no heroin case had ever been dismissed in the courts; acquittals were snatched from the accused when the public prosecutor lodged his automatic counter-appeal. I had bouts of homesickness, and sometimes woke crying from dreams of Blackburn.

Margaret Cole and Lucille Lunceford had left promising to visit again. When they appeared the next week, I found I had even been looking forward to their coming. When they asked me how I was, I told them. 'I'm lonely and I hate being here.'

The odd thing about them was how ready they were to talk about God. After three visits I had begun to respect them; they were remarkable people. But I was disconcerted by their openness. I wasn't used to hearing God talked about on weekdays. It was a long time since I'd heard him discussed much on Sundays, come to that. It struck me as being in rather bad taste. But when I was with them it seemed the most natural thing imaginable, to listen to their stories of how God had done something special for them that week, or to hear them quoting Bible verses which they thought I would like to hear. When Margaret talked about Jesus Christ it was like talking about a close friend. In some weird way, her experience reached out and involved me as well. I asked her, 'Why do you come, really? I can sense . . . it's, well, like you love me in some way. Why would you want to love me?'

Margaret smiled. 'That's the love Jesus has planted in me,' she said gently. 'And it's projected through me, to you. God loves you too.'

I must be getting soft, I thought to myself. *I'm swapping pious thoughts with a missionary.*

When they were gone I felt warm and almost contented for an hour or so. Then it wore off. I told myself I shouldn't be stupid. It would take more than religious talk to sort out my problems. I brooded on the forthcoming sentencing, going over and over in my mind the things I'd heard from the other prisoners and the lawyers. It was all too complicated. So many hopes, so many promises. And now I was facing what could be a fifty year sentence.

I wrote endless letters home, full of desperate attempts to pull off a victory against what I believed to be only a relentless machine, the Thai judicial system. I knew nothing about English law, let alone Thai law, but I was convinced that I was being robbed of my rights and dealt with inhumanly. I would hear no arguments otherwise. My mind was made up.

I wrote to an Interpol officer, shrewdly composing the letter to give the impression I was about to confess, so that he would come to see me and I would get a chance to argue things out once again. I conceived a plan to hire a private investigator to check the Bangkok banks in case Simon or Alan Soon had deposited large amounts of money. I worked out schemes to get even with James. I contemplated trying to persuade somebody at the Embassy to do some unofficial spying for me. I begged Mum to point out to David Allin the advantages of uncovering information that would lead to my release: 'Tell him it will make him a world-famous investigative reporter overnight,' I said.

I plotted and counter-plotted. At night I lay on my bed and wove ever more complicated webs of intrigue. Always at the back of my mind was the fear that the decision I had made, to continue with my not guilty plea and refuse to appeal against my sentence, might have been a terrible mistake. I flung myself into speculation and the composition of agitated letters. My inner turmoil was made worse by the scarcity of information and the frequency with which rumours changed. One week I was told that David Allin was in Hong Kong and had found Simon Lo in prison; the next, it turned out David had not been to Hong Kong at all.

As the time drew near for my final court appearance when I would finally hear the verdict, I nerved myself for the end of one fight and the start of another; the end of the court processes, and the launching of what I hoped

124

would be an international campaign for my freedom. I felt I had been abandoned by God, by so-called friends, and by justice itself. I was more than ready to cast myself in the role of the wronged martyr at the centre of a world crusade. I hoped the world would oblige.

14 Martha

Please rest easy, Mum, the hard part is over.
Letter to Mum, 13 October 1977

On December 9th I was to go to court to be sentenced.

When my name was called I was surprised; it was earlier than usual. I wasn't expecting visitors to be allowed in until later. I wondered if it was the two missionaries, Margaret and Lucille. I wasn't sure if I wanted any visitors at all.

The visitor's enclosure was empty apart from one person. I could see the litter and dirt blowing round her feet; empty, the room looked grimy and depressing.

She was an old lady, frail and snowy-haired, dressed neatly and prettily. She leaned against the barrier and looked straight into my eyes. She was accompanied by an English missionary who introduced himself as Jim. The old lady spoke with a broad Lancashire accent.

'I'm Martha Livesey. I've just come to see you, love, because I'm from Blackburn, too.'

I looked back at her and burst into tears. I saw her giving a bag of food to a guard for me, and then the other visitors came in and the clamour began. I stood at the barrier, clutching it, crying my eyes out. Through my tears I saw her looking disconcerted and trying to make herself heard above the shouted greetings. Though

I couldn't hear her I could read sympathy in her face. I could only sob helplessly. 'I want to go home . . . I want to go home . . .'

I wasn't capable of saying anything else, and she couldn't make herself heard, so after a few minutes she left. I made my way back inside, and numbly took the bag she'd brought me from the guard. Still crying, I went to the kitchen. There were several people preparing food. They looked up as I came in and banged the bag down on the table.

'What's up?' asked Hannah in surprise.

I couldn't explain. I didn't know the words. That woman was from Blackburn. She'd be going to see my Mum when she got back there . . . Suddenly, as if a dam had broken its banks, everything came flooding back; that there was a Blackburn, that it was all still there after nine months in prison, that there was a world outside where people had names like Livesey and lived in Blackburn. I'd never forgotten these things, but the old lady had brought them to my mind with a terrible clarity. She had been so sweet and frail, stepping in from another world into the dirt of the prison.

'I had a visitor . . . from Blackburn . . . an old lady. I can't stand it any more, Hannah. I want to go home, I really do. I've spent nine months in this Godforsaken hole and I want out, Hannah, I want to leave, it wasn't my heroin and nobody will believe me . . . Oh, Hannah . . .'

'Don't come that old innocent victim stuff again!' Hannah knew my tantrums. 'We don't want to hear it. We've all got our problems here, you know.'

Something exploded in me. I swore at Hannah and the others. I shouted obscenities at the top of my voice. As I stormed out I grabbed at the bag I'd brought in, intending to take some fruit. Instead I found a booklet which had been put inside. I stuffed it in the pocket of my jeans. I was desperate to get away, to be on my own, to try to sort my head out and think things through.

When somebody is crying in prison a crowd soon gathers, jeering or simply curious. There are no official places for prisoners to be on their own. Even the toilets in Lard Yao were doorless. I knew of only one place where some privacy could be found. Underneath the hospital building, which like the others stood on stilts, was a dark shady place avoided by everybody because in the daytime snakes came in from the bushes to shelter from the heat. I didn't care.

I sat in the cool darkness. The music on the loud-speakers was drowned by the sound of my own pulse in my ears. My heart was pounding. I gulped lungfuls of air in between retching sobs. I was shaking all over. Huge questions battered my brain. Why? Why had it all happened? Why was I in prison? Why did my mother and family have to suffer? I hated being hurt myself, but knowing they were being hurt too was even worse. Why? . . . Why? . . . Why? . . .

Memories of the past eighteen months came back to me, each with the same burning question-mark hanging over them. Why hadn't I been happy in Hong Kong? Why did James single me out to deceive and lie to? Why didn't I realise what was going on? Why was it me that had to go through all that hell?

I put my hand in my pocket, looking for a tissue. I pulled out Martha Livesey's booklet. It was a small pocket-sized pamphlet, and on the cover were the author and title: it was by somebody called Laidlaw, and it was called *The Reason Why*.

I began to read. As I read, it seemed as if every word in the booklet had been written with me in mind. Had I been the victim of my own foolishness and the wicked-ness of others? But, I read, that is exactly the problem of the world. Everybody is selfish, nobody ever does

128

good things by nature. Was I angry at God, and bitter towards him? Yes, said the booklet; that is what everybody in the world is like, if they do not know who he really is. In simple language the author explained that there is a thing that the Bible calls sin, that sin makes it impossible for people to have any kind of relationship with God because he is perfect and holy, and that we are all born with it.

As I read on, I realised what sin was. I suddenly saw, as I'd never seen before, my selfishness and hardness. I remembered my marriage. I'd always acknowledged that there were faults on both sides, but now I remembered specific things I'd done and said, and I was ashamed. I thought of the Kokusai, of times when I'd proudly thought of myself as sophisticated and clever when in fact I was being cruel and heartless. More and more things came into my mind, episodes I'd tried to forget. 'Sin' was an old fashioned word, but I knew what it meant, all right.

It was the reason why; the reason why the world was in a mess, why my life was in a mess, and the reason why God had done something about it.

For – I discovered as I read on, absorbed – God had done something about it. He had sent his own son into this messed-up world, to suffer in it and live among the selfish human race; finally even to die for it – and by coming back to life, he had destroyed death.

Suddenly there was an explanation for everything. My unhappiness in Hong Kong when I knew something was missing from my life, but not what it was; the reason for my restlessness and searching. God had been missing in my life, and I saw now that what I had been looking for was something that only he could bring me: forgiveness, peace, love. All my searching for love had led me nowhere. But God was telling me now that there was real love – his love – that made sense of all human loving.

I'd been taught it all before in Sunday School but hadn't understood it. I knew the right words, I could even string together an intelligent conversation with the Martins, but it was only empty words. All the time while I'd prided myself on being a good, decent person born in a Christian country, I'd been keeping God out of my life. But he wasn't going to be kept out. Apparently he wasn't the sort of God you turn your back on so easily. He had come after me. He had even come into Lard Yao prison to find me here under this hospital hut. And he wanted something from me; he wanted my life, to put it right.

I felt a surge of shame. I had suffered and been degraded and disgraced, but so had Jesus Christ; he too had been taken to trial and publicly punished. But unlike Jesus, I was hard and selfish. I had lived my life for my own satisfaction; he had lost his life to save people from their sins. I had given nothing, done nothing, in return. But God had given his son for me.

I couldn't remember when I'd last prayed seriously. But now I felt an urgency to talk to God, to respond to the amazing things I had read in the booklet. I closed my eyes.

'Oh God . . .'

I hesitated. Who was I, to be talking to God?

Then the words spilled out. 'I'm sorry for the mess I've made of my life. I'm sorry I've not wanted you. Please come into my life and change it. I want to give it to you . . .'

Again, I hesitated. Here I was, giving my life to God; but what was the gift worth? Probably a life spent in prison for the next few decades, a life spoiled and disgraced. What sort of a life was that, to be giving to God?

And then, deep inside, the certainty: *I made you. I*

*know you. Give me your life, and I will change it. I want
you for myself. I love you.*

I must have sat there for ages. Eventually I emerged
from under the hospital hut and went inside it. I sat
down in the waiting area and gazed out across the compound, blinking in the suddenly bright sunlight. *It's not
just us who are in prison*, I suddenly thought. *The whole
world's in prison, and I've just been shown the way out.
I've been in prison all my life.*

On the far side was the Warden's office. I could see
her standing at the window, looking at me. Hannah
appeared from the office doorway and came across the
grass. The Warden must have sent her to find out what
was going on.

'You all right?' Hannah sounded placid and un-
alarmed. She was used to my moods.

As I looked at her I could see past her to the prisoners
in the factory buildings. The loudspeakers were relaying
a march; a rhythmical clash of cymbals and a drone of
wind instruments. A guard was leaning against the doorway of the nearest building, reading a newspaper. The
smell of the sewer was strong in the sultry heat. From
the gatehouse block an odour of fish wafted across; there
must have been a delivery.

Hannah raised her voice. 'Come on, Rita. Let's get
back to work. Maybe I shouldn't have shouted at you.
I can see you're upset. OK, so I should have kept my
mouth –'

I broke in gently. 'It's all right now. It's really all
right. Really. All of it.'

'Huh?'

'I've just understood something that's been staring me
in the face for my whole life.'

'You're cracking up. Come on, there's enough to do
in the kitchen . . .' She turned to lead the way.

'I've become a Christian. I finally realised, you see, about God, about Jesus, how it all fits together –'

'Hah!' grunted Hannah, and strode off lost for words.

Later that day I went to the prison library and borrowed a Bible. I began reading it that evening in the dormitory. I had no idea where you were supposed to start, so I opened it at the beginning, at the book of Genesis. The others saw me reading but didn't comment. I read a few chapters. I remembered the creation story from Sunday School. Now it was different. The God who made the world – who had put the sun and the moon in the sky and all the rest of it – was the same God who I had met that afternoon. I didn't understand much about Genesis and had to stop reading because I lost track. But I closed the Bible feeling happy. I might not know much about God, but now I knew who he was.

I was ready for sleep. I prayed again. I talked to God silently, nothing fancy, just telling him about things that had happened and pouring out some of my fears and doubts. I didn't know what the correct way to pray was. I didn't know if I should be kneeling or putting my hands together or what. It didn't matter. As I talked I knew God was listening. I knew I didn't have to go into long explanations about things, that he knew perfectly well what the situation was. And as I told him everything that was trapped inside me, things that I had never been able to tell anybody before, the loneliness I'd been experiencing disappeared.

As I fell asleep a last recollection from the day came briefly into my mind. It was of Hannah, looking at me perplexedly in the hospital hut. I remembered what she'd said: 'You're cracking up.' I shut the memory out. Whatever had happened in the hut had been real. God had done something amazing. I knew things were going to be different now.

132

Over the next few days I was troubled by frequent doubts. Had I really only been clutching at straws? Hannah made it clear what she thought, in a kind enough way.

'I'm not denying it's important to you, Rita. I don't doubt that it's made a difference. But don't bank on it lasting. I've seen too many girls get religion in this place. It's wonderful for a while. But you're in here longer than a while. It takes a pretty good religion to see you through a place like this.'

I spread my hands. 'I can't argue, Hannah. I don't know enough about it. But I know it's real. I'm not fooling myself.'

Hannah shook her head pensively. 'I don't want you to crash any harder than you need, that's all.'

Afterwards, struggling through the middle chapters of Genesis and trying to make sense of unpronounceable Hebrew names, I thought of what she'd said. Was I settling for an emotional trip, something to blot out the harsh realities of prison life?

But I held on to the conviction that if what God had said was the truth, then it could be tested and checked out. As I prayed, I saw things happening. I saw myself changing. I found that I saw things differently. People I'd taken for granted suddenly became important to me. I was grateful for kindnesses I'd previously ignored. I was learning to love people. In many little ways I was changing. There was no mistaking it; my life was beginning to turn round. God's promise to me that day under the hut was actually coming true.

My doubts often returned, but when I considered what was happening in my life, they lost their power. It wasn't simple heavenly-mindedness, burying my head in the sand like an ostrich. This was something so real, so exciting and unlike anything I had ever come across in my life before, that – incredibly! – it might even have been worth coming to Lard Yao to find it.

I was very concerned about my family. One of the worst things about being in prison was wondering what the effect would be on them. It was easier for me; I had regular visits from officials and lawyers; they had to make do with what they could pick up from Embassy letters, occasional telephone calls and reports from people who'd been in Bangkok and come to see me. Mum's visit had left her grieving for me, and the effect of my imprisonment on her was one of the things I hated most about Lard Yao.

So as soon as I could after I had become a Christian, I put Robert Laidlaw's booklet into an envelope and sent it to Mum. At the back of it here was a page headed 'Decision', with a place to sign your name if you wanted to become a Christian. Now my name was written on the page, and I was so sure that Mum would see things as clearly as I had that I had no doubt she would sign alongside my name automatically.

It didn't happen like that. I was frustrated, and pleaded with God: 'It's so easy for you,' I prayed. 'Please make her see. She needs you just as much as I do. Please, God, do something special.'

As time went by, Christians I got into correspondence with went to see Mum and reported some good conversations. But I was so impatient. I wrote enthusiastic letters to her, and she replied carefully, obviously distressed that she couldn't commit herself to something that meant so much to me. 'I do pray, Rita. And what I pray for is that God will bring you home.' It was as if that was the condition which had to be met before she would commit herself. I could understand why she felt that way. A month ago, I would have felt exactly the same.

15 Sentenced

*Today, at around eleven am, I got a twenty
year prison sentence. It didn't come as a
shock, but it certainly came as a surprise, I
was expecting over thirty . . .*

Prison Diary, 9 December 1977

So December, the month I had been dreading for so
long, found me quite a different person. I had no way
of knowing what was going to happen, I knew that all
attempts to track Simon Lo down had failed, and I
realised that there would be no affidavits from Hong
Kong to support my innocence. Mr. Puttri was preparing
me for a severe sentence, and Mr. Lyman was talking
about appeals and amnesties, which assumed I was going
to get thirty years or more. After the months of hard
work by my lawyers, the Embassy officials and people
in other countries, everybody had settled down gloomily
to expect the worst.

Yet I had the most incredible feeling of peace. It
wasn't that I floated round Lard Yao with a seraphic
smile. Neither was it a torpid lack of interest in my fate.
I cared very much about my future, and I still lost my
temper and grumbled and criticised. What was different
was the fact that I knew God was in control. When I
found myself becoming angry and selfish, I was aware
him helping me. I'd never experienced anything like it.
It was as if somebody was standing by my side all the

time, and when storms threatened, tugged my sleeve and drew me back. Suddenly all the 'religious' phrases made sense: 'the Lord is my Shepherd', 'Jesus is in my heart', and so on. I'd heard them and laughed at them before, but now I knew what people who talked like that were talking about.

It didn't matter what the outcome of my trial might be, my life was God's now and he was quite capable of doing what he wanted with it. When I remembered this it made me see the forthcoming sentencing differently.

'Please, God,' I asked, 'give me the strength not to despair. Don't let me be bitter. I'm not strong enough on my own.' It was a prayer I had to pray often as the tension built up, but he answered it.

5th December is a national holiday in Thailand, celebrating the King's birthday. Most of the capital is decorated. Pictures of the King, coloured lights and flags are everywhere. In the prison the holiday was preceded by elaborate preparations by staff and prisoners. Marchers drilled, dancers practised, and decorations appeared on every prominent part of the buildings. The general excitement was heightened by the fact that the royal birthday is traditionally the time of the royal amnesty, when reductions in sentence ranging from a third to a half were given. It would mean that over 300 prisoners would be released. The music blared even louder on the loudspeakers, making reading and even sleeping impossible. It was announced that the music was a special treat for us because it was the King's Birthday.

'It looks very pleasant, Miss Nightingale,' said the English visitor. I'd seen him strolling round with the Warden earlier. 'The grass is trim, the paths well-kept – I'm going to be able to take a good report back.'

He was right. The grounds did look particularly attractive. Prisoners had been set to work tidying and trimming for days in preparation for his arrival.

'Now then.' He looked round cautiously. The guard was standing stony-faced at the door. She didn't appear to be taking much interest. 'I shall be reporting back when I get to England. You know, I've some influence in certain quarters. What I'm saying,' he said, leaning forward intently, 'is that I can drop a word or two in the right ears. Tell me, are you happy with the way things are going? What about Mrs. Castle? Do you think she has helped your case? And what do you think the King will do? Will he intervene?'

I recognised the gambit. Lately a variety of people had visited me in prison, taking an unusual interest in my welfare. There had been a few like him around, trying to trick me into making wild statements and hopefully embarrassing both the Thai and British governments.

'No,' I replied sweetly. 'I wouldn't expect the King to intervene. I'm grateful to everybody who has helped.'

Not long after, an open invitation was issued to the world press to visit the prison, to see for themselves what conditions were like. Again, the prisoners were detailed to get the place into good shape. We became used to seeing small groups of journalists touring the factories. I had to fend off several who wanted to interview me. My reputation as a trouble-maker had increased with the press coverage of my case, and I was very unpopular with the Warden and her guards. It was also the beginning of my rift with Hannah, who bitterly resented the influx of visitors and the fuss that my case was arousing.

At home, the Bishop of Blackburn wrote to the Foreign Office on my behalf, a number of fund-raising schemes were started by the same people who had collected 20,000 signatures on a petition for my release, and I had letters of encouragement and a few Christmas cards. By now I was resigned to the thought that I would not be released. I began to feel that Christmas in prison might not be such a bad experience after all.

The night before I was due to go for sentence, one of the Thai girls in the dormitory approached me hesitantly. She had something in her hand.

'*Khor thot* (Excuse me),' she said. 'I made it for you.'

It was a crocheted necklace, beautifully made in black thread. Many Thai prisoners made such chains to wear instead of jewellery. The Thai people are famous for their skill in handicrafts, and I had admired the patient skill of the girls in the dormitory. I took the necklace gratefully.

'Busaba, it's lovely. Thank you.'

She pressed her palms together in the traditional Thai salutation. 'I wish you great luck tomorrow, Rita.'

'Thank you . . . look, I'll show you . . .'

I rummaged in my box of possessions. Somebody not long ago had sent me a tiny silver-plated cross taped to a letter. I found it, and fixed it to the chain. 'I'll wear it with the cross tomorrow. It's lovely.'

The 9th began like every other day when the doors were unlocked at six am. By seven-thirty all those due to attend court were lined up by the gate. After a roll-call had been taken we were all searched. Often prisoners going to court smuggled letters out for other prisoners, and the guards were looking for these. Then we were crammed into the visitors' enclosure. We waited in the airless heat for an hour. Finally, after another roll-call, we were herded onto the prison bus.

At the courthouse we were put in the Holding Room, which was windowless, about forty feet by thirty, containing four rickety benches and the usual toilet area. In my several visits to court, I had learned its nickname – the 'Hat-Box'. It was the filthiest room I have ever seen.

The toilet stank, and a cracked pipe from the one upstairs periodically leaked into the room, frequently on to some unsuspecting girl who had the bad luck to be standing underneath. Once I was in that room for eleven hours with seventy girls.

Unless people came to visit you there you were given neither food nor drink. On a previous visit I bribed a guard to get me an iced coffee by promising to make her a cake back in prison. Fortunately, on the day I went for sentencing I was called into the court after only half an hour in the Hat-Box.

I was astonished at the number of people in the courtroom, far more than for a normal hearing. A tall Englishman shook hands. 'Hello, Rita,' he said. 'I'm Jim Biddulph; BBC.' I saw television cameras nearby. As we talked bright lights shone on us and the cameras whirred. I was shaken. My mental preparation for this ordeal hadn't included the idea of a full-scale television interview. I began to realise to what degree the press had become interested in my case. I can't remember what I said in the interview except for my reply to his question, 'What do you think will happen to you today?'

'I don't believe they'll let me out,' I asserted. 'They're going to sentence me to imprisonment.'

Afterwards I sat with Mr. Puttri on the bench that had been assigned to us. Behind were a number of spectators. Among them were Mr. Lyman and Leonie.

I was grateful for Mr. Puttri's presence. He of all people had never tried to raise my hopes; but he was sympathetic and explained matters to me. Mr. Lyman had tried to enthuse me and make me excited about my chances, but by that time I only wanted to be done with the courts and find out the worst. Mr. Puttri was realistic and I appreciated that.

As I sat down he looked at me directly. 'They are probably going to give you life, Rita.'

I knew what that meant in Thailand: 100 years.

'If we are lucky,' he added morosely, 'we will get fifty years.'

There was nothing to say. I stared ahead.

A hush fell over the room. The cameramen drew back, the conversation subsided to a murmur. Everybody stood. Judge Udom Tuchinda and his two colleagues entered and took their seats. The court business began. An official rose to his feet and began reading out a lengthy document in Thai.

I closed my eyes. I tried to think of home, family, anything but the Central Criminal Court, Bangkok. The pictures refused to come. My mind was a blank. Suddenly, without conscious thought, I began to repeat to myself under my breath, 'The Lord is my shepherd, I shall not want . . . Even though I walk through the valley of the shadow of death, I fear no evil . . .'

It wasn't something I recited following some notion of what a Christian should do at such a time. I hadn't had time to memorise any Bible passages; I'd only been reading it seriously for a matter of days. The words of Psalm 23 had come to me from childhood, from the past, from home; I remembered that I'd learned them as a child. With a thrill of excitement I realised that God was reassuring me. All those years ago, he had known that this was going to happen, and had planted his words in my mind. I only grasped this fleetingly; my mind was too numb to think about it; but it was enough. I knew God was with me.

The judges were standing up, collecting their papers together. The hubbub of conversation rose again. Mr. Puttri turned to me and permitted himself a smile. 'Twenty,' he said. He seemed relieved. I raised my head and looked round the room. Leonie left her seat and came to hug me.

140

My initial reaction was one of tremendous relief. Twenty! Not thirty, not forty, not fifty – but twenty! Why, with remission for good conduct –

Then anger gripped me. I began to weep. 'Why only twenty?' I demanded. Leonie looked perplexed.

'Rita, it's wonderful news. We were expecting . . .'

'They gave me twenty because they know they're in the wrong . . . it's a stupid sentence, nobody gets twenty for heroin, it should have been at least twenty-five. Don't you see? It proves I'm innocent. I'm innocent, and they've admitted it . . .'

Leonie held me in her arms and let me cry. I sobbed out to her and to the newsmen standing round us, 'It wasn't me, it wasn't me . . . they just took away twenty years of my life, and it wasn't me . . .'

The horror of the sentence swept over me. The prospect of returning to Lard Yao for one day, let alone twenty years, was sickeningly, frighteningly vivid. The guards, perhaps reading my thoughts, moved closer. One grasped my arm. Leonie pushed her away roughly. 'Just give her a minute, give her a *minute*.'

Then all of a sudden the realisation of what had happened to me under the hospital hut flooded over me. Into my mind, unbidden, came the thought, *It doesn't matter. Whatever happens to you now, you've given your life to Jesus. He'll always be with you. You won't be going back there on your own.*

I wiped my streaked cheeks and squared my shoulders. I looked at Mr. Lyman. I could hardly meet his eyes, he looked so sad. I realised that it wasn't just a defeat for him as a lawyer. He genuinely cared for me. He swallowed, and grinned at me determinedly. 'We'll appeal, li'l honey.'

The peace that had descended on me was the only thing that could get me back into that Holding Room. The judges had left, the court was emptying, and I was taken back to the hat-box to be greeted by cries of 'What did you get?' 'How many?' When I said 'Twenty,' there were cries of amazement. '*Chock dee*! (You're lucky!)' came from all sides.

Back in the prison, I was distraught from the tension of the day and the knowledge of my sentence. I agreed with those who told me that twenty years was less than we had expected. But twenty years was twenty years, and the guards had already begun to hint that remission for good conduct was unlikely for a notorious trouble-maker like me.

I began to realise the implications of the sentence. Instead of travelling the world and having a good time, I would be a prisoner in a foreign country for twenty years. I would be over forty when I was released. I would have become middle-aged in prison. My friends would have forgotten me. My uncles and aunts would be old, or dead, when I came out. I might even die in prison myself, far away from friends and relatives.

It was impossible to come to terms with the thoughts that now assaulted me. Things I'd pushed out of my mind, because of hopes that I might still be found not guilty, now returned to dominate my thoughts. I found myself contemplating the worst possibility of all; that one day I would open a letter and read that my Mum had died thousands of miles away in Blackburn. When I thought about it I broke down and cried.

Yet it was not long before that wonderful peace flooded my heart again. Even the damp, drizzly weather that followed my court appearance couldn't dampen it. The day after, Hannah had a visit from Gladys Martin, the missionary. Various problems in the prison had interrupted the Martins' monthly sessions inside the prison, and Gladys, who kept an eye on Hannah's son and reported about his progress to her, had to follow the normal procedure for visitors. Even so, Hannah managed to pull strings as usual and secured the lawyers' room; and the meeting lasted much longer than the regulation ten minutes.

Gladys asked for me to come too, as she had read about my sentence in the newspapers. It was Hannah's meeting, and I hardly knew Gladys, so I didn't feel able to talk about my new-found faith. It was frustrating: Gladys was the first Christian I had seen since I became one myself. I promised myself that soon I'd make sure I had some time with Jack and Gladys on my own.

'Nightingale to the gate-house block!'

It was my day for visitors. I wondered who it might be.

As I entered the enclosure, I saw Margaret and Lucille among the visitors. Lucille saw me first. 'Rita – we read in the newspapers about your sentence . . . We're so sorry.'

I found it impossible to look serious. I was bubbling inside. They looked at my face in astonishment. Then Margaret, awed, said: 'Rita, you're not angry any more. Something's happened.'

I nodded happily. 'You remember you were telling me that God loves me? And about Jesus – I just couldn't see it? Well . . . I can see it now.'

A look of delight spread across their faces. They looked at me, and they looked at each other, and for a while we could only laugh and jump up and down. If the barrier hadn't been there we would have been hugging each other, but we let off steam anyway, to the amusement of the people nearby.

When we calmed down, Lucille said, 'Rita, can we pray together?'

'Oh, yes!'

So, separated by that seven foot gap, we prayed. Margaret and Lucille both prayed aloud, shouting so that I could hear over the uproar of all the other conversations going on around us. They thanked God that he had shown me the truth; they asked him to help me as I entered this new stage of prison; and they prayed for my family. It was the first prayer meeting I'd ever been part of. I can't imagine an odder one! When they'd finished, I said 'Amen' with a full heart.

It was very hard to see them go, and return to my daily routine. I half-expected the reality of my new faith to fade as Hannah had said it would; not that I doubted that God's promises were true ones, but I didn't see how he could make much of a change in Lard Yao. I gradually discovered that, on the contrary, he was changing me.

One problem I'd battled with was nightmares and sleepless nights. It happened regularly enough to make me worried; in Lard Yao, sleep was important. You needed all your reserves, and the cumulative depression caused by several bad nights could take a week to disappear. I would often wake up to find one of the Thai prisoners, anxious that my soul had strayed into danger on some dream-expedition, shaking me: 'Where is your spirit walking?' they would say. One morning, I woke up with swollen eyelids.

'What do you think's the problem?' I asked Hannah. 'My eyes look awfully funny.'

'I'm not surprised,' Hannah replied drily. 'Apparently you kept the dormitory awake half the night. I've never heard you so bad. You were sobbing like your heart would break. Do you have to let yourself go like that? There's others need to sleep . . .'

'You mean I was crying last night?'

'Oh, come on, Rita: you know you were.'

But I didn't know. So far as I was concerned, I had slept soundly. I didn't even remember dreaming. As I slept, God had enabled my mind to be at peace and let my body handle my sadness on its own.

Canon Taylor, the Bishop of Bangkok, visited the prison regularly. He was a very friendly man, who made it his business to introduce himself to all the foreign prisoners and also had good relationships with the Thai people in Lard Yao. He once mentioned, his eyes twinkling, that he saw me as one of his 'parishioners'. He arrived on one of his regular visits shortly after I had become a Christian, and I told him about it.

Before Christmas I went through a time of depression. Of course separation from my family was especially poignant at that time of year. I was also being closely watched by the guards. Now that I was no longer 'on trial' and was a fully-fledged prisoner, their attitude towards me changed. A rumour that I was about to commit suicide reached the Warden's ears, and she ordered a special watch to be kept on my movements. One day I was standing near the gatehouse block when a guard shouted out to her colleagues, 'Get her further inside! She has got twenty years – she might try to run away!'

All this emphasised that fact that I was a prisoner, answerable to others and watched from morning to night. It was amazing, however, how God seemed to know exactly how much I could stand; when I had had enough and couldn't take any more, mail began to arrive for me – piles of letters and Christmas cards. Many of those who wrote said they were praying for me. My spirits rose. I'd always known I could depend on my family's support, but here were hundreds of people I'd never met who were concerned for me. God answered their prayers. I still became depressed, but it was as if God was waiting at the end of every tunnel to comfort me.

'The choir's arrived!'

Jenny's head appeared round the kitchen door. 'Canon

Taylor's here. He's come for the service. Wow, I do feel Christmassy!'

It was Christmas Eve, and pouring with rain. Christmas is not widely observed in Thailand except among the foreign population, but we were allowed to celebrate it in Lard Yao. We were well into our festivities. The Thai prisoners and the guards looked on in amusement as we prepared a Western Christmas with all the trimmings – a member of the Embassy staff arrived a few days before Christmas with a chicken, salads, mince pies and fresh cream. Other goodies arrived from friends. We had almonds, jellies, fruit, coffee, biscuits, jam, chocolate . . . it all looked quite strange in such a hot climate, but was none the less welcome. Leonie had sent in a Christmas pudding that day, and a jar of mincemeat. Six of us were making mince-pies; a Chinese girl called Lily, Georgina from Canada, Chris and Jenny, Hannah and myself. The final touch of festivity was provided by my forty-two Christmas cards, which we displayed in the kitchen.

'Merry Christmas!'

Canon Taylor appeared at the door, soaking wet, a flurry of wet umbrella and handshakes all round. He twirled his umbrella gaily. 'And how is everybody today?'

'Mind where you're splashing!' warned Hannah, and took it from him. He beamed at her.

He had come with the Christ Church choir to hold a carol service. It was lovely. Georgina, Chris, Jenny and Hannah didn't want to go to the service, so I went with Lily and really enjoyed it. The service ended with communion – my first as a Christian. A Catholic priest spoke to the Thai prisoners, and also chatted to Maria in Spanish.

I was very weepy. I was missing my family, and uncertain as to what the future held. That afternoon I started a letter to Mum, in which I warned her that the Embassy had told me that my hopes of a successful appeal might be affected by the amount of press publicity there had been. 'It's not going to be easy and I don't know what it's going to do to me,' I wrote, 'but I have strong faith now, and also I have you and the family.'

At four pm an announcement was given over the loud-speaker. 'Everybody must report outside their huts for a roll-call.' Amidst loud groans we all obeyed. After three separate roll-calls it emerged that somebody was missing and the guards thought she had escaped. While I was washing later, a call went out for everybody to report to their dormitories to be counted. Apparently the roll-call had revealed that we had two more prisoners than the official count, and the guards were panicking. It got sorted out eventually. A typical ending to the day, I thought. Merry Christmas.

We had a hilarious evening in the dormitory. Maria had a wonderful sense of humour when she chose to use it, and it was good to unwind. I stretched out on my bed feeling pleasantly drowsy, and reached for my diary.

'Well, it's Christmas,' I wrote. 'Today has been better compared with the last few, and for that I know I must thank the Lord, because now I know he's helping me. And this peaceful feeling could only have come through him, so who says prayers aren't answered? Not all prayers, it's true, otherwise I wouldn't be here, but who am I to question his reason for me being here, although I think I know why . . .'

I woke early. It was a grey drizzly morning. I lay under my mosquito net listening to the rain. The net was a fairly recent acquisition. I'd paid a small fortune for it, but it was bliss to be free of the mosquitoes.

Under the net was a lovely surprise – a parcel from Lily. I didn't open it then, because I wanted to save it

147

for later. I went to the kitchen to start work, though I doubted whether there would be much work done that day.

An official was sitting with Hannah when I arrived, which put a damper on things. The others arrived. Lily had to ice a cake before coffee. We busied ourselves in small tasks until eventually the official left.

We hugged and kissed each other. We exchanged little gifts. I was given makeup, a T-shirt, soap – much-appreciated luxuries. After coffee and sweet bread I changed into a lovely new dress Mum had sent, and I even put my shoes on. They felt awkward after months of going barefoot or sandalled. We sat around the radio and listened to Christmas carols. Chris and Jenny wept, and as the familiar strains of 'Silent Night' echoed round that unlikely setting, I busied myself making the fruit salad, glad of an excuse to conceal the lump in my throat.

A power cut finished the carols. We had Christmas dinner early at eleven am. Roast chicken with stuffing, mashed potatoes, greens – a traditional Christmas feast. Officials were coming and going all morning, staring at the food. In the end we sat down to a cold meal because so many guards had been inspecting the oven and the fridge, making excuses to hover. After the meal nobody spoke very much. We all fell silent – too silent; I know where I was, and it wasn't in Lard Yao.

We baked nothing for sale in the prison shop that day. In the afternoon we had mince-pies and cream. I was feeling so peaceful I even offered a mince-pie to my least favourite guard, an enormously fat woman who had watched over me in court.

That night I continued my letter to Mum. It was the hardest part of the whole Christmas for me. I could picture them so clearly at home, sitting round the television, Uncle George playing with the kiddies. 'I am with them,' I wrote in my diary. 'Oh, Lord, how I'm with them – letters just aren't enough . . .'

I wrote to the Embassy, thanking them for the food. I wrote out a well-loved poem:

> And I shall flee from the darkness, from the cold place of silence;
> for my heart wants flowers to hold in my hand.
> Beautiful songs, beautiful flowers . . .

I allowed myself to think briefly of all that had happened in the year that had passed. I contemplated the future. *God could burst open the doors of this prison, I thought, and I could walk free tonight. I wonder if he will . . .*

I reached for my diary and added a final sentence. "I've kept it at bay all day; but what a desolate loneliness I feel inside – will it pass?"

16 Growing

*Terrible letter I wrote you and Ann last
week, but I'm pleased to say, I'm back on
top again, not all my own doing, the Lord
Jesus has helped me and I know he will
continue to do so, so I ask you only not to
worry about me, OK? . . . It'll be
Christmas when you get this . . . I want
you to have a good time Mum, and please
don't worry so much, I'm reading my Bible
a lot and keeping very much to myself, I've
found a quiet peace of mind and I'm not
thinking about the future in any way . . .*

Letter home, 18 December 1977

Incredibly, I woke up on Boxing Day with that deep
sense of peace. It had to strengthen me through some
setbacks. I heard that I had to return to court the next
day.

My decision to appeal against my sentence had been
a difficult one to take, because previously I had decided
against doing so. Mr. Lyman, however, advised me very
strongly after my sentencing that I should appeal.

'You've got fifteen days to sign an appeal affidavit,' he
explained. 'Don't you think you ought to try every possible avenue of release? How are you going to explain to
your family that you had the opportunity of registering
an appeal – and didn't?'

I thought about it. 'Perhaps you're right,' I said.

'I surely am right,' he declared. 'And another thing. If you don't appeal, it's going to look as if you think you got off lightly, and that will make the Official Prosecutor think again.' I realised the force of his advice and took it. The affidavit was submitted within the time limit.

The Official Prosecutor has the option in Thai law of appealing against a judge's sentence if he considers it too light. The summons to court which I received on Boxing Day could only mean that he had lodged a counter-appeal. Such turned out to be the case. He was appealing for an increase to thirty years; his argument was that I had clearly intended to distribute and sell the heroin.

Mr. Lyman responded characteristically. 'His appeal is a reaction to our appeal for a reduced sentence,' he told the press. 'It is tit-for-tat. I personally do not think that he has a cat in hell's chance of pulling it off.'

Though it was normal procedure, Mr. Lyman thought it strange that the Prosecutor had appealed. A large body of public opinion supported me; there was even some support for me in Thailand. One thing the Prosecutor's action did achieve; it made me determined to go ahead with my own appeal. Mr. Lyman was optimistic about its chances.

So, all things considered, 1978 began on a high note. If all went well, I would be home before another Christmas.

Another foreigner, Jenny, arrived. Her pliant personality made her particularly badly fitted to adapt to prison life. Her arrest had been almost identical to mine; she had been found in possession of three kilos of heroin at the airport. She was Dutch, and became friendly with Chris. Jenny thought she was German at first, because she heard her speaking the language fluently. It was an odd relationship; in many ways they were quite different.

Jenny was an avid reader, for instance, and would devour any reading matter; Chris read nothing but romantic novelettes, which she preferred in English because she found reading Dutch difficult. Their stormy friendship was punctuated by frequent arguments and torrents of flowery Dutch, rising to a crescendo of screams and usually ending in blows. Chris was so big and strong that none of the guards dared to interfere, so it was usually me who tried to separate them.

Jenny's case was typical of the arbitrariness I saw in prison. Her case was virtually identical to mine, and moreover she pleaded guilty. She was expecting a light sentence, and we all thought she would get one. When she returned after being sentenced her face was white.

'How was it?' we asked her.

Jenny's reply was a faint whisper. 'Thirty years.'

The news was met with disbelief. 'It can't be right. You've made a mistake –'

'It should have been sixty,' whispered Jenny. 'They halved it to thirty because I pleaded guilty.'

That night Jenny broke down and was hysterical for several hours. When she finally slept we discussed her sentence. Nobody could work out what subtlety of law had determined that sentence, when the normal sentence one might expect would be forty, maybe fifty years.

The next day was Jenny's twenty-fourth birthday.

I was sitting in the dormitory reading my new Bible. It was a present from Lucille and Margaret, and I was reading it with the help of some Bible reading notes that Gwen Abbott had sent me from England.

Gwen was a Christian who had seen me on the television news and couldn't forget me. She seemed to hear a voice inside her insisting 'Write to that girl.' She'd never had an experience like that before and wasn't sure what to do about it. After some weeks of the insistent demand, she struck a bargain with God. 'Tell me her address in Bangkok and I will write to her!' The next day the newspapers printed the address of Lard Yao. She wrote to me regularly and prayed every time she sat down to write, that what she said in the letter would be helpful. God answered her prayers, because her letters were just what I needed. She also sent me helpful booklets and devotional material such as Selwyn Hughes's *Every Day with Jesus*.

I looked across at Maria. I'd been praying for her for some time. I felt very fond of her, partly because she reminded me of my mother, and I couldn't forget that she had a family outside as well. She was a very religious woman, but also a very sad one, and I wanted her to know the joy I'd found. The problem was, I still didn't speak much Spanish, and her English was very poor. I was helping her with it each evening, but the results were slow.

As I sat watching her reciting her rosary, I racked my brains to think of a way I could share my Bible reading with her. Suddenly, I hit on an idea. I went to Maria's bed, and pointed to a Spanish Bible that she owned. I indicated mine, and placed the two side by side. Then I showed her the passage I'd been reading in my English Bible. Maria caught the idea. Leafing through her own Bible, she found the same passage. She read it and clapped her hands. 'Good! Good! We read together.'

We began to spend time together each evening, sharing with each other Bible verses which we found helpful. It was extraordinary how much we could share with so few words. It was also a very frustrating way of learning which we both found agonisingly slow. Of course I couldn't explain the verses to her, only show her where they were in the Bible, and I couldn't lend her the material Gwen had sent because it was in English.

In the end I wrote to Gwen, explaining that Maria was

a Spanish Roman Catholic and asking if she had any booklets in Spanish. 'Please send anything you can get hold of,' I requested. She did. Now Maria was getting Christian literature to read as well as her Bible.

It was hard to accept the sight of a woman in her forties lying on the floor, sharing our rough life-style, and bathing with a crowd of others in the morning and evening. We younger people could put up with it; Maria was different. I felt very sorry for her. After a while I could understand her mixture of languages and enjoyed her company even more. She had a sharp sense of humour, and was quite a character as well. At night she would build what she called her 'parapets' round her bed, to keep the mice away. She would stuff an old bolster with clothes and odds and ends, and carefully position it round her. Not until it was settled to her satisfaction would she settle down to sleep.

One of the unexpected bonuses of my new, 'sentenced' status in prison, was better sleeping quarters. Hannah arranged for me to share her room, which only had eight other girls in it. I asked if Maria could be moved over from the 'on trial' room as well. This was because she was still unable to speak much Thai, and I was one of the very few who could have any sort of conversation with her. The Warden gave permission.

The new quarters were much more pleasant. We were no longer shut up at six o'clock, because some of us were late getting back from our work. My status in the kitchen changed too; I was now officially working there. Before, I had worked there from choice. Once again Hannah's influence made sure things worked out as we wanted them to.

Sitting up in the evenings was a new experience. Sometimes I would sit with Hannah and one or two others in the kitchen, listening to cassettes on her player. Often, too, I would sit with Maria in the twilight outside our door, laughing and chatting until bedtime. The others used to laugh at me.

'What are you doing talking to that crazy woman? She's mad – doesn't understand a thing anyone says to her!'

'That's the very reason we should spend time with her,' I retorted, but they only laughed.

I was a young and inexperienced Christian. My initial sense of peace was still very strong, but as I prayed and read the Bible I began to understand that God was doing much more for me than simply calming my anger. He had forgiven me. I had been proud of the fact that I was wrongly arrested, that though others in the prison deserved to be there, I didn't. But as I found out more about Jesus and saw his life in contrast to mine, I became increasingly aware of the things that needed sorting out. As I talked to him, God made me realise my selfishness, my pride, and many other things I had to face up to. I might have been wrongly arrested for one wrongdoing, but there were many other things I had done for which I had never been punished. And as I realised that, I asked God to forgive me, and he did.

I had always been moved by the plight of my fellow prisoners, many of whom were in prison for some act of stupidity or anger and had been abandoned by their relatives. I wished I could speak Thai more fluently, so that I could talk to some of them in detail; I was very glad that the Martins were around, because they were able to help the Thai prisoners. I developed a deep concern for prisoners in general, not just those in Lard Yao, but all over the world; sometimes I would lie awake thinking of the hundreds of thousands of people in prisons near and far. One old lady had brought me a booklet; a few missionaries visited regularly; but it was a handful of people, and there were so many that needed to know what Jesus had done for them. I began to pray for prisoners, those I knew in Lard Yao, and those all over the world who I didn't know anything about personally.

My Christian life was unusual already. My friendship with Maria was the nearest thing I had to Christian fellowship on a day-to-day basis; and we could hardly speak each other's language! A great many things which new Christians learn quickly and relatively painlessly were hard for me to learn, because I was in prison.

I took many of these problems to Jack and Gladys Martin. I had always had a quite civil relationship with them; I'd even been to their meetings. But I'd brushed aside their friendly conversation-starters, and had assured them that yes, of course I was a Christian, thank you very much. But now I really was a Christian! Their work was mainly with the Thai prisoners, and at the meetings Jack showed films in Thai and talked to them. The Martins had quite a shock when, as soon as the ban on their work was lifted and the monthly meetings restarted, I turned up with my Bible, anxious to learn as much as I could. They were thrilled; they hugged me, and when I tried to apologise for my off-handedness in the past, they brushed my apologies aside. 'We've been praying so hard for you,' they said.

They came only once a month, but I saved up my questions, and they sat down with me and helped me. They were the only Christians who ever had regular close contact with me at normal speech levels. Margaret Cole was once allowed into the prison to see me in the lawyers' room, but Lucille only ever saw me through the bars and across the seven-foot gap.

Lucille's faithfulness was something which taught me many things about what the Christian life involves; in her love for me I saw reflected the love of Christ. She was not young, did not have much money, and was in indifferent health. Yet she came to see me regularly, making the tedious journey from Bangkok and often waiting for up to two hours to see me for ten minutes. When Margaret eventually left Thailand, Lucille continued to come on her own. She put up with frustrating difficulties to make her weekly visit. When I was forbidden visitors for various reasons, she would still queue patiently for two hours or more just so that she could leave a gift for me. She brought me food and various necessities, and Christian books. I would have hesitated to ask my own mother to do what Lucille did for me while I was in prison. Indeed, the other prisoners referred to her as my 'mother' – 'Hey! Rita! Your mother's here!' was a familiar cry on Thursdays. Lucille did in fact write to Mum regularly; often brief, terse airmail folders, but always containing exactly the information Mum wanted. When I was unable to write because of a mail embargo, she wrote and reassured Mum.

'Please, Lucille,' I urged her after a particularly rowdy visiting session, 'don't come every Thursday. I can't bear to think of you queuing for so long, only to end up having to shout like this. It isn't worth it.'

She shook her head. 'Rita, it is worth it. It's worth it to come here and remember what you used to be like. That makes it really worth it.'

If opportunities to spend time with other Christians were scarce, church worship was non-existent. Canon Taylor held a monthly communion service in the prison, together with a Catholic priest who spoke Thai. I attended many of those services, and the Easter and Christmas services were highlights too.

So, though Christian fellowship was non-existent in the sense that young Christians usually know it, God compensated by providing me with wonderful Christian friends outside the prison, and by supplying the answers to my most important queries.

My attempts at Bible reading were a case in point. I was fortunate to have a Good News Bible, a modern translation which was much easier to understand than the Authorized Version in the prison library. I began by studying Genesis, but soon ran into problems. I kept wanting somebody to explain things to me. As I read further, I became more and more perplexed, and by the time I was into Exodus I was ready to give up. Then Gwen Abbott's letters began, and I used the devotional booklets she sent.

I still had problems, however. One day I talked them over with Jack and Gladys.

'I want to read the Bible properly,' I explained. 'I'm enjoying reading a little piece every night, but I want to read it right through as well, like any other book.'

'Great!' said Jack. 'What's the problem?'

'Genesis is,' I replied gloomily. 'I can't make head or tail of a lot of it. I tried jumping ahead to Leviticus – that was even worse.'

'Do you know how the Bible is made up?'

'Not really. I know that the Old Testament comes before the New and that's about it.'

'It's a collection of books, Rita, written at different times. There are history books, poetry books, letters, law-books, hymnbooks – all collected into one volume. They're all part of God's true word to us, but you don't have to start at page one and read all the way through to the end. Would you read a hymnbook right through like that?'

'No, of course not!' I was much relieved.

Jack and Gladys suggested I should start with one of the Gospels, and that's what I did. I loved to read about Jesus's life, the things he did and the things he said, and as I read about his death and coming back to life again, it was wonderful to know that the old story was true.

He had really died and been raised to life, and now I knew him and could talk to him.

One of the most exciting things about being a Christian was the way the time-worn 'religious' phrases became real and meaningful. I was 'saved', I was 'born again', I had 'asked Jesus into my heart' – I'd smiled at such things when I heard people say them in the past, but now I knew what they meant.

I had no commentaries or Bible dictionaries. When I came across something I didn't understand, I made a note of it and asked Margaret or Lucille when they came, if it was a minor problem, or saved it up for Jack and Gladys if it was complicated and needed an extended chat. My Bible reading really got under way when Jack gave me an American Bible study correspondence course. I worked at it every night, and Jack collected my papers each month and marked them for me. It was very helpful to have to follow a system of study. I was so excited by the Bible that I was always dipping in here and there, finding out what was in the various books. I didn't stop doing that, but it was good discipline to have to read a particular topic as well.

I was in the kitchen working with Jenny and some of the other girls.

'Jenny,' I demanded suddenly, 'you know all that about the Ark and the Flood?'

'Huh?'

'You know – the flood that drowned everybody in the world, and God told Noah to build an Ark to keep his family safe.'

'Oh!' Jenny registered recognition. 'It's a story in the Bible. Sure, I know it.'

'Well – it's true!'

Jenny raised her eyebrows. 'No, Rita, it's a story. It couldn't have happened.'

I launched into an animated argument about the flood. The Martins had given me a book on biblical archaeology, and I was fascinated by it. I was fired with the excitement of my new knowledge. Jenny listened patiently, interrupting with an occasional query. At the end she sighed.

'Yeah – I'm really pleased for you, Rita. It's really nice, it's good that you have this thing.'

As she turned back to her work, I noticed Hannah frowning at us. She found my new enthusiasm for the Bible irritating. She mistrusted it. As my faith grew and didn't wither away, I hoped that she would be sympathetic, but she remained sceptical.

'Oh, people in prison do turn to God; of course they do. They've got nothing else. You were at rock bottom. You saw something you thought you could hold on to. Yes, I can understand.'

I tried not to be hurt by such comments, and to think instead of the things I could see in my life which had changed. I had evidence that Christianity was true. I *was* evidence.

I was so sure that anybody who would seriously consider Christianity could not fail to be convinced by it, that I constantly told people about my own experience of God and showed them Bible passages which had meant a lot to me. Mostly they nodded appreciatively and let me finish. I was disappointed that nobody became a Christian upon hearing about what had happened to me, but I found that they gradually accepted that it seemed real and valuable for me at least. Sometimes, when one of the girls was distressed about her case, or was worried about their home and family, I hesitantly suggested, 'Would you like me to pray about it?' Often they would say yes. Also as the months passed some of them began to talk to me about their problems.

I sometimes wondered whether I should be more

160

aggressive about my faith. I read Christian books about people who had helped dozens of people to believe in Jesus. It seemed to be something which every Christian should be trying to do. I was living among Buddhists, atheists and drug addicts; people were sharing my life who didn't know about Jesus. What should I be doing?

One major barrier to communication was my poor knowledge of Thai. I was able to make small-talk with the Thai prisoners, but I couldn't imagine explaining the Bible to them. I just didn't have a large enough vocabulary. So I concentrated on building relationships, trying to put right my earlier dislike and harshness towards them. As I got to know them better I became very fond of many of them. I shared with them what I could about Jesus, and prayed that God would override any difficulties my inadequate Thai had introduced into the conversation.

Most of the foreign prisoners knew I was now reading my Bible and praying, and that I was meeting with the Martins and other Christian visitors. They were amused by the amount of studying I was doing, and the fact that my life was so full. 'Why don't you lie on your bed and be bored, like everybody else?' I was often asked.

But there was so much to do that I couldn't be bored! Every night I followed the same routine. First I exercised for a quarter of an hour, which was a long time in the sweltering evening heat. I really needed it, and it worked; I kept to the same weight for my whole time in prison and stayed in good health. So I put up with the fact that the guards and the other prisoners laughed at me for doing it.

Then I wrote up my diary. My diaries were odd documents; a mixture of my new experiences as a Christian and the resentments and frustrations with which I was still battling. There were many things which I still had to sort out in my head and I knew that I must sort them out; I prayed about these things, but it was a help also to write them down in a book which nobody else read. Praying to God was just like talking to a close friend about anything I wanted to. Writing in my diary was helpful in a different way; the act of writing it down helped to release the tension. Even so, as I looked back over entries in my diaries, I could see the change that had taken place. One striking change was in my handwriting. Before, I'd scored the page with the force of my bitterness. Now, my handwriting was clearer, neater, and more even. It was a reflection of the way I'd changed as a person.

I wrote letters next. When anybody in the family had a birthday or anniversary, I would make a special card, using dried flowers from the prison grounds and bits of coloured tissue. I spent hours on little details, lettering and so on. I'm not a very good artist, but I enjoyed making things. The other girls began to ask me to make cards for them, too.

A large part of the evening was spent reading my Bible and Christian books. I was hungry to find out as much as possible, and the Martins had a knack of producing just the right book at the right time.

I gave Maria help with her English in the evenings too, and we'd share our Bible verses, pointing them out to each other in our respective Bibles.

Finally, I settled down to sleep. At first, I prayed only in the evenings, telling God what had happened that day, talking to him about problems that I'd had, praying for other people like Maria and Mum, and thanking him for the things I'd discovered in that evening's Bible reading. It was a good way to end the day. Later on I began to pray in the mornings as well before I got up.

Sometimes I remembered the evenings I'd spent stretched on my bed, cursing my misfortunes and blaming God for abandoning me to Lard Yao. Now I was talking to him, as a Christian! The wonder of the transformation shook me one day when I found myself praying the unthinkable: I was thanking God for allowing me to be imprisoned.

'I would never have found you outside, Lord,' I confessed. 'I had to come here so you could show yourself to me. Thank you for bringing me to Lard Yao.'

I always prayed silently. It was just as well. If any of the others had heard that prayer they would have thought I was going out of my mind. As it was, I smiled at the irony of the situation and fell asleep.

17 Forgiving

*I do try and I do pray, that I will
completely put all my trust in Him and that
I accept that however long I am to be in
here is for my good and it's to fulfil His
purpose, because I know He has a plan for
my life. I just pray for the courage to accept
His will. I'm all talk, because I'm still so
self-centred and proud, and He's done so
much for me.*

Prison diary, 28 March 1978.

The beginning of 1978 was dominated by my appeal for
a reduced sentence. Unlike the sentencing procedure,
this only involved two appearances at court: once to
register the appeal and then to hear the result. The first
hearing was the one immediately after Christmas, at
which I heard that the Official Prosecutor had lodged his
appeal to increase the sentence, and that the results of
both appeals would be given on the same day. I didn't
forget that the appeal was being processed, but I was
able to put it out of my mind for long periods.

Letters continued to arrive from home. I found one
of them very interesting indeed.

'A firm of lawyers in London want to take up your
case. They've asked for all the details. They are international lawyers. They really do sound as though they
might be able to do something.'

It was an exciting piece of news. The lawyers had offered to assist on humanitarian grounds, without charging any fee or expenses. The head of the firm personally handled a lot of correspondence and paperwork for my mother, who trusted him completely.

The firm strongly advised that we should do everything possible to avoid stirring up any adverse publicity against the authorities in Thailand, and that my best interests would lie in using every possibility open to me under the Thai judicial system. In their opinion my best hope of release would ultimately be in securing a King's pardon. I saw this news as confirmation that my appeal had been a wise move.

In Blackburn, an old lady handed over a weekly fifty-pence gift for me at my aunt's shop, as she had done for months. There were hundreds like her in different parts of the world. I was grateful for them all.

The press continued to draw attention to my situation. In February news came that David Allin had been awarded a commendation in the British Press Awards for his work on my story. The Lancashire Evening Telegraph pointed out that the paper would continue to reflect the 'intense community interest' in my case, and this it certainly did. 'I only hope the commendation will attract more attention to the unhappy plight of Rita,' David commented, and continued with his three stories a week about me.

It was during a time of very bad tension between me and the Warden that I went to the Martins in great distress.

'I can't stand it.'

Jack and Gladys were collecting their belongings together after their monthly visit. Gladys looked up from packing hymnbooks into a carrier bag.

'Whatever's the matter, Rita?'

'It's the Warden. I've tried so hard. I don't know how

to forgive her. I don't want to forgive her. She hates me. I know she hates me.'

Jack and Gladys sat down. Gladys reached for my hand. 'Talk about it, Rita.'

'I can't help it; I can't forget all the things she's done to me. She's branded me as a trouble-maker, and it's not fair. I'm always getting into trouble.'

Gladys held my hand as I released my frustration in a heated tirade. 'She wouldn't let me put my arms round my Mum . . . I had to see her in that filthy visitor's enclosure . . . Oh, I hope somebody does something like that to her some time in her life. And there was a beating on New Year's Day – you don't know what it's like in here after you've gone, they're always beating people and it's all the Warden's fault.'

Gladys and Jack looked at me thoughtfully. I waited defensively for them to make the obvious comments – both they and I knew that there were things to be said on both sides of the issue. I knew that though I was genuinely trying to relate to the Warden differently, I was still tormented with bouts of resentment and my behaviour was still very erratic.

Gladys's reply was quite different to what I had expected.

'You haven't forgiven her yet, Rita.'

I gasped. 'But I have, I really have! You have no idea how much I've prayed . . . But God hasn't changed her.'

'*How* have you prayed, Rita?' interjected Jack.

'What do you mean?'

'You see, there are two ways of praying about a problem like this. You can try to enlist God's sympathy on your side against the other person. Or you can ask God to simply change the whole relationship you have to her. You must choose whether you change or she does.'

I fell silent. Into my mind flashed an image of the severe-faced, crisply-uniformed woman who ran Lard

Yao. I tried to think of her as a friend, as a human being like myself, but shook my head in despair.

'I can't do it, Jack. I've such bitterness in me.'

'That's right. You can't do it. But Jesus can.'

Suddenly remembering the changes in my attitudes which I could already recognise, I nodded slowly. Gladys smiled.

'It won't happen overnight. You have to go on forgiving. Jesus told his disciples that they should forgive seventy times seven times. Keep bringing her to God, Rita. Tell God about your feelings. Don't try to be something you're not. Ask God to change you into what you want to be.'

'Satan is trying to make things as difficult for you as possible,' added Jack. He grinned. 'He's letting all this anger build up, until your own bitterness hurts you. You're doing his work for him, Rita.'

God followed that conversation up swiftly. Jack and Gladys gave me a book, *The Freedom to Choose*. It was tremendously helpful as I began to put forgiveness into practice. I was finding that forgiving somebody was much more than having warm thoughts about them. It was hard work, an effort of the will. In that hard work the book played an important part. I think I underlined every paragraph in it. What made me particularly happy was that the book dealt with problems which loomed very large in my life and which I hadn't had time to ask the Martins about. God had supplied the answers anyway.

As I learned about forgiveness, my understanding of what was involved expanded, sometimes painfully. Passages in the Gospels seemed to leap from the page and bore into my brain. As I read about the attitude Jesus had towards his enemies, I was ashamed of the state of my heart. I found it hard enough to forgive the Warden, because it meant accepting that I too had been in the wrong. But gradually I had to face up to the fact that I had to forgive James, Simon Lo, and Alan Soon as well. I couldn't put the matter out of my mind. God kept reminding me that it needed sorting out. I argued with him as I prayed.

'Why do I have to forgive them, God? They used me. I didn't do anything to deserve it. Surely I don't have to forgive them. They deserve to be punished and humiliated, not forgiven!'

As I fell silent, I was aware of God's answer. He was not going to let me forget. Pictures and memories filled my mind. I saw James, proposing marriage to me. I remembered a contemptuous denial in a hotel room: 'Who are you?' An image of Alan Soon, silent and arrogant in the Interpol interrogation, swam before my eyes. Try as I might, I couldn't ignore them. And, as more and more of my deep resentments were brought to light, I had to face up to the fact that I had been nursing bitterness against the police, because they had arrested me and let Lo and Soon go.

It was a slow and painful progression. Each person had to be prayed over, agonised over, and forgiven. When I thought I had really forgiven somebody, I would find myself resenting them two or three days later, and have to forgive them all over again.

It was only as I looked back, as the days became weeks and the weeks months, that I saw that my attitudes were changing. I was learning how to forgive.

I had periods of doubt and uncertainty; my Christian visitors had warned me that I would. I never doubted the reality of Jesus, but I often stretched his patience; I demanded the most stupid things, just to test him. He even gave me some of the things I'd asked for.

I was also periodically oppressed with loneliness, when

the distance between Bangkok and Blackburn seemed infinite. I feared that somebody would kill me in the prison. There were plenty of assassins inside – convicted murderers who had killed ten or more people for the equivalent of twenty English pounds each. I was unpopular with some of the guards. Sometimes I would be unable to shake off the fear that one of them had paid an assassin to despatch me. The fear was in all probability irrational. But that didn't make it any less real.

It was especially hard at such times to know that all my Christian friends were outside. Jack and Gladys suggested I should pray in the mornings before the day began, so that I could bring all my worries and fears to Jesus. I began to do so, and it helped.

In all these matters I realised more and more that being a Christian wasn't just believing in a philosophy or a set of religious statements. It wasn't a matter of signing a membership card or joining a church, neither of which I could do anyway. Becoming a Christian was entering a relationship. It was getting to know somebody, and it was getting to know yourself. As I found out more and more about God and what he had done for me, I discovered things about myself I'd never realised. It was this process of discovery, which often involved realising things I didn't want to realise, that convinced me that Christianity was true.

18 · Rejected

*April is the hottest month of the year here
and we're all just about suffocating at
present . . .*

Letter to Mum, 23 April 1978

'Liar!', said Maria. I gritted my teeth.

'You're imagining it, Maria. It isn't true. They – are
– not – talking – about – you. Do you understand?'

Maria shrank back against the wall. There was a crafty
look in her eyes. 'Why they not speak English, then?
Hah! They speak Dutch. Why should they speak Dutch,
if they not talking about me?' She stamped on the floor,
like a judge rapping his gavel on the bench. She waited
for my answer.

'Maria, they are Dutch, you know. Jenny and Chris
are Dutch, that's their nationality. For heaven's sake,
Maria, they can surely speak Dutch together and not be
talking about you.'

Maria scanned the room fretfully. Hannah, Lee, a
Chinese girl, and a few Thai prisoners all ignored her.
Jenny and Chris stared back at her. She dropped her
eyes and muttered angrily.

I was becoming very worried about Maria. She was
growing edgy and suspicious. She jumped to conclu-
sions, thinking that anybody chatting quietly in a corner
must be discussing her. The episode with Jenny and
Chris was the latest in a long line of incidents.

I did what I could to reassure her, but she was becoming more difficult to reassure. 'Why do I bother with her moods?' I asked myself sometimes, but then I reminded myself that her case was still uncertain and information was difficult to obtain. She must have been frantic with worry.

She became obsessive about cleanliness. Cleaning the room and wiping it down was one of the prison chores, but Maria went further. Everything had to be just right. I was sleeping between her and another, very untidy girl, who left books and clothes strewn everywhere. Maria's complaints developed into a vendetta. Often, when matters boiled over into bitter argument, I thought 'This isn't like Maria. She wasn't like this when she first came in.'

The times spent sharing the Bible, learning English and joking together grew fewer and fewer while her outbursts became more frequent. A minor mishap at a mealtime would provoke a fury. I became more worried. I wondered it it was the change of life; there was *something* changing her personality. I prayed for her every day. Maria's friendship had become very important to me, and I was deeply concerned.

People came and went; new prisoners arrived, others left. I found time passing very slowly. Though I had lots to do, I lost the sense of time passing. Sometimes I would leaf through the pages of my diary and think, 'I'm sure time passed much more quickly last year.'

Hannah's attitude towards me was changing. She had accepted the fact that I was now a Christian, but she disliked hearing me talk about it. She was extremely sceptical about my appeal. Whenever a fresh burst of publicity blew up about me, she was sarcastic and pessimistic. She felt that I was making a great to-do about

171

something which I should have accepted gracefully; after all, my sentence was only twenty years.

One night in July I was working through an English lesson with Maria when the door of the dormitory was unlocked. A guard began reading out a list of names: mine was among them. 'To go to court tomorrow,' she explained.

I was frightened. 'It's the appeals,' I said. 'There can't be any other reason. They're going to tell me the results.'

Maria put her arm round me. 'It'll be all right, don't worry. It'll be all right. You'll see.'

Hannah, across the room, gave a short ironic laugh. 'You're for it now, you silly cow,' she called out. 'Now you'll get what's coming to you. All this talk and public protests . . . you'll see where it's all got you now.'

I couldn't reply. I lay on my bed and prayed silently, for strength to face whatever was going to happen next day.

At the court house I had to wait several hours before I was called. The Hat-Box no longer existed; I was told to wait in another room. The Hat-Box, I was told afterwards by a prisoner, had been removed because of the foreign interest in my case and the journalists who were covering it.

I sat on the floor with the other prisoners awaiting their hearings. I had a book by a Dutch Christian, Corrie ten Boom, in my pocket. I turned the pages and began to read.

At the head of each chapter was a verse from the Bible. Each one of them, as I read it, was like a message from God to me.

I began to pray, my head bowed, as the conversation flowed around me and people shifted around restlessly in the heat. My prayer wasn't hopeless and despairing. I looked around the room and prayed for each of the other prisoners one by one. I prayed for their families, and for their cases. I prayed that God would make himself known to them as he had done to me. Then I prayed for the guards. I told God about the things that were making me resent the guards, and I talked about them with him. As I prayed I realised that I felt differently now.

I opened my eyes. The Thai girl sitting near me was staring at the floor. 'Sawadee (Hello),' I ventured. She smiled at me shyly. I asked her what she was coming to court for, and she embarked on a long story only part of which I managed to understand. But it was an opening.

Others nearby saw us talking and joined in. We exchanged simple Thai sentences. They told me about their families; I told them about mine. In other court appearances I had been preoccupied with my own problems. This time God brought me out of myself. I even smiled at the guards as they went back and forth. When my name was finally called, I went quietly. This time I didn't need to be pushed into the courtroom.

Mr. Southworth, the Embassy official from Blackburn, greeted me. Mr. Puttri came over and shook hands.

'Is Mr. Lyman here?' I asked anxiously.

'It was difficult to find out what is happening,' said Mr. Puttri. 'A messenger has been sent: I think he is on his way.'

I sat down with Mr. Puttri. The judge came in. We rose as he entered. When we sat down again a court official read out a document. This time my Thai was adequate to grasp what it meant. Mr. Puttri confirmed it.

'Your sentence stands, Rita: our appeal has been rejected.'

I felt sick. I hardly registered the fact that the Official Prosecutor's appeal had also been rejected.

Reporters from the Bangkok papers swarmed round, asking questions about prison conditions, lesbianism and beatings. I ignored them. I was used to trick questions by now. I went over to Mr. Southworth. He looked very dejected. 'I don't see how I can have faith in anything now,' I wept.

Inside, I knew that nothing would shake my faith in Jesus. My despair was for those who had worked so hard for my release, and the impossibility of further court applications.

Mr. Southworth put a hand on my shoulder. 'You have an excellent case. You could appeal higher, to the Supreme Court.'

I shook my head. 'I had the strongest possible case when I first came into this court, Mr. Southworth. I was innocent. No, I'm done with courts. I will not appeal to the Supreme Court.'

Mr. Puttri held an impromptu press conference. 'No further appeals,' he stated. 'The next step is to apply for a King's Pardon. This we shall do as soon as possible.'

There was a flurried entrance at the door of the court room. Mr. Lyman, breathless and annoyed, entered. 'How did it go?' he demanded.

'It was rejected,' Mr. Southworth replied. 'So was the Official Prosecutor's application.'

Mr. Lyman looked at me squarely. 'The Supreme Court?'

My face told its own story. Mr. Lyman nodded. 'OK, li'l honey, we'll go flat out for a King's Pardon.'

The guards approached to take me back to prison. 'A King's Pardon!' repeated Mr. Lyman.

What none of us referred to was the one fact we all knew. In Thai legal history a pardon for a convicted heroin offender was unheard of. Such an amnesty had never been granted.

19 Ann and June

*How can you comfort friends who've just
had such heavy sentences passed on them?
The sentences are getting heavier . . . I'm
afraid my calm optimism has taken rather a
severe blow. But don't worry kid, I'm not
half as upset as I sound . . .*

Letter to Ann, 8 July 1978

The big event of the summer was the arrival of my
sisters, who came to visit me. Their journey was paid
for by the generosity of the Portia Trust, an English
charity which helped women in trouble and had interested itself in my case.

'One thing's for certain,' I said to Hannah. 'There's
not going to be any repeat of what happened with Mum.
I'm going to see the Warden.'

'Hope it goes well,' she grunted. 'You never know
your luck.'

When Embassy officials made one of their regular
visits, I asked if they could also discuss my sisters' visit
with the Warden. They said they would do what they
could. When Lucille and Margaret came on Thursday,
we prayed about the arrangements.

When I asked the Warden if special arrangements
could be made for the visit, she agreed that Ann and
June could visit me for an hour each weekday, in the

175

office used for Embassy visits. I was thrilled, and very grateful to the Warden.

I was so excited on the day they were due to arrive that I kept jumping up and down like a schoolgirl. At last the loudspeaker blared my name, and I rushed to the Embassy room.

Just as I'd done with Mum, I rushed round the screen and hugged them. They were laden with presents – a lockable cosmetics bag, English tea, my favourite liquorice – and they'd brought some things I'd requested for Maria: cigarettes, some nighties, and other odds and ends. I didn't give the gifts a glance. The sight of my sisters was marvellous.

'You're so grown-up!' I exclaimed, over and over. It was true. June had left her schooldays behind. It made me realise how long it was since I'd seen them. 'And Ann – you've not changed a scrap! You look great!'

They were enthusiastic in their turn. 'You look so well,' said Ann. 'And you're so happy,' they kept saying. They couldn't get over it. 'We've never seen you look like this before . . . When you came home from Hong Kong you didn't look like this – it's really from inside . . . You look marvellous.'

'Make sure you tell Mum,' I insisted. I repeated it several times in the week they were in Bangkok. I couldn't forget how I'd looked when Mum saw me in prison, and I wanted to be sure that she would know I'd changed.

'How is Mum?' I demanded. 'And Uncle George and Auntie Mary and everybody? What's it like at home? What sort of a trip did you have?' The questions tumbled out.

'She's great,' they assured me. 'She's keeping busy. We have reporters all over the place now. They keep ringing up – Mum's had the phone number taken out of the directory! We can't go anywhere in Blackburn without being recognised. You wouldn't believe it!' they laughed.

I drank in every detail, and inspected them minutely. It was so long since I'd seen them.

'Your skin's so fair,' I told them wonderingly. I was amazed at their English complexions. I'd got used to seeing dark skin all around me. I was very tanned myself. The girls in the prison who saw my sisters arrive commented on the same thing. 'Your sisters are really pretty! And they have such light skin!'

Each day Lucille took an hour off work to bring them to Lard Yao, and all my friends helped to make them welcome. Jack and Gladys took them out sightseeing, so they saw something of Bangkok. I had told my sisters in letters that I was now a Christian, and I was very glad that they were able to meet my Christian friends.

Among the first people I asked my sisters for news of were my Uncle George and Auntie Mary. Ann and June had been dreading the question. My uncle and aunt had been our next-door neighbours since I'd been born; they were the closest to us after our mother and father. Shortly before Ann and June left for Bangkok, Auntie Mary, who had suffered from arthritis for years, took a sudden turn for the worse and was rushed to hospital. Within days her liver and kidneys had failed and she was in a coma. Doctors said that there was no more they could do for her, and advised Uncle George to prepare himself for her death.

Ann's husband John said that they should tell me she had died. It was inevitable, and it would be better if I heard it from my sisters than if an official brought the news. But when they arrived neither could bring herself to say it.

'How is she?' I asked anxiously. I had already heard she was in hospital.

Ann looked uneasy. 'She's very ill.'

'But she's going to get better . . . isn't she?' I insisted. Ann and June didn't speak. A cold fear seized me. Then I heard myself saying calmly, 'Yes; she is going to get better.'

That night I prayed with all my heart that if Auntie Mary were to die, it should not be until I returned home. I couldn't bear the thought of her dying without knowing Jesus, and I wanted desperately to have the opportunity to share my experiences with her.

A day or two later, back in Blackburn, my aunt moved in her bed and opened her eyes. 'Please, could I have a glass of water?' she asked an astonished nurse.

She made a full recovery.

It was a wonderful week. We shared all sorts of family gossip, and caught up on the things you can't put in letters. Ann saved a special surprise for me until the last day.

'I went to the doctor before I left England,' she said. 'It's been confirmed, the tests are OK. I'm pregnant! I wanted you to be the first to know,' she added. 'I haven't told anybody else yet.'

As the idyllic week came to an end and we said goodbye, June was in tears. 'Don't cry,' I comforted her. 'I want you to go home. I don't want you to see me here again, because I'll be seeing you in Blackburn. I want you to tell Mum how happy I am, and I want you to keep her spirits up.'

I wasn't crying. I felt peaceful and relaxed. Then, as they disappeared out of sight, through the gate, I turned and went to my room. I pushed open the door and lay down on my bed. *Then* I cried – for a whole morning.

God arranged the visit perfectly. Not only were the

arrangements totally different to those when Mum had visited me, but the timing of the entire visit was very precise. The Warden was helpful and sympathetic; she granted the special favours I asked of her. But only a week or two later, I received the news that a public charity in England had decided to launch a new political party: the Rita Nightingale Party. They felt that public sympathy might secure enough votes for me to be adopted as a candidate for the parliamentary seat recently vacated by Barbara Castle. The theory behind the plan was that the Thai government would never dare to hold a British Member of Parliament prisoner.

It was a foolish scheme, if only because of the effect it had on me in prison. My reputation as a trouble-maker, which I was trying to shake off, was dramatically enhanced. The publicity generated was not all favourable towards me, and it embarrassed Barbara Castle, the British government's representatives currently handling my case, and the Thai government. The Telegraph in Blackburn quoted (in translation) a leading article from the principle Thai newspaper, the Siam Rath:

> It would be a great historical achievement in the annals of Thai history to have a British MP in Lard Yao gaol . . . If she is elected there must be no thought of paroling her or reducing her sentence under any circumstances – let her stay in prison, in Thailand.

I appreciated that the campaign was undertaken and supported out of sympathy and concern for me, but it was one of several examples of organisations not well-placed to see the results of their efforts. The Warden was very angry about the publicity, and about the new wave of press coverage it generated. Articles appeared which quoted criticisms I was supposed to have made of the prison. I never said the things they quoted, but the Warden didn't believe that. My relationship with her slumped dramatically. I do not believe that a request for special visiting privileges then would have been successful.

The increased hostility from the guards made life difficult, and it took a while for life to get back to normal after Ann and June's visit.

My fragile friendship with Hannah broke down completely when the new publicity campaign began. Things became so fraught with tension that I had to stop working in the prison kitchen. This meant that my privileged food arrangements came to an end, and I had to use the prison shop like everybody else. I was put to work in Factory No.1, where I operated a buttonhole machine. We made children's clothes and sometimes army uniforms. It was hard work when there was a big army contract to fulfil; I went to sleep at night with my fingers rough and aching. When things were slack, however, we were allowed Saturday and Sunday off. A radio played constant Thai music as we worked. Occasionally I persuaded the guard to tune to a Western station playing music I liked. The result was usually a very tearful Rita Nightingale, wallowing in some sentimental ballad from home, until the other prisoners decided that enough was enough.

Now that I was no longer in the kitchen where most of the foreign prisoners worked, I had less opportunity to speak English. I had to set to and learn Thai properly. I helped one girl to read the letters she received from her English boyfriend (they married eventually and set up home in Birmingham, England).

Even so I often thought I would never understand the Thai people. I no longer called them animals and fools. I found that like me they had their strong points and weak points. I discovered I had been wrong in many of the judgements I had passed in my bitterness before I became a Christian. But I was still perplexed at many of the differences between Thai and Western attitudes.

The factory was built of cement blocks, with a wire-covered gap near the ceiling. Often, birds would find a way in and fly around for a while until they could escape again. One day I was unpicking some stitching when a small feathery bundle dropped on to my hand. A bird had flown inside and blundered into one of the newly installed electric fans. Now it lay in my hand, breathing rapidly, a fatal gash in its skull.

I looked down at it and watched it struggling in its death-throes. Suddenly one of the older Thai women rushed over, took the bird from me, and cradled it in her hands as its life ebbed away.

'What was all that about?' I asked one of the English-speaking Thai girls.

She smiled gently. 'She did not want the bird to die in the embrace of a foreign spirit,' she said softly.

I knew little about Buddhist attitudes to the spirits of animals and birds, or about their belief in reincarnation, and I found the incident perplexing. My perplexity increased when a week or two later a girl received a serious head wound from one of the fans while cleaning it. Nobody paid any attention. I was the only one who even reacted. I took her to the prison hospital, and she had to go to an outside casualty department in Bangkok to have the wound properly stitched.

20 Valerie

*Maria never speaks a word to me, she never
said good morning let alone Happy
Birthday on Friday.*

Letter to Mum, 17 October 1978

I was becoming more and more worried about Maria.
The mystery over her sentence did not clear up. The
brief radio announcement that she'd been given life was
never followed by any official mention of the matter; and
she wasn't called to court.

Her behaviour was increasingly strange. She had been
cheerful when my sisters were visiting. That time, in
fact, was one of the best I ever had with her; every day
after they left I sought her out to share the delicacies
they'd brought and tell her all the things they'd said.
That was how close we'd grown. I didn't relate in this
way to any of the other girls. I really liked her and felt
terribly sorry for her. It was so hard for her, not knowing
English well. At least the rest of us could argue with our
lawyers.

I doubt if Maria had realised, even then, that she had
been sentenced to life imprisonment. She was obviously
distressed because she had no visitors and because the
legal machine seemed to have ground to a standstill.
Because of prison regulations then operating, which said
that letters could only go in and out if they were in Thai
or English, she had no letters either.

One day I was sitting with her, sewing. Maria was very edgy. She was picking up bits of thread I'd dropped, and winding them into tiny skeins. As I watched her, I made a decision.

'Maria, I'm going to write to your son. He should know what's going on. He may be able to help.'

Maria looked up in alarm. 'No, no; my son is good boy, don't bother him.'

'But he must be told. He'd want to know.'

'My son is good boy. Doing many things for me. No write to him.' She began arranging the skeins into rows, carefully aligning each one with the next.

I finally managed to extract an address. I wrote a long letter to her son, explaining the situation and pointing out that as we were unable to get information ourselves she needed outside help. The letter was returned two months later. Across the address Maria had given me were scrawled the words 'No such address'.

I wondered what was going on. Had Maria given me a false address deliberately, or had it been a lapse of memory? It was one more disturbing incident.

After many months, Maria's case began to move forward again. The usual process of preliminary hearings began, and eventually she was told she would be going for sentence. I sat up with her the night before she went to court. She was very distressed. When she came back next day, she said that nobody had mentioned life imprisonment at all. She had been sentenced to forty years.

We didn't know what was going on. I didn't know whether the original rumours had been true or false. We weren't well-placed to assess the situation.

I tried to cheer her up. When she came back I treated the sentence as good news. That was a bad mistake. Hearing sentence passed had made Maria realise the reality of imprisonment for the first time. And forty years is a very long time.

As a convicted prisoner she was put to work in one of the factories, but before long she began to refuse to work, staying in her room instead. I tried to argue with her.

'You must go to work, Maria. It's not good for you to spend so much time alone.'

'I'm all right. Not want to go out,' she replied stubbornly.

'I feel like that, many times,' I reasoned. 'But you are doing it so often.'

It was true; sometimes it was good to stay in all day, just so you could be on your own. Every six weeks or so, when things got on top of me, I stayed in myself, just to be alone. But if you did stay in, it always involved an argument with the guards, and you were locked in, so it was effectively self-imposed solitary confinement. It wasn't long before Maria was staying in every day.

She stopped going with me to the prison shop; she stopped wearing shoes; her obsession with cleanliness and tidiness became fanatical. I was going through a difficult time after the Rita Nightingale Party episode, so I found relating to Maria made me even tenser. The other girls were also becoming impatient with her. In addition to her other idiosyncrasies, when we were settling down for sleep Maria would start speaking to herself in Spanish. A torrent of protest invariably greeted this: 'Shut up, you silly old bag!' – or worse. Maria, whose grasp of English was adequate for her to realise she was being vilified, only spoke faster and louder. Eventually a guard would appear to find out what the uproar was about. 'Hah! It's Maria – that crazy one,' was the usual reaction. The guards usually left us to get on with it ourselves.

Further up the corridor was a group of four small

cells, making a unit. Two girls from there had been released recently. 'Maria,' I suggested, 'Wouldn't you like to move in there? Then there wouldn't be so many people around you.'

She looked at me doubtfully. 'You too?'

'Sure,' I replied, and went to see if Hannah could fix it up with the Warden. Hannah was only too glad to be rid of Maria, and the Warden gave permission when she was approached. 'But it must be a permanent move,' she stipulated. 'You cannot go back and forth. If you go there you must stay there.'

The changes in Maria meant that we were much less close on the spiritual level. I'd really appreciated our Bible reading; and she had been a help to me in many ways. As she became more distressed I began to pray specifically that I might have a Christian companion inside the prison; somebody who could help me to help Maria, and with whom I could pray and read the Bible. I had no idea how such a thing could happen. I couldn't pray that a Christian would be imprisoned in Lard Yao: I wouldn't have wished the place on anyone. But I was desperate for Christian fellowship. I knew I wasn't mature enough to help Maria on my own. 'Please, Lord Jesus,' I prayed, 'send somebody to help.'

It seemed impossible, unrealistic. And then, when I had almost given up hope, Valerie came.

Valerie was a prisoner. She arrived with two other girls; they had been held in a prison in Northern Thailand and were moved to Lard Yao while they were on trial. I liked tall, cheerful Valerie right away.

'Where are you from?' she asked me.

'I'm from England. I lived in Darwin, then Hong Kong.'

'I'm from Adelaide,' she said. 'Couple of Aussies, we are! OK, Rita, tell me what's what.'

I spent some time with her, helping her to settle in, and we became friendly. After a few days it seemed as if we'd known each other for years.

One day we were sitting on the steps of the hut. I was explaining something about prison routine. I realised she was looking at me thoughtfully.

'What is it about you?' she said. 'You're different. You walk round this place and you're contented. You've got twenty years – what on earth have you got to be contented about?'

I took a deep breath and launched into my story. 'Well, about a year ago – before I was sentenced, in fact – I was really angry and bitter. I'd been set up to take drugs through customs in Bangkok. I got caught, and ended up in prison while the guys who set me up got away scot free.'

Valerie nodded. 'Yes . . . It's always happening. You carried the can.'

'Didn't I just. I was told I was going to get fifty years, or life . . . I thought I'd go out of my mind. And then I had an incredible experience. I found out about Jesus.'

Valerie looked up suddenly. I continued. 'I'd known about him when I was a kid. I thought I was a Christian. But I found out I wasn't. And I had to sort it out. In the end I told God I was sorry for everything. I became a Christian . . . now I feel peaceful inside. I never was before. Even before I was in prison, there was something missing.'

There was a brief silence. Valerie's normally humorous face was thoughtful and serious. Prisoners nearby were arguing vociferously about something; the music on the loudspeakers changed to a different march. We sat wrapped in our thoughts.

'I had an experience too.' Valerie spoke slowly, as if she was choosing each word before she said it. 'It was

186

up in the other prison. I was in a cell, and I began thinking about my life.'

I didn't say anything. I listened intently as she told me about herself.

'I was married when I lived in Adelaide. One day I just left my husband and took off with a rucksack. I was looking for something; that was why I started to travel. I don't know what I was looking for but I knew I was looking for something. I read books – about Buddhism, all sorts of things. One of the things I got into was drugs. I thought they might help me. In the end I bought some stuff from a pusher. The pusher turned out to be a police agent.'

I groaned sympathetically. It was incredibly bad luck to have been arrested for drugs when you'd never even tried them.

'So I ended up in jail. One day I was in the loo, or something – anyway, there wasn't any privacy, there never is. All the other prisoners were standing round laughing and talking and smoking cigarettes, and suddenly I blew up at them and started swearing. I went berserk. Everyone ran for safety. They thought I'd gone crazy. Anyway, I stayed in the room all day. And I thought and thought about my life, about the foul things I'd done – I don't mean the drugs and the trial, but everything in my life – and I found myself saying "Sorry" over and over again. I couldn't stop. I just kept repeating "Sorry", I don't know who to.'

The other girls, said Valerie, hadn't been able to make sense of it at all. Evidently it had been a deep and catastrophic experience for her.

She asked me more about my experiences. I told her how I'd found the Bible was true, that God existed and loved me. We talked on, until I had to go. I went off to work in the factory. When I returned that evening Valerie came running to meet me. She had a Bible in her hand. 'Look! Look!' she cried. 'Look what I've found in the Bible!'

It was the story of Nicodemus. Valerie was beaming with joy. 'It's true, Rita! It's true!'

I was overjoyed. We threw our arms round each other and for a time we stood hugging each other as prisoners pushed past us, stolidly ignoring our cries of delight. Strange things were always going on in prison.

We prayed together. I asked God to give Valerie a deep understanding, to teach her about himself just as he had taught me.

Valerie spent the next morning in the prison library, reading solidly. There were some Christian books there; some were ones I'd been given and had put in the library. She buttonholed anybody within reach, pointing to something that had impressed her, saying 'Hey! Look at this amazing thing I found in the Bible!' The other girls groaned. 'Oh, no . . . now another's gone like that!'

Her arrival was a definite answer to prayer. But though it was wonderful having her in Lard Yao, I didn't want her to get a long sentence. She thought she'd get twelve months, but I tried to encourage her, saying 'No, you'll get less than that.' But somebody else with a very similar charge was sentenced to a year around then, so it was a hard time for Valerie. We spent a great deal of it in discussion. I think she must have read the whole Bible in a couple of weeks. Her mind was razor-sharp; she'd read the prophecies of Nostradamus and all sorts of other weird books, so she had a lot of hard questions to find answers to. There were no Christians close at hand to whom I could go for help. We were able to ask Lucille and Margaret or Jack and Gladys about some of the questions. For the rest, I could only tell her what I had learned from my own brief experience as a Christian and my sketchy knowledge of the Bible.

188

'Perhaps,' she said once during a complicated discussion, 'God could have been an astronaut.'

'He couldn't be!' I protested, quite sure she was wrong, and not at all sure how to prove it. I made a quick silent prayer for help.

'Well,' continued Valerie, 'not in the sense he wore a glass helmet and a suit and all that, but still, when you think of all the planets in the universe . . .'

'I don't think so,' I countered, and tried to point out Bible passages which seemed to indicate God wasn't an astronaut.

These debates weren't destructive or bitter. Valerie really wanted to know the answers, and she had a backlog of questions to ask. For me, it was great; I really enjoyed having my mind stretched. And it was exiting to find, as we studied the Bible and prayed together, that though it was uncomfortable to be challenged to think through what one believed, the Bible really was true and did have answers.

Most of all, I was grateful that God had provided me with somebody to share my faith with and to help me help Maria. That was what I'd prayed for; it was what God gave me. Valerie became fond of Maria too, and because she was concerned for her, she was able to comfort me when I was distressed about her.

'I was up all night with her,' I sobbed one day as we were reading our Bibles together. 'I don't know how to cope. I explained to her, people aren't persecuting her. I spent all night explaining it, and this morning it's made no difference at all . . . I've had no sleep all night.'

As I wept, my gaze fell on the Bible in front of me. It was open at the passage where Jesus promises that where two or three people are gathered in his name, he will be present with them. I showed the passage to Valerie.

'Maria,' she said at once.

I nodded. 'Yes. Maria.'

'We've got to pray for her, Rita.'

So we prayed for Maria, that God would give her troubled mind peace and that he would help us as we talked with her and tried to help her.

21 Changing

Still with all that I'm happy! Yes sir! No
way will I get down over these things
again. Maria and I are back friends,
although not as close as before. Valerie,
Aussie girl still here, but probably leaves
some time this week . . . I really thank God
for the time we've had together.

Letter to Mum, Ann and June, 12
November 1978

'She's got a knife!'

A guard ran across to where Valerie and I were sitting
on the steps of our dormitory hut. 'Maria's gone mad up
there! She's got a knife!'

The shimmering, hot afternoon seemed suddenly chill.
A crowd gathered, as people emerged from the other
buildings and girls in pyjamas on their way from their
baths stopped to see what was going on.

The guard was frightened and angry. 'Do something!'
she ordered. She pointed at me. 'You're that crazy
woman's friend. You go and talk to her.'

Valerie pulled me back. 'You *can't*,' she said. 'Maria
will never take it, not from you.'

She was right, I realised. Maria thought I was going
to murder her anyway. There was no knowing what she
would do to me in that state, if she had a knife.

The guard stood over us, waiting. 'I'll go up,' said Valerie. 'But we've got to pray about it, Rita.'

That morning, we had shared Jesus's promise that he would be present where 'two or three gathered' in his name, and the words came back to me vividly as we sat on the steps and prayed that in some way Valerie would be able to reason with Maria, despite the language problem and Maria's disturbed state of mind. The crowd watched us with interest. Then Valerie went up the steps and into the building.

The minutes passed. I wasn't able to hold back my tears. Prisoners talked animatedly as I sat with my head in my hands, praying and sobbing alternately. I imagined the worst, that Valerie was lying up there wounded. 'Do something!' I urged the guard. 'She might be in terrible trouble!'

But the guard did nothing. I wondered if I should go up. Then I realised that if there were a delicate situation going on upstairs, my appearance up there might be disastrous. So I waited and continued praying.

I heard Valerie's footsteps clattering down the steps. I looked up: she was radiant. Her excitement was so great that she could hardly speak. The people standing round pressed close. 'It's not a knife!' she stammered. 'It's a crucifix! And she understood me! She understood every word I said!'

This was a miracle. Maria had never been able to understand Valerie's Australian accent, and when the three of us were talking together I frequently supplied a 'translation' for her. And now, though highly excited and overwrought, Maria had understood Valerie's words and they had calmed her down.

We both went back upstairs, embraced Maria, and kissed her. We told her gently how harmful it was for her to be on her own so much, and reassured her that people weren't talking about her behind her back.

'They're bad,' she complained fretfully.

'They're not,' we insisted. 'You mustn't mind them.'

'When did you last eat?' asked Valerie. Maria shrugged.

'We'll make you something,' we said. We persuaded her to eat a little, though it was difficult for her after starving herself. For a few days afterwards, she seemed to be improving.

Valerie and I often talked about Valerie's future. She wanted eventually to go back to her husband. He was still writing to her, and he'd said she would be welcome if she came back. 'It's not that I didn't love him,' Valerie explained. 'I just had to get away, you know? I realise now what I was looking for. I had to come to Lard Yao for the reason you did – to find Jesus.'

She had been God's special gift to me, too. My first regular Christian fellowship! What made it such a special relationship was the way we'd become friends. Her experience in the northern prison was unmistakeably the work of God, who was beginning to reveal himself to her. I thanked God that he allowed me to put some of the pieces together for her, and be a friend at the point where she willingly and completely committed herself to Jesus and became a Christian.

She had such a rich personality, with many gifts. She was an accomplished artist – she drew a magical portrait of Maria which caught exactly that undercurrent of madness that ran in her features at that time.

It was a useful talent, too. Her hair was long, and when she arrived in Lard Yao it needed attention. We persuaded her to have it cut. We warned her not to expect too much from the prison hairdressers.

'They're not very brilliant,' Chris warned her. 'Forget what you've heard about the genius of Thai hairdressing. Our lot missed out on it.'

'That's OK,' Valerie said. 'I'll draw what I want.' And she drew a beautiful portrait of herself, complete with earrings, the way she wanted to look. Then she went off to the hairdressers.

An hour later we heard her cheerful whistle. When she appeared we gasped in admiration. She looked stunning. Her hair was short, framing her slender strong-boned face and emphasising her startlingly blue eyes. It was the sort of haircut you would have been happy to have anywhere in the world. We couldn't believe Lard Yao had managed such an amazing result.

We talked together to some of the other girls about Christianity. Many others listened in to the conversation – in the crowded prison rooms it would have been hard to avoid overhearing! There was one girl in particular who was a friend of Valerie's. When she was about to be released I gave her a booklet about Jesus, writing inside it, 'Hoping that the things you've heard Valerie and me talk about will give you food for thought, if not now then in the future – think about these things, love, Rita.' But her release was unexpectedly delayed, and the booklet I thought she would read out of prison was in fact read in prison. When she finally did say goodbye, she grasped my hand.

'Rita, that book has given me something to think about. I did listen to a lot of what you and Valerie talked about. But I'm not going to do anything about it now. If I did, people would say it was only a reaction to prison. When I get home, I'll make up my mind about it.' So we had somebody else to pray for together.

It was not very long after the incident with the crucifix that we saw, sadly, that Maria was deteriorating again. A blank, strange look had come into her eyes.

One morning we were queuing for our hot water together.

'See – they're doing it again: I see them,' muttered Maria.

'Huh?' I responded absently.

Maria pointed at Chris and Jenny. They were talking Dutch. 'They talk about me. They are speaking *Dutch*.' She looked cunningly at me. 'They speak Dutch so I will not know. But I know.'

Behind us in the queue somebody laughed. 'Maria's flipping again.'

I lost my temper. 'I spent half the night telling you, Maria, people don't talk about you behind your back. But it's just a waste of breath! I'm sick of you saying it. I won't listen to you any more, I won't, I won't!'

Without a word, Maria seized the pan of near-boiling water and flung it at my face. I only just managed to dodge; drops of the scalding liquid spattered my face. Valerie pulled me out of harm's way.

'You can't stay here.' She was white-faced. 'I'll queue for you. She's out of her mind.'

I went to find Hannah, who was angry. 'I told you,' she said. 'You go in with a crazy one like that and that's what happens. Didn't I tell you so?'

The result of the episode was that the Warden forbade the guards to allow Maria to stay in her room all day. She wandered round the prison instead, shoeless, dressed in an old sarong. Eventually the authorities took action. She was committed to a mental hospital in Bangkok, and was there for two months.

The day for Valerie to go for sentencing arrived. We prayed together before she went. She was quietly confident. 'I feel I'm going to be allowed home, because I've found what I left Australia, my husband, everything for.'

She was given a light sentence because of the small quantity of drugs involved and the circumstances of the

195

arrest. They gave her three months, and allowed the time already served in prison to be taken into account. She was to be released in a week's time. When I knew she was going out, I gave her some of my prison diaries to take out with her and post home for me. I'd kept the diaries a secret from the prison authorities, and smuggling things out of prison was forbidden. I worried about breaking the rules in this way, but in the end I just couldn't resist seeing the diaries sent safely home.

Lucille and Margaret had prayed with us that when Valerie left I wouldn't feel it as badly as I expected, that I wouldn't be shattered. It really did happen that way. I was sad when she left, but not devastated. I was happy for her, and I could see that her time for release had come and mine hadn't. I didn't know why the long negotiations for a King's pardon hadn't made any apparent progress yet, but I simply carried on with my various activities and thanked God for giving Valerie to me for as long as he had. I was surprised to find myself reacting like that. I had feared that I would be heartbroken. Observing my peaceful acceptance of Valerie's departure, I saw it as one more example of the way God was controlling my life.

In one connection, however, I missed her especially: my relationship with Maria. We'd prayed together, and we'd seen God working in so many ways. But now Valerie was gone, and Maria was in hospital. What was God doing? Why had he not at least given Maria peace of mind, if for some infinite reason it was right she should stay in prison?

But he hadn't. She was in hospital, living in some weird mental nightmare, out of my reach and beyond our help. I did not know what would happen. Of all the hard things I had to accept in prison, Maria's suffering was one of the hardest to bear.

So 1978 drew to a close. I had been a prisoner for nearly two years and a Christian for just over one of them. My case was still regularly discussed in the newspapers. I was visited by various important people, who seemed anxious to hear my version of the story; on one or two occasions I was summoned to meet them in the Warden's office, and found silver tea-things set out.

One evening, some weeks after Valerie had gone out, I was on my way up to the dormitory when I found my way blocked by a guard.

'Stop!'

She stood in the corridor between me and the room. I stopped.

'Whatever's the matter?' I said innocently. The guard folded her arms.

'You cannot go in.'

I scratched my head. I couldn't think of anything I'd done wrong lately. It was hard to take the situation seriously. The guard wasn't one I knew very well, and my rather perplexed smile was meeting with no response.

'Why can't I go in?'

'You are being punished.' A thin sneer spread across her face. 'You in big trouble. You had letter.'

By now completely confused, I was about to demand further information when I saw movement behind her. Two more guards were carrying things out of the dormitory. One had my box of possessions, the other my bedding. They dumped their loads unceremoniously in the corridor and walked past us, not looking at me.

'Those are *my* things. What is going on?'

'Your things are being searched.'

I turned my back on her and ran downstairs and out to the kitchen. Hannah was clearing up.

'What on earth's happening up in the dormitory?' I said breathlessly. 'All my stuff's been thrown out!'

'And so have you,' returned Hannah equably. 'You really are in for it now.'

'What am I supposed to have done?'

'Don't you know? You gave Valerie your precious diaries to take out. And Valerie wrote you a nice letter telling you all about it. Went into all the details. I expect you'll be able to read it after the Warden's finished with it.'

I couldn't believe it. Not Valerie. She had been here, she knew the score; she of all people wouldn't have done such a stupid thing.

But she had. As it sank in, my name was called on the loudspeaker.

My interview with the Warden was not pleasant. She was extremely angry.

'You will lose all mail privileges and all visiting privileges for three months after Christmas. You will be moved from your dormitory. Do you understand?'

That night I entered my new dormitory, the most unpopular person in the prison as, amid protests and scowls, I lugged my pile of belongings into a cramped little floor space such as I hadn't seen since I became a member of Hannah's privileged entourage.

Yet in spite of the punishment hanging over me, it was a wonderful Christmas. Canon Taylor organised special services with his Roman Catholic colleague (a Thai-speaking American who had made his home in the Bangkok slums in order to be near the people he had come to serve). Jenny and Chris came to the carol service and met a Dutch lady in the choir, and just like the previous year we ended up crying as we sang the carols.

My second Christmas in prison was a much more significant experience than the first. It's true I had been a Christian twelve months before; but I was moved then more by the familiar traditions and symbols, bringing the world of home sharply into my mind, than by what those traditions were talking about. A year later, I could look back on God's presence in my life, the reality of Jesus Christ, and the ways in which he had changed me. Christmas was now not simply an age-old festival of well-loved carols and Bible stories. It was a celebration of the birth of somebody who had become the most important person in my life.

We received gifts from each other and from visitors. One of the gifts I received was a book of Christmas carols. On Christmas Eve I took it with me to work. The machine I operated in the factory didn't need continuous attention; I propped the book against it, and for the whole day I sang carols at the top of my voice, tunelessly and joyfully. My Thai fellow-prisoners must have thought I was crazy. Tears were streaming down my face; tears not of sadness but of joy, because for the first time I was singing the familiar words with a real understanding of what they were talking about.

On Christmas Day I woke up depressed. The trouble with the Warden dominated my mind. I lay in bed as the others got up, and I relived the episode over and over again. I knew I should not feel bitter towards her. Jack and Gladys had told me that, and I had found it to be true. So I consciously forgave her for her harsh punishment.

But another thought intruded; an unwelcome one. Smuggling things out of prison was against the rules. *It's a silly rule*, I thought fiercely. Unbidden, part of me responded with: *But do I, as a Christian, have the freedom to pick and choose which rules in this place I'm going to keep and which I'll break?*

It's an unchristian rule, I argued with myself. *It's petty and it doesn't make sense.* Again, I heard myself arguing back. *Of course it makes sense. Just because you're not doing something really wicked doesn't mean that others might not be. Do you expect the Warden to trust everybody to do the right thing? This is a prison, for heaven's sake!*

I sighed in frustration. It was a familiar experience. Ever since I became a Christian I had been aware of that voice. Before, I had seen myself as fighting a just war against every aspect of the prison. Now I was reluctantly being forced to admit that, for all Lard Yao's severity, depersonalisation and brutality, Rita Nightingale wasn't exactly a model prisoner. The Warden whom I had just so painfully forgiven might have some justice on her side after all.

Lord Jesus, I thought gloomily, *when I asked you to change me I didn't want you to change me as much as this!*

I got up and joined the queue for washing. Afterwards, the foreign prisoners headed for Hannah's kitchen, taking the Christmas goodies which had been sent in. There were cooking facilities there and Hannah's radio, a source of blessedly Western music. I picked up my own Christmas things, started after them, hesitated, and changed my mind. Instead, I went off to the library. As I went by the kitchen I heard somebody saying, 'Where's Nightingale off to?'

In the deserted library I sat down and spread out the Christmas cards I'd received. There were fifty. As I looked at them I began to relax. A feeling of contentment flooded over me. 'Why do I need to dwell on trouble and friction?' I asked myself. 'Look at all these cards. Some of them are from people I've never met!'

I examined them again, one by one; the pictures of holly, the Dickens coach-and-horses outside nostalgically English inns, the funny cards, the solemn ones. I read the messages inside. Some were intimate, loving assurances from members of my family, others were a few words from people I didn't know, others were from officials and other individuals who were helping me in

200

my case. England and the English Christmas were very near at that moment.

Outside the building the usual prison noise went on and on. It was beginning to be a hot day. I daydreamed for a while, and then began talking to God. I took each card, and prayed for the person who had sent it. As I prayed, and thought about family and friends and home, I realised that God was with me.

It's difficult to describe. It was as if somebody was sitting with me in that room. I felt the way you feel if you are sitting facing away from somebody who is perfectly motionless. You can't see them, you can't hear them, but you are aware of the fact that there is somebody there as well as yourself. It was like that. I knew that Jesus had come to be with me.

I sat for what seemed a very long time, talking to him and thanking him for everything. Eventually I went to the kitchen, and the Christmas festivities were in full swing. All told the day went really well; Hannah was in a good mood, we laughed a lot, reminisced about the past year, and hugged each other a great deal.

Christmas was always at heart a sad day in prison. The Thai prisoners didn't celebrate it, though it was a holiday for Western prisoners. At such times, imprisonment was hardest to face. There were many thoughtful faces around, and not a few tears.

But that was a wonderful Christmas. Not because the realities of prison life were any less evident; they weren't. It was wonderful because for the first time I really understood what Christmas was about, and because God came to me in prison.

22 Anita

*God is watching over it all, so it's not our
place to worry.*

Letter to Mum, Ann and June, 28
December 1978

1979: a new year. The first of January celebrations meant
special food and other concessions. On New Year's Eve,
I was alone with Jenny. We could hear rowdiness in the
men's prison some distance away. A passing guard asked
us what we were doing. 'We're thinking of all the things
we would be doing, if we weren't here,' said Jenny. The
guard grinned, and nodded in the direction of the men's
prison. 'You're best off where you are.'

In the dormitory I scratched two marks in the floor
near my bed; a calendar. There were just over eighteen
years of my sentence left. I tried not to think about it.
I worked out the time difference between Thailand and
England, and at the right time I imagined the church
bells ringing in Blackburn to welcome the new year.
Happy New Year, Mum.

During the first months of the year, while I was being
disciplined over the incident of the diaries, Lucille came
to see me each week even though I wasn't allowed visitors. Each week she made the tedious journey out to
Lard Yao so that she could leave me food or some other
small gift. After a few weeks the officials decided to put
a stop to this, so they refused to accept the food for me

and left it uncollected, to rot. Even so, Lucille continued to come each Thursday. I could scarcely believe such sacrificial love.

Also during those months Margaret Cole wrote to the King of Thailand. She explained that as a missionary her reason for being in Thailand was to work with impoverished Thai communities. She pleaded with the King to be allowed to serve my sentence herself so that I could go free. 'I am an old woman; I am almost at the end of my life. Rita is a young woman. I believe that she has a work to do for God, among prisoners in many prisons.' She did not argue that I was innocent, but drew attention to the fact that my life had changed. I do not know whether the King personally read the appeal or whether it was dealt with by a government department; in either event, it was rejected.

When I heard about the letter I was shattered. I had not known that anybody could contemplate such a thing. I tried to find words to thank her, but she wouldn't listen.

'I would be as happy in there as out here, Rita,' she explained.

'I'm as happy as anybody could be in this prison,' I insisted gently.

'No, Rita,' Margaret said. 'I would be happier than you are. I would have the extra happiness of knowing that you were free.'

More foreign prisoners were arriving in the prison. Tall, beautiful Anita, a Greek with a model's figure, came in before my disciplining was lifted. She was unbelievably good-looking – thick, henna'd hair framing classically perfect features. Anita was her nickname; her real name was Diana, and I could never remember her Greek surname. She spoke English perfectly with a faint accent.

She was only twenty-two, but looked much older. She had been using heroin since she was fourteen.

Chris and I, who weren't users, had little in common with the prisoners who were – we couldn't sit and talk about our trips and the highs we'd had. Consequently we didn't get to know Anita very well. She became friends with Ilse, a Viennese girl. When she went to court she told them she was an addict, and they gave her one year. She accepted the sentence philosophically. She knew that she hadn't done badly.

People like Anita had no option in prison but to go 'cold turkey' – come off heroin. The guards were expert at finding any drugs that were smuggled in. Once, when cigarettes were banned, a quantity of marijuana was brought in by a visitor. Within hours it was confiscated. For this reason Anita didn't relish the thought of a year in Lard Yao.

One evening in February I was sitting on the steps of the dormitory hut in my pyjamas, ready for bed.

'Rita.'

I looked up quickly at the familiar voice. A forlorn and ill-looking figure was crossing the grass. 'Maria!' I cried. We embraced. I was thrilled. She had recognised me.

I held her at arm's length to look at her properly. I gulped. 'Maria – your hair! What happened?'

All the hair on one side of her head was gone. Her scalp was scratched and grazed. The remaining hair was wild. Maria's eyes shifted uneasily as I looked. Her shoulders were trembling.

'Is nothing,' she said, looking down at the ground, running a hand through what hair was left in an attempt to cover the poor ruined scalp. Later I was told that in hospital they had had to strap her down; Maria had managed to get one arm free, and had clawed at her head until she had made herself bald.

It was not long before the old pattern began to reappear. What improvement there had been lasted for at most a month. The decline that followed was rapid. One day she was coherent and lucid; the next, she was saying that the hospital staff talked about her behind her back.

'No, Maria,' I insisted. 'It's not true. Stop. Think; this is how you began to get sick last time. Think about yourself, not about other people . . . Think about God, about your life; talk to me – don't let yourself be ensnared again.'

She listened, and it was obvious that the words were making sense to her. But she couldn't help herself. Before long, she had to go back into hospital. When she came out again she was desperately sick in her mind. She didn't recognise me, and she was violent with the guards. She craved the dark, and took to staying in the old punishment block, where she lived like a filthy animal. When I visited her there she would occasionally recognise me; usually she ignored me.

It was heartbreaking to see her deteriorate. Before, she had always been neat and tidy; one of the first signs something was wrong had been the development of this into an obsession. But now she lived in her own dirt like an animal. The authorities had done what they could; she had been to hospital twice, but it had not cured her.

Somebody who took a great deal of interest in Maria's sickness was Anita. Desperate to get out of prison, she thought that anywhere in the world would be preferable to Lard Yao, even a mental hospital where, indeed, it might even be possible to get drugs. When she found out that the authorities had actually sent Maria outside to hospital, she was very excited and asked numerous questions.

Anita suffered from epileptic fits. The Thai prisoners were terrified when she had them, and Chris was usually summoned to deal with her. It needed Chris's strength.

Anita was phenomenally powerful during a fit; she once threw me across the room with a single twist of her body. This was not sufficient to merit being sent to an outside hospital, however; there were medical facilities in the prison. So Anita, whose behaviour was always unpredictable and was more so now she was withdrawing from heroin, devised a way out.

She came rushing into her dormitory with her hair wildly on end. As the other prisoners sat rooted to the spot, she seized a mirror and smashed it on the floor.

'You fool!' I shouted. Anita ignored me. Bending down, she selected a razor-sharp sliver of glass. She stood up. Glaring at everybody, she quickly and expertly slashed her right arm. Blood trickled slowly down.

Two or three girls jumped on her and forced the glass sliver out of her hand. A piece of cloth was ripped into bandages, and somehow or other the wound was dressed. Anita stood passively, breathing heavily, watching the proceedings with contempt. When the bandaging was finished she left the dormitory without a word.

We followed her to see where she would go. She was walking slowly and deliberately to the Warden's office, her bandaged arm held like a weapon across her body. She went in. We waited breathlessly; later we found out that Anita was demanding to be sent to a mental hospital. The demand was refused.

When she reappeared she was glowering. She marched up to the dormitory again and came out with another sliver of glass. Before we could stop her she had slashed her other arm. She rushed to the main gate and stood against it. Ripping the dressing from the arm that had been bandaged, she stood with blood pouring from both arms, screaming. The guards stood round her, waiting for a chance to overpower her. In the end it took several of them to drag her to the ground. Her wounds were

forcibly stitched. She achieved her wish to be hospital-
ised; when she came back after six weeks, she was more
cheerful and served the rest of her sentence without
further incidents.

It was so sad, though. I said goodbye to her on the
day she was released. 'I hope you'll be all right outside,
Anita.'

She smiled. 'Yes, I think I'll be OK. I should be able
to pick up some dope outside the gate.'

When the mail ban was lifted, I once again had the
support and encouragement of friends who wrote to me
from all over the world. I had only known a few of them
before my arrest. Some who wrote to me sent prayers
and love, others were working for my release in various
ways. Through their letters, I came to know them as real
friends.

A Liverpool man, Albert Downing, hitch-hiked from
Melbourne to Bangkok simply to talk to me for ten
minutes. His hobby was travelling, and he was in Australia when he heard of my imprisonment. He also travelled to Lourdes to pray for my release. Blackburn
residents sent funds raised through various projects. Little children all over the world wrote to say they had
heard of me and wanted to send me a letter. In Adelaide,
Australia, a lawyer who had begun writing to me the
previous year was organising numerous funds and func-
tions to support me. Margaret's church in America sent
me a cassette recorder (I wasn't allowed to have it in
prison, but was very moved by the gift). A Londoner,
Frank McManus, wrote me wonderful letters to which
I looked forward. There were many others. I valued
them all.

In America, a group called the Prison Fellowship began to write to me and send me their newsletter. This
was a group founded by Chuck Colson, a special aide to

President Nixon who had been sent to prison himself for his involvement in Watergate. He became a Christian during the Watergate investigations, and when he was a prisoner he felt tremendous concern for those in prison with him. The Fellowship exists to show the love of Jesus to people inside prison. I was thrilled that such a group existed. It was an answer to all the heartsearching I'd had about the plight of prisoners; God was doing something, he had started such a group.

My application for the King's pardon was made during the first part of the year. There were a great many forms to complete. Mr. Lyman was brisk and decisive. 'We have the papers here, Rita. Now we have to have them signed. This is the formal application for the King's pardon. We have to do it exactly right.'

Mr. Puttri produced the papers from his briefcase. 'You sign here . . . and here.'

I bent over the forms and signed my name where Mr. Puttri indicated. Mr. Lyman clapped his hands. 'Well, that's that. Now there will be more forms for you to sign later; the prison has to authorise the appeal too.'

When I went to the prison offices to sign the next forms, the official dealing with me read out the questions.

'What is the reason for this application?'

Something snapped inside me. 'I've had enough,' I replied simply. 'I shouldn't be here in the first place, and now I've had enough. And I miss my family. I want to go home. That's the reason for this application.'

As the official began to translate what I had said into Thai and write it on the form, I left.

I knew that in deciding not to appeal to the Supreme Court and to appeal to the King, I was asking for something unique, so I had been told, in Thai legal history.

I did not like to think of my chances of success. The prisoners ridiculed the idea.

My faith in God was growing all the time, but I refused to allow myself to think that the appeal might be successful. Even those closest to me wouldn't commit themselves. I could only wait, for however long it might take.

As summer came and went, the number of foreign prisoners continued to increase. There was a shift in the government's policy, stronger measures were being taken, and more drug offenders were being sent to prison. Most of them were in for comparatively minor offences and did not get long sentences. I was quite friendly with all the foreign prisoners, though it was always a wrench to see them leave; they were going after such a short stay, and I was sentenced to twenty years. But I knew that the future was something that God knew about, and that I didn't need to be afraid. If he wanted me to stay in prison for twenty years, he would make those twenty years as fulfilled and significant as the rest of my life. I knew it; I believed it; but all the same, it was hard to see others going out. At such times I still felt very lonely.

Two new prisoners, Mary and Linda, arrived. They were Americans, stunningly attractive black girls. Mary was in her thirties, short and very pretty. She had a nice Afro hairstyle when she came in, but let it grow out. Her clothes were lovely. Linda, on the other hand, was tall and well-built, a very jolly girl who laughed a lot. On the evening they came in we talked together in the dormitory.

'Hey,' giggled Linda. 'Where's the wardrobe?'

She peered round the room comically. I laughed. 'There isn't one in this suite, I'm afraid.'

'Waal . . . I'm afraid this is gonna get all creased.' She rummaged in the bag she had brought in with her, and produced a beautiful evening dress. We were very impressed; the Thai prisoners clustered round and passed it from hand to hand, exclaiming over the quality of the needlework – high praise, because Thais are usually accomplished in that art. Linda rummaged again. 'I got these too, girls . . . when do we get any dancin' done in this place?' She handed me a pair of expensive high-heeled shoes. These too were duly examined by everybody, but Linda was so big that her shoes didn't fit any of us when we tried them on. She rolled her eyes humorously. 'I'll keep 'em safe for when we go visitin' ', she promised, folding the dress and placing it back in the bag.

'You gonna have to keep that dress safe for a while, then,' said Mary. She was combing her hair with a plastic Afro comb. She looked troubled. 'Sure hope this business don't go on too long.'

'It depends,' I volunteered. 'The courts move terribly slowly, you have to go through the procedures . . . sometimes they pass light sentences.'

Mary frowned. 'Hope so,' she muttered. 'I got six kids out there. Being looked after. Hope they're all right.'

She brightened after a while, and began laughing with Linda.

To my surprise, they turned up at Jack and Gladys's monthly meeting. In conversation afterwards, I discovered that Mary had been brought up as a churchgoer and that Linda was interested in Christianity and wanted to know more about it. Like Valerie had been, she was curious to know how I had managed to retain any peace of mind in the prison. We had some good talks after that, and I told her how I had become a Christian. I began to pray for them very specially. The three of us became close friends and spent a lot of time together. It was good to talk again about Christianity with sympathetic friends in prison. Our relationship wasn't so clear-cut as mine had been with Valerie, who had become a Christian in Lard Yao. Mary and Linda were very willing to talk about Christian things, and I didn't probe beyond what they were prepared to discuss. I prayed for them, and tried to answer their questions as completely as I could.

Poor Mary found prison life very heavy going. Like many extrovert people, she was a sensitive person when you got to know her. She loved reading the Bible, and would often sit pouring over it during her free time. But the obscenities which were part of the general conversation in the dormitories were a great trial to her. She hunched over her Bible, hands over her ears, vainly trying to concentrate while all around her people were talking and shouting and swearing, and occasionally a couple who couldn't restrain their affection for each other began kissing in full view of the outraged Mary.

'It's terrible!' she complained to me. 'Those women! They're swearin', and makin' blasphemous jokes, and I don't know what else!'

'Yes, I know,' I said peaceably.

'But do you know what they're sayin' in there?'

'Of course I know what they're saying – and doing!' I retorted, perhaps more sharply than was necessary. 'I've lived here for over two years. I know what goes on. But you're making yourself worse than they are: you're trying to make them change. You can't. But you can change yourself, you can see them as people not monsters.' I was especially sorry for Mary because I had had to go through the same adjustment myself.

'But the noise,' repeated Mary. 'It's plain ridiculous. I can't even read my Bible with all that goin' on.'

'Yes,' I replied, 'I've been though that problem, too. You just have to change your routine, study in the day-time, in the library.'

Mary took time to find her feet in prison. I was often

frustrated, because I wanted her to make faster progress. She easily became tense, especially when she was worried about her children. But when she did begin to settle down, she became much more peaceful.

Ubol was a high-born Thai of striking good looks; she was in prison for cheque embezzlement. Her English was impeccable. I was chatting with Mary one day when she approached us. 'Please, I want you to pray for me. Will you pray?'

I was surprised; it wasn't the sort of request you expected from Ubol. I looked at her, concerned. 'Why, Ubol, what's the matter?'

'I have had a letter from my sister. She says that my husband is planning to take legal custody of our children. If you pray I know it will be all right.'

I had only every prayed out loud with one person – Valerie. I hadn't done so with anybody since she left. I looked at Mary. Mary, always anxious for her own children, nodded to Ubol, and she sat with us. We held hands, and I prayed, and so did Mary, and Ubol said a few words.

Afterwards we didn't release our hands immediately. Ubol thanked us quietly. 'I really think it will be all right now.'

Later that morning I hesitantly said to Mary and Linda – I don't know why I felt so embarrassed about it – 'Why don't the three of us get together to pray each morning?'

'Oh, Rita!' beamed Mary. 'I've been waitin' weeks for you to say just that!'

I felt terrible. I had been thinking of myself as a sort of 'older Christian', but I hadn't suggested such a simple thing until then.

We met each morning on the grass behind the hospital hut, before we had to go to work. People picked their way past us; it was like having a prayer meeting in

Piccadilly Circus or Times Square! We didn't mind the curious stares or the crowded situation. We had some wonderful times. Our relationship became very close, and we began to be very open with each other. One example of this was the morning when Mary was struggling with her problems. She was agonising over her children. We'd prayed about the situation, but Mary talked on and on about it. It was as if she wouldn't leave the matter in God's hands – she kept putting it down and then picking it up again. I wondered how to talk to her about it, prayed about it, and in the end decided on a rather aggressive approach.

'Mary, you are so immersed in your own problems – have you even thought of praying for me this morning?'

'What do you mean?'

'Well, I'm waiting for a King's pardon,' I said. 'I'm waiting to hear whether I'm going out or not.'

'Oh, you'll get that,' retorted Mary irrepressibly, as if it were the easiest thing in the world. I shook my head.

'It's not that simple. I've been here a while and I know how easily things go wrong. But it's in God's hands; we can pray about it. But we haven't, have we?'

I wondered whether I should have spoken so strongly, but that morning Mary did pray for me; it was lovely to hear her pray.

A Thai girl, who went to Jack and Gladys's meetings, was with us that morning too. When Mary had finished praying, she prayed. 'Lord, thank you for what Rita has come to mean to us. Thank you for her pardon.'

It took a moment for it to sink in. She was praying about my pardon as though it were already granted.

Why had I been so slow to suggest that we meet for prayer together? It was something I'd dreamed of when I first became a Christian, when I was one of a few foreigners in Lard Yao; so why didn't I?

I don't really know. Why are Christians so shy to speak to strangers in the street about Jesus? Why are we embarrassed to pray aloud in public?

I don't know. But I wish I'd conquered my shyness sooner. It was such a wonderful thing, to be part of that group.

23 Pardoned

Freedom hope for drug girl in Thai jail
Daily Mail article caption, December
1979

During the eight months or so that it took for my application for a King's pardon to go through the official channels, I never allowed myself to build up any great optimism. I knew that the government of Thailand had been placed in a difficult situation over my case. They were constantly being urged by the West to be uncompromising in their treatment of drug-traffickers, and I had been found guilty in a Thai court of that offence. The publicity generated in the press around the world over my arrest and imprisonment only made it less likely that I would be released. If I were, the government would appear to be weak in enforcing its controls and there would be no deterrent value in my sentence; there would be a grave risk that the impression would be given to any drug-smuggler that the only action needed to secure release was to stir up sufficient publicity.

I knew, too, that the things which I had said in the past – and even more, the things I was wrongly reported to have said – had not increased my chances of an amnesty. The prison authorities often saw statements in the Western press which distorted or falsified things I had said, and there was no way I could mend matters. On top of that, I was hardly Lard Yao's most docile prisoner at the best of times, and in the first months of my imprisonment I had built up a record of disobedience and intransigence which would not easily be forgotten.

It was such a messy situation, seen from my viewpoint. The government had a difficult situation to deal with; but against that, I knew I was innocent. The prison authorities had good grounds for complaint about my attitude; on the other hand, like all prisoners, I had seen brutality and discrimination so often in the prison that I wasn't going to readily see the authorities as faultless. In other words there was no clear argument that I ought or ought not to be freed – except that I was innocent, and that argument had been defeated in the courts.

Even when my lawyers did permit themselves the luxury of cautious optimism, or when I heard rumours that my application was receiving favourable consideration, I refused to get excited and did my best to forget the whole thing. I had left it in God's hands; now I had to learn to leave it there.

It was easier to say than to practise. At the back of my mind there was always the thought, 'Maybe . . .' But I forced myself to keep remembering the other possibility, 'Maybe not'. I tried to prepare for the worst, to accept that my life would be lived in prison for the next eighteen years. It is easier to write these things now than it was to do them at the time, but I honestly tried to think only that God was in control of my life and would make it a wonderful life wherever it was lived.

He encouraged me in countless ways. He sent people to talk to me at the very times I needed them most, he provided me with books and other help when other Christians weren't around, and when I read the Bible certain passages seemed to be written directly for me; I would read them with the same excitement that I read letters from home. I loved St Paul's letters, many of which were written in prison; through them God taught

216

me things I could never have learned elsewhere. One day I opened Paul's letter to the Roman church, and read these words:

> We know that in all things God works for good with those who love him, those whom he has called according to his purpose (Romans chapter 8, verse 28).

The words were a special encouragement. Paul had been in prison; he knew how difficult it was to believe that God was working for his good when he was locked up and separated from his friends and family. Yet he was able to write 'we *know* . . .' – not 'we hope' or 'we believe'. I accepted the words as God's message for me, and thanked him for them.

Another encouragement was the knowledge that by now hundreds of Christians all round the world were praying for me. When Martha Livesey had left Bangkok after visiting me, she had gone on to Australia, where she received my letter telling her I had become a Christian. From there she went on to America and Canada. Everywhere she went, wherever she addressed meetings, she talked about me and asked people to pray for me. 'Prayer chains' were set up, and I heard about them from Gladys and others. Gladys often reminded me that every hour of the day somebody, somewhere was praying for me.

The letters kept coming. I wasn't allowed to have them all, because they had to be scanned by the prison censors, who were getting swamped by the quantity of mail I was receiving. Eventually Christians aware of the situation appealed to people to stop writing to me. That appeal might usefully have been listened to by some organisations in the West which mistakenly thought that the best way to get me released was to flood the authorities with letters pleading for my release and sometimes accusing the authorities of injustice. Apart from the obvious deterioration that this brought about in my relationship with the authorities, it created a practical problem by swelling the volume of mail that was arriving.

But even when I wasn't allowed to have the mail to read, I was moved and thankful that so many people were praying for me and writing. Some people wrote to Gladys and Jack, and though they would always strictly observe the prison rules – it would not have crossed their minds to smuggle mail in to me – they did share some of the contents of these letters with me in conversation. (It was very noticeable that God honoured their care to follow prison regulations. None of my Christian friends ever broke them; when my mail ban was operating earlier in the year Lucille never tried to break it, though other prisoners thought I was stupid not to try to persuade her; yet she managed to pick up enough information about me from official sources and the Embassy to be able to write to Mum and keep her in touch, even though I was forbidden to write.)

I did receive one letter which had been through the censor's office; it was on the official writing paper of the Vatican. It was from the Pope's office, and it said that my imprisonment had been brought to his notice and he would be remembering me at Mass.

I was overwhelmed by the kindness people showed me. Somebody regularly sent me the novels of Morris West, which I really enjoyed. I never found out who the sender was – labels and letters often got detached and lost in the censor's office. Hampers from Jacksons of Piccadilly, a first-class London food store, arrived at intervals from another friend whose identity was never revealed. In this case I wrote to Jacksons to express my gratitude, but they wrote saying that they didn't know who had ordered them and could not find out without an invoice. So the hampers remained a mystery, like

218

many other gifts I received. I always wrote to thank people for any present which arrived with the sender's name and address attached. But many well-wishers must have wondered whether I ever received their gifts.

There were many encouragements. But I was worried for Mum. She must be finding the uncertainty unbearable. When I wrote to her I tried to encourage her to think my way.

'Don't listen to rumours, Mum. Just forget them. The people over here don't know what's going on, and they often don't know how applications are dealt with anyway . . . We can only pray now, Mum. It's all we can do, and it's in his hands anyway . . .'

Mr. Lyman gave me what information he could.

'December 5th – the King's birthday. That's the big day, we'll hear then. Now you hang on, Rita. We've done all the formal application. I heard the other day that there's a good chance we'll pull it off.'

'It's always the same,' I said. 'Just hints and possibilities. Nothing certain, ever.'

Mr. Lyman looked at me sympathetically through the grille. 'I know, li'l honey. It must be really hard for you, not knowing. Well, just as soon as we hear anything, anything at all . . .'

'Don't worry,' I assured him. 'I'm not pinning my hopes on anything. I promise you that.'

He tried to cheer me up. 'We'll celebrate when you get out. What we'll do is –'

I cut him off short. 'Don't say that!'

He looked hurt. I apologised.

'I'm sorry. But I don't know if or when I'm going to be released. I might have to go on living here for another eighteen years. Please don't talk about getting out. I'm really trying not to build my hopes up.'

I found it difficult to pray. I would talk to God about the future, and I would try to talk about a future in Lard Yao, but all the time the possibility of release was distracting me. The prospects of release dimmed and brightened and dimmed again. Though I refused to raise my hopes, I couldn't help seizing on every rumour and wondering what lay behind it.

A Chinese girl, Su, had become very friendly with me, and she became very protective. She understood my confusion, and helped me through some bad times. Our prayer meetings continued. Mary and Linda were praying hard for my release. We learned a lot about caring for each other; I found that with others bearing some of the load of my worries I was able to spend time praying with Mary and talking about her children. Hannah, her natural pessimism colouring her view of what was happening, nevertheless tried to be enthusiastic. Most of the other prisoners avoided raising my hopes.

Mr. Coleshill, the British Consul, arrived one day in November. He was very depressed.

'I'm not at all sure things are going well,' he said. 'Bangkok is full of Western reporters. They're waiting for the King's birthday. It might go against you.'

'How?'

'It's the kind of publicity the government would wish to avoid. It could decrease the chances of an amnesty.'

I could understand this. Mr. Coleshill said very little about it, but I supposed that with the international implications of releasing a convicted drug smuggler, the Western press might ruin my chances just by what they wrote. Mr. Coleshill would not confirm this. I was impressed by the way he gave me what information was relevant to me but avoided discussing the wider implications. It gave me confidence that the small encouragements he did give me could be relied on. I tried to be detached about the possibility of anything happening on 5th December.

All the same, when the 5th came and went without any announcement about me, I was devastated. Mr. Coleshill assured me that the application was still alive. 'We'll hear something any day now . . .'

Something had changed in me. December 5th had been the day when I had been sure that God would do something special. Either he would let me go home, or he would give me the spiritual ability to rejoice in my imprisonment. I had expected wonderful things to happen. I had looked forward at the very least to my doubts and fears falling away, and for a quiet acceptance to fill my heart. That was what had happened in the lives of great Christians I'd read about. Why hadn't it happened to me? *Oh God*, I prayed, *What's going wrong?*

Christmas was a blur, dominated by my obsession with release. I stopped eating. Su tried to make me eat but I refused. I began to make excuses to avoid praying with people. Worst of all, I stopped praying on my own.

There is a classic symptom of prisoners called 'gate fever'. I had heard of it; now I knew exactly what it was. I found myself thinking for hours about nothing but the gate. I opened my Bible, and saw only dead words. I tried to pray, and as I called out to God, all that was in my mind was that iron gate and the dusty road behind it. I wasn't even thinking of home and family. It was the gate that dominated my waking thoughts and my dreams; the gate, symbolising all that Lard Yao was and all that prevented me from walking out to freedom.

It was a catastrophic spiritual crisis. I poured it all out to Jack and Gladys. 'I can't think, I can't read my Bible, I can't pray, I can't do *anything*,' I sobbed. 'I know that's wrong. I know God is in control. I just can't help it – I can't get that gate out of my mind. It's not the uncertainty that's the worst thing. It's not being able to talk to God about it.'

Then Gladys said something which cut through the fever and went straight to my heart. 'Rita, I don't know why I'm saying this — I believe the Lord is saying it through me. Rita, this is your last hurdle. You must let go completely. In prayer, in your heart, you have got to let this fever go.'

Her voice held a quiet authority. Nobody knew yet what the outcome of my appeal to the King would be, but I heard her words of assurance and believed them. I didn't know what 'your last hurdle' meant, but I knew that God had spoken to me through Gladys.

'I'll try,' I promised. My voice was quavery. Like the embers of a dying fire, doubts and questions still thrashed around my brain. That night, I talked to God. I cried so much at first I could hardly form the words, but when I calmed down I told him everything. Memories came back to my mind of bitternesses and resentments that were still unresolved. I thought of the Warden, the symbol of the prison authority. Had I really forgiven her? More, had I asked God to forgive me for my attitude to her? I talked each problem through, and as I talked, I was aware of God showing me more and more things that needed to be faced and prayed about. When I finally fell asleep, exhausted, it was as if a burden had been taken from my back. When I woke the next morning, the gate fever was gone, and in its place was the peace which I had not experienced for many weeks.

I began to work hard at the Thai language. The prison authorities allowed foreign prisoners time off work once a week in order to learn it. I'd gone along from time to time, more to get away from work than for anything else; I'd picked up a working knowledge of Thai from the other prisoners. But now I set to enthusiastically,

222

and each week a few of us gathered in the prison library to study.

It was during one of these mid-week study sessions that the door of the library opened and two women came in. One was Gladys Martin; the other was an American. Gladys spotted me and introduced us.

'This is Kathryn Grant.'

I liked her at once. She was a missionary, on her way back from a visit to Japan. We began chatting, and the other girls joined in. We couldn't work out how the visitors got inside; it wasn't the regular day for missionaries to visit. But they had applied for permission in the normal way and had been granted it. 'We were really praying about it back in America' laughed Kathryn. 'So many people have tried to get permission to enter the prison to see you, we didn't think we'd much chance, but they let me come in with Gladys!'

'How did you know about me?' I asked.

'It was Prison Fellowship', she said. I recognised the name at once – that was a group that Chuck Colson, the Watergate ex-prisoner, had started, and which had been corresponding with me. He had given Kathryn a copy of *Life Sentence*, his autobiography, as a present for me. 'Chuck knew I could break my journey from Japan and stop over in Thailand. "Make sure you see Rita", he said, and here I am!'

I was thrilled. God was breaking wide the prison doors not to let me out, but to let Christians in. *I don't have to go outside to meet him*, I reminded myself contentedly. *He's here inside with me*.

Kathryn talked about Prison Fellowship, the work it was doing and the vision it had for the future. It was wonderful to see in detail how God was reaching out to prisoners all over the world. He had given me a deep concern for prisons ever since I became a Christian, and now here he was, showing me in a visible way that he was dealing with the problem.

When we parted, we prayed together. It was a sober moment. Kathryn was leaving behind somebody with almost 18 years to serve in prison; I was saying goodbye to someone whom I had suddenly grown fond of. We were both in tears; not hopeless tears, but tears none the less, because prison is a place of separation.

Life went on in the familiar routines of prison. The prisoners often told me, 'There's no chance of your getting out.' But I was able to handle the thought now.

'Nightingale to the gate-house block!'

The familiar summons echoed round the prison. It was a fortnight or so after Kathryn's visit, but it wasn't my visiting day. I was taken to the Embassy room. Mr. Coleshill, the Consul, was there. The muscles in my stomach tensed into a knot. He had been to see me only yesterday. It must be really bad news if he had come back so soon.

'Is there something wrong?' I cried. 'Mum – is she –'

He shook his head and smiled. 'Everything's fine,' he said. 'Come and sit down.'

I sat down opposite him. Between us, the metal barrier was solid and permanent. Mr. Coleshill reached his hand forward and pushed his fingers through. 'Hold my fingers while I talk, Rita.'

I took hold of his hands through the barrier. I had no idea what it was all about. 'Let me read you the front page of the Bangkok Post,' he said. As I clutched his fingers, he read the news of my pardon. I burst into tears.

He read on. One word leaped from the article – 'unique'. It was, according to the Bangkok Post, a unique pardon. *That's God*, I thought immediately. *It was impossible without him.*

Mr. Coleshill finished reading. He laid the newspaper down. 'It was in today's paper,' he explained. 'We can't find any more information. I've tried to find out what's going on.'

The feeling of deflation was like a physical blow. All my excitement drained from me. I looked at him with a dull, blank face.

'It was a hoax. They didn't mean it. It's just a joke.'

The Consul shook his head. 'No, Rita. It's no joke. You know the Thai people; they're not joking. This is the Bangkok Post, Rita. It's true.' He took a card from his wallet and pushed it through the bars. 'We've asked for information to be given us as soon as it's available. But that may not be possible. Take care. When you are released, this is the telephone number you must ring.'

When I emerged into the prison yard I was trembling. I began to laugh, a huge, violent laughter that was dredged up from deep inside me. I looked up into the blue hazed sky, and I let out a great scream of joy. Then I began to run at top speed, still laughing uncontrollably. Running was not allowed in the prison grounds, but I flew the length of the compound to the building where Chris worked. But she had seen me already; she started running to meet me, and we met half-way. There were no explanations needed. 'I knew you'd go out, I knew, I knew!' shouted Chris ecstatically, hugging me in her crushing grip. We wept, and laughed, and wept again.

'Maria,' I said. 'I must go and tell Maria.' So we went to see Maria, sitting in her dark room alone.

She had been locked in at her own request. I pressed my face to the bars, ignoring the stench, and I wept. I called her name. 'Maria! Maria – I'm going out – I'm being released!'

There was no response; nothing. She sat in silence, her face turned away, as if nothing was happening. And

225

that was how I parted from Maria. It was as if all the wonderful things, the Bible readings, the prayers, the miracle that Valerie and I witnessed, the improvement after her first visit to hospital – it was as if they had never happened. I did not doubt God, but I did not understand what he was doing then. 'Maria!' I called again. 'Maria!' There was no answer.

Chris gently took my arm and led me away. We went to tell the other girls. The news had already reached them. Most were thrilled. One or two wouldn't meet my eyes. It was too much to handle. I knew how they felt. I'd felt the same when people were released.

The Thai lady who had looked after me burst into tears and hugged me. A girl whom I often paid to queue for hot water for me came over and hugged me too. We all talked at once, as the celebration rose in volume.

There was a sudden hush. The Warden had appeared. She stared at us all, tightlipped, and her gaze travelled around the group. When she looked at me I looked down at the ground, but could not stop laughing. She went away again without a word.

I began to thirst for details. What day was I going out? What would happen? Where would I go? Mr. Lyman had tried to tell me about the procedure for release, but I had always shut him up because I hadn't wanted to raise my hopes. This was different. Now it was official. I went to the Warden's office.

The Deputy Warden was there. I suppressed my simmering excitement and greeted her with the appropriate formality. Vainly trying to appear casual, I remarked 'I've got a pardon – I'm going out!'

'What?'

'I've got a pardon from the King. I'm going out. When am I going? What date has been given?'

She laughed. 'No, no. You haven't got a pardon. Not a chance! You won't be released. You have twenty years!'

'I have a pardon, I have!' I insisted. 'It was in the newspaper!'

'No, no, no! You haven't got a pardon,' she repeated. 'Not Nightingale; no pardon.'

'Well,' I said tightly. 'Just suppose, for the sake of argument, suppose that I *had* got a pardon, and it was in today's newspaper – when would I go out, if that were the case?'

She went and consulted colleagues. I heard their laughter. Nobody would believe it.

Finally she said, humouring me, 'Not before weekend. Impossible. Paperwork . . .' It was Wednesday. I nodded delightedly. 'OK! OK! That's fine by me, just fine! I only wanted to know!'

After that, my appetite disappeared again. Su sat beside me at supper, feeding me tasty delicacies of fish, but I couldn't eat.

That night I sat up talking with the other girls. My mind was a jumble of all sorts of emotions. Jenny, with her thirty year sentence, sat holding my hand. I fumbled for words. 'Jenny . . .'

'You don't have to say anything. I'm so happy for you.' Her sad face belied her words. 'You're going out. And I'm here, I'm still here . . .'

I knew she was happy for me, but my heart ached for her own sadness. I was frightened for her and for others I was leaving behind. We sat up all night, and I held Jenny's hands the whole time.

'I don't know what it will be like outside,' I told her. 'I'm frightened. I don't know whether there'll be trouble still waiting for me, in Thailand or even in England. But if there's anything I can ever do to help you, Jenny –'

She nodded thoughtfully. 'You cared for people, Rita. You were one of the few. And that's why you're going out.'

In her own way she was acknowledging God's providence. I would never say that my pardon was God's 'reward' for anything – the Bible tells us not to look for rewards, and there are a great many Christians serving him faithfully in dreadful situations from which he hasn't released them. But Jenny recognised that God was supremely involved in my release.

Next day I went with Chris to the prison hospital, to arrange for the transfer of a supply of headache pills I had from my name to hers. Afterwards we sat on the hospital steps.

'Think of it!' exclaimed Chris. 'You'll be on a plane soon!'

I buried my face in my hands. Suddenly everything was too much to cope with. 'Don't, Chris,' I pleaded. 'I can't imagine it. My mind won't go outside these walls.'

I went and did some packing. I decided to give the rest of my books to the prison library. I wanted to keep my Bible and some other things. I would give my blanket to an old Thai lady whom I had got to know; it was a European, expensive one; she'd never seen such a thing before. That was all the sorting out I did then. I believed I had until the weekend. I did no work that day and ate nothing.

I met with our little prayer group, not knowing it was for the last time. They asked me, 'What will we do now you're leaving?'

'You must keep the group going,' I replied. 'I could have suggested we meet like this months ago, and I didn't. Now we have started it, it mustn't stop. The best thing you can do for me is to keep praying. It doesn't matter that I'm going. It matters that you're praying together as Christians. You don't even need to pray out loud if you don't want to.'

The loudspeaker was calling my name. 'Nightingale

to the Warden's office,' the disembodied Thai voice announced.

I discovered that my knees no longer obeyed me. I couldn't stand up. 'Lord,' I prayed frantically, 'please, just get me to that office.' The unknown future, which I'd successfully kept at bay in a flurry of goodbyes and packing, was suddenly upon me. Somehow I managed to get to the office.

On the way, a prisoner called to me, 'Tell her, Rita! Say what you think of her! You can give it her straight, now – you're leaving anyway!'

I was torn by a mixture of emotions. The old resentments flared up again. 'Lord, hold me back,' I prayed. But I couldn't help myself; I remembered all the grievances I'd held against her, the anger I'd felt over Mum's visit, the visiting ban and scores of others. I was going to leave prison. She would no longer control me. *Now, surely, I can tell her what she's done to me?* There was no answer; I wasn't listening for one. I had become determined to have my last fling.

The Warden was waiting for me with several prison officials. They were shrinking away from her; she was very angry indeed. She glared as I walked in: Rita Nightingale, the most difficult prisoner in Lard Yao, the one who would never be paroled or pardoned – now to be set free.

When I had been at my most rebellious, I had expressed my rebellion most aggressively in my attitude to the Warden. When she refused to speak to me in English, I refused to speak to her in Thai. To speak English to the Warden became a symbol of my anti-authority stand. I also refused to give her the respect that was usual in the prison. I would not make the deferential bow and press my palms together in the Thai gesture of greeting; while most prisoners, because of the Warden's rank, actually sank to their knees on entering her presence, I had made a point of drawing myself up a couple of extra inches.

Since my conversation with Jack and Gladys about this, I had made a great effort to conform. But she was so much a physical embodiment of the prison and the authority which had imprisoned me that I fought a constant battle with my resentment. I had taken no other problem to God so often as this. But as I entered the office, my awareness of her as a fellow-human being was replaced by a sudden and uncontrollable surge of the old bitterness.

I opened my mouth, determined to take maximum advantage of this opportunity to say all the things I'd suppressed over three years.

But before I could get a word out, an extraordinary feeling of peace descended upon me. I hadn't slept, I had been in a state of nervous excitement for many hours, and I had been rushing around doing a hundred things simultaneously. Then my walk across to the office had brought me to a fever-pitch of excited resentment. And now it had vanished. In its place was an absence of hate for the Warden. It was more even than that. After three years of bitterness, after months of prayer which I thought had only been partly answered, I had finally come to feel love for this woman for whom Christ had died. As the realisation swept over me, I found myself sinking to my knees before her, my hands clasped, my head bowed, in the traditional Thai gesture of respect towards a superior.

'Yes, Warden?'

I hardly noticed that I spoke in Thai, or that she replied in English. She waved a document at me. Her normal icy restraint did not conceal her anger. 'Do you know what this is?'

I could not answer.

'It is a pardon from His Majesty the King. Sign this document.'

I had to sign in several places. I didn't know what I was signing. She was trembling. I was still aware of that amazing peace. She gestured angrily. 'Now get your things, and go.'

I ran to the dormitory. Already some of the guards were trying to pack my things for me. They were being helpful, but they were packing things like jars of coffee and plastic crockery that I wasn't going to take with me. 'Let me do, let me do,' I protested, and packed a few things – letters, some clothes, things like that. I stuffed them all into a holdall. The Warden appeared and stood watching me. 'Be quick! Be quick!' I was beyond being upset. It was like a dream, in which I was carried peacefully along.

When I appeared at the door of the building, packed and ready, all the people I'd come to love were standing at the foot of the steps – Jenny, Chris, Su, and the others. The Thai prisoners were standing a little farther away, because the Warden was watching. I took each of my friends in my arms one by one. I thought my heart would break, leaving them behind. I hugged Jenny the longest. She had the worst sentence, and that made the various frictions we'd had seem irrelevant.

The Warden moved me along. I was smiling radiantly. At the end of the line stood Hannah: Hannah, with whom I had been on bad terms for several months, ever since our row over my newspaper publicity. I was suddenly confused, not knowing how to speak to her now I was leaving.

She was saying goodbye. I heard her words of farewell but couldn't respond. She was too bound up with Lard Yao. Hannah had always been the one you could rely on to get a favour for you from the Warden. She knew the system. She made it work for her. Seeing her standing there I realised that, in many ways, she was the prison. It was her life.

I felt pity . . . contempt . . . a mixture of conflicting emotions. I looked into her eyes and could not read what I saw there. In the end I gave up trying to find something to say. I left Hannah without a word, passing silently by her words of farewell.

It seemed a long walk to the prison gates. One of the guards carried my bag. As we walked past one of the buildings Mary and Linda shouted down to me. 'Wow! Great! Good luck, Rita!' The Warden glared up at them. 'Who's making that noise? Be quiet! Stop it at once!' From the factory, as we passed, came cheers from some of the Thai prisoners.

We were at the gate, and the moment I had dreamed of for nearly three years was actually happening. I walked through the small door cut into the gate. I stood on the dusty road. In all that long walk from the dormitory steps, I had not turned round once.

I was put into a van with two junior guards. It had been used not long before to take a woman to her execution. The Warden watched me get in. Nearby stood the one high-ranking official who had been genuinely kind to me. Crying, I pushed open the van window.

'I'm going out,' I sobbed. 'For three years I was in there. And you were the only one who was good to me . . .'

In the van, I realised I was still holding a pair of earrings I'd intended to give to Jenny. I gave them to one of the junior guards, asking her to give them to Jenny later. The Warden peered into the cab. 'Hurry! Hurry!' The engine coughed into life. We drove away.

For about fifteen minutes we drove through heavy traffic. Then the van pulled up by the road side.

'Get out,' said one of the guards. I clambered down.

The guard tossed my bag after me. 'Bye bye! Write to us!' I watched the vehicle lumber off, back the way we had come.

I had no idea what was happening. I hadn't imagined that it would be like this, dumped on the side of the road. Too happy to be frightened, but very confused, I began praying. 'Lord, please help me.' I picked up my bag and started walking. Almost immediately, I came to a small police station. I walked in. There was a policeman on duty.

'Hello,' I announced. 'I'm Rita Nightingale. Can I use your phone?'

24 Home

*I am Rita Nightingale, and I have been
reborn again.*

Interview with David Allin, Lancashire
Evening Telegraph, 24 January 1980.

The police were very friendly. 'Hey! Look at this!' they
joked. 'Nice-looking foreigner who speaks Thai. You
want a coke, something to eat maybe?'

'I want to use the telephone,' I insisted.

'Oh, sure,' they agreed, and waved me over to the
phone. I was clutching Mr. Coleshill's card. I dialled the
number. The phone was temperamental, and I was still
dialling and re-dialling when one of the policemen tapped
me on the shoulder.

'Are you Rita?'

He pointed to another phone, with its receiver off the
hook. 'For you,' he said laconically.

It was Mr. Puttri. 'Rita? Now, listen. Stay exactly
where you are. Don't move from the police station, don't
go anywhere until we come. We have been told that you
were being brought there. We are on our way.'

I put the phone back. Somebody gave me a Coke and
I began to relax. The police joked with me. 'My, you're
a pretty girl to be speaking Thai!'

'Well,' I countered cheerfully, 'you're not so bad-look-
ing yourself.' We bantered for a few minutes. I felt
light-headed and very happy.

There was a shout from the road. I went to the front and looked out. Mr. Coleshill, the Consul, was standing outside. He hugged me, and for the next few minutes we talked nineteen to the dozen.

I am so grateful to him. He was always very proper in his dealings with my case, and in every way he provided the assistance that anyone would look for from a Consul when in trouble abroad. But the care and support he gave me and the way he sheltered me during those first few days of freedom went far beyond the demands of duty. In the news photographs taken at the time he is nearly always to be seen, well out of the limelight but always near at hand.

Then Mr. Puttri arrived; dear Mr. Puttri, who had worked so hard on my case and had as often as not had little thanks from me in return. I don't know what he did for me, because he was always speaking Thai in court; but I know he was regarded as a fine lawyer, and he was very kind to me. He brought Leonie with him. She had brought me a fresh strawberry, which was a real treat at that time in Bangkok.

I was leaping up and down joyfully, tremendously excited, praising the Lord and unable to believe what had happened. Mr. Coleshill stayed protectively close, which must have been like escorting a whirling Dervish.

Officially, I had to report to the Immigration Office, but Mr. Coleshill had insisted that I be allowed to go to the Embassy first. When we walked through the door, another world I'd forgotten confronted me. Wallpaper . . . carpet . . . a chair . . . People greeted me pleasantly, but I was staring open-mouthed at everything.

Mr. Coleshill winked at me conspiratorially. 'Now,' he beamed. 'I've something rather special you'll enjoy.'

He took me down a corridor, and opened a door. 'Just stay in there as long as you like,' he said. It was a bathroom. It had a European toilet, and pink wallpaper and tiles, and a mirror. The people in the Embassy must have wondered what the wild shout of joy was that came from the bathroom as I rushed in joyfully. For at least fifteen minutes I luxuriated in the opulence of a Western bathroom, flushing the toilet, turning the taps, looking at myself in the mirror; I couldn't believe it.

Eventually Mr. Coleshill took me, clean and glowing, to Immigration. As we arrived an enormous crowd of reporters from different countries surged forward with cameras and taperecorders. Mr. Coleshill squared his shoulders. 'We'll get you through this somehow,' he promised.

We began to make our way through. I felt no tension. There was a clearing in the crowd. I saw dear Mr. Lyman standing there. He had, I found out later, been waiting there for me since I left the police station.

His sight had deteriorated in the time I'd known him. Now he peered anxiously in my direction. I flew into his arms and hugged and kissed him. He gripped my shoulders and laughed with me. 'We did it, li'l honey! I *knew* we'd do it! I knew we would!' He whirled me round, and we shouted joyfully.

It was getting dark. I was being moved on to the offices. I held Mr. Lyman a moment longer. 'I'll do my best to see you again before I go,' I vowed.

Albert Lyman had been my lawyer from the beginning. He had put up with my bitterness and anger. For nearly three years he had championed my case, and for most of the time he had no help from me. I owe more to him and his firm than I can say, and I was so glad to see him there.

In Immigration, Mr. Coleshill asked me: 'Now, Rita. Do you feel able to talk to the reporters?'

'Sure!' I said happily. I was still on cloud nine.

'Be very careful,' he advised. 'Don't be led into saying anything you don't want to say.'

236

I can't remember anything I said. I do remember that in my dazed state the hardest thing was to construct English sentences. I'd been among Thai speakers for so long. My accent had become very peculiar. 'I thought you were English!' remarked one reporter.

Somebody asked me who I would like to say thank you to. It was quite a question to be asked in my state, but I tried to list everybody. I ended up repeating over and over, 'I want to thank God . . . I want to thank him for everything he's done in my life. I want to thank all the Christians who have been praying for me.' I saw Mr. Puttri glancing anguishedly at me. I remembered just in time. 'And I want to thank the King for pardoning me.'

I was truly grateful to His Majesty the King of Thailand, and I still am. I am well aware that though amnesties for lesser offences are a traditional feature of the Thai royal calendar, the act of clemency shown to me, who had been found guilty of smuggling drugs, risked international criticism as fierce as that which followed my arrest. Whether it was a personal intervention on his part, or a decision made at ministry level, I am deeply grateful to His Majesty King Bhumibol. At that moment, however, I was so thrilled by God's goodness to me that somehow my answer to the questioner came out rather one-sided.

Mr. Puttri and Mr. Coleshill accompanied me into Immigration. It was the same office where I had been arrested. Some police were there, but there were no big guns to be seen, just small arms carried in shoulder holsters such as all Thai police wear.

There was a big discussion about where I was to sleep that night. I gathered from what was being said to Mr. Coleshill in Thai that I would not be permitted to sleep in the Embassy. I didn't mind. A girl who'd been released from Lard Yao a few days earlier was being detained in Immigration while some details were sorted out. 'Get me in with Rosemary,' I assured Mr. Coleshill, 'and I won't mind sleeping in a cell.'

So I ended up in a cell with Rosemary, sharing it with a number of Khmer refugees from Cambodia. It was quite noisy, but my meeting with Rosemary was noisier. 'I couldn't believe it when I saw it in the papers!' she screamed.

Mr. Coleshill was allowed to see me in the cell. 'I know I can't get you out tonight,' he said, 'but I can bring you anything you want to eat.'

'I want a steak!' I cried ecstatically. 'And I want a salad, and a cold drink, and I want a roast potato . . .' Mr. Coleshill went off to get it.

Later a guard called me to the door. To my surprise he dumped a suitcase at my feet. 'For you.'

I opened it. On the top was a press photograph from the Daily Mail, showing Mum and my sister Ann raising champagne glasses to the camera. They had obviously heard the news. There was also a letter from Mum, brief but heartfelt. She mentioned that Ian Smith of the Daily Mail was in Bangkok, and that on my behalf she had accepted the paper's offer of help to get me home. She explained that I wasn't bound to say anything to anybody, and that if I didn't want to I didn't even have to meet Mr. Smith.

I barely took the details in. I stared at the photograph. My heart was full. Up to that moment, the whirlwind of events had pushed my family to one side of my thoughts. Now, looking at the photograph, I knew I wanted to go home.

By the time Mr. Coleshill arrived with the feast I had pulled myself together. Rosemary and I sat down and ate and ate. We tried to share the food with the refugees, but they didn't know what it was and wouldn't eat any. I couldn't resist trying a bit of everything; it was so long since I'd had that sort of food. I paid a price for it later though. My insides were churning round for days, and I was for ever having to leave important meetings suddenly . . .

I wanted to shower before I left. The shower was actually private; it was possible to wash without an audience. But as soon as I was inside I was transfixed by fear. It took a few minutes for me to realise that the fear was because for the first time in three years, I was in a dark place. There had been nowhere really dark in the prison. In the end, I had to ask Rosemary to stay with me and keep me company while I showered.

Next morning a number of people came to the cell to see me, and then I went to the Immigration offices. As I went down the steps, I saw Gladys Martin. We ran to each other. 'Oh!' she exclaimed. 'I'm so glad to see you!' She had been refused permission to see me earlier and had decided to wait there until I went past. My time with her was all too brief. In no time at all I was in Immigration, being asked innumerable routine questions and being put through the proper procedures. There were scores of photographers there, and for the first time I became irritated as I was pulled this way and that as they all competed for photographs of what was happening. Mr. Coleshill efficiently made sure that I wasn't overwhelmed.

'I've got permission for you to have an hour or two free – you can rest in my apartment,' he told me afterwards. 'There'll be a couple of police standing by, but don't worry about that.'

As we drove through Bangkok I stared like a child at everything we passed. On the way, we stopped at Mr. Lyman's house and stayed with him and his wife for half an hour.

'Please visit us at home when you come to England,' I begged.

'I don't think I'll ever make that journey again,' he said regretfully. 'I'm getting to be an old man, li'l honey.'

And so we said goodbye to each other.

Mr. Coleshill's apartment was blessedly free from photographers. I washed my hair, glorying in the luxury of that splendid bathroom. As I emerged, damp and very happy, there was a knock on the door. 'You open it,' said Mr. Coleshill. I did. Lucille was standing there.

For all that time she had visited me faithfully, supporting me, encouraging my mother, caring for me in thousands of ways; and this was the first time I had been close enough to touch her. I was overwhelmed. As I was recovering from that excitement, Jack and Gladys arrived, bringing Margaret Cole with them. Then one by one other people who had played a part in the whole story came in: Mr. Lyman, Canon Taylor, and several others. It was wonderful; I hadn't expected anything like it. The meal we had together was a lovely, precious celebration.

It had to finish eventually. It seemed hardly any time had gone by before I was saying goodbye to everybody. Lucille and Margaret and Jack and Gladys prayed with me for the last time, and I shared with them my hopes and fears for the future. The euphoria was beginning to fade, as I realised I would soon be back in England. 'I don't know any Christians there,' I told Jack. 'I don't know which church to go to or anything like that.'

'You'll be all right,' he replied. 'The Lord has his hand on your life, we know that. He is going to protect you and use you.'

The emotional distress of saying goodbye to my friends showed when I got upset with photographers a little later. After guiding me through that bad patch, Mr. Coleshill said, 'We have to decide what you're going to do, Rita. You must leave Bangkok today. Where would you like to go?'

I believe God guided me very clearly then.

'Mr. Coleshill, there's nothing I want more than to go home and be with my Mum and my family. But I can't go straight home. I want to go to Kuala Lumpur, to sort myself out and settle down.'

Doctors working with freed hostages and prisoners now insist that the captive should go through an interim period of adjustment before being allowed to go home. I didn't know about this 'hostage psychology', but I believe God planted that instinctive decision in my mind to protect me from emotional problems which would otherwise have spoiled my homecoming.

We went to the airport in best James Bond style to avoid publicity (rather spoiled by my discovery that the bag I was carrying, a present from a friend, bore my name in bold letters for any passer-by to see!). We got there with a minimum of fuss. However, as we emerged from a lift, Ian Smith of the Daily Mail and a photographer were standing waiting to enter. 'It's her!' they exclaimed, and so the Mail got a scoop photograph.

I travelled first class to Kuala Lumpur. When I stepped down from the plane, I saw groups of Europeans waiting for their flights. I froze.

'What's the matter?' asked Mr. Coleshill.

'All those people!' I said. 'They're so big . . .' I had grown accustomed to Easterners, who are on average much shorter than Westerners.

Mr. Coleshill, who was staying at the Embassy, left me at the hotel with strict instructions to answer the door to nobody but himself and to speak to nobody who telephoned. I hung the 'Do not disturb' sign on the door, shut it, locked it, and sat down.

Immediately, an indescribable fear swept over me. I couldn't handle it; I knelt down and prayed. *Lord, what is this feeling? What's happening?*

And then I realised what it was. I was alone.

For nearly three years I hadn't experienced quiet and solitude. I had already faced the dark, but this was much more of a shock. I was alone with myself, and it was quiet.

When I realised what the fear was, I rejoiced and praised God. Now I knew that I was free.

Nevertheless, I wasn't used to it. I opened the window to let the traffic noise in, and curled up on the soft bed with the radio on quietly to give a background noise. But I couldn't sleep. I tossed and turned. It wasn't the heat – the hotel air-conditioning was bliss after Lard Yao's sticky nights. It was the softness of the bed. In the end I got out of bed and curled up on the floor, and managed to doze.

I persuaded Mr. Coleshill to let me visit the hotel shop next day. I bought some sweets and wandered away to stand at the edge of the hotel pool, watching a crowd of bronzed swimmers. I was laughing to myself out of sheer happiness. I kept thinking about Jenny and Hannah and all the others, but I had to push the thoughts out of my mind; I wasn't capable of handling them, there was so much going on in my head.

Behind me, Mr. Coleshill was urging, 'Come on! Get back inside the hotel!'

'Oh, please let me stay,' I implored him. 'Nobody's going to recognise me.'

'With hair like that?' He pointed at my long, wild hair. 'Everybody will recognise you! Come inside!'

We drove to the house of a lady from the Foreign Office for lunch. She was really lovely to me. When I sat down at the beautifully laid-out meal table, I broke down and had to leave the room. It was an hour before I could return. I had never seen anything so lovely.

These stages were all important, and I'm still glad that I asked Mr. Coleshill if I could have that period of adjustment. But now I was beginning to want to go home.

I knew that Ian Smith had flown to Kuala Lumpur, and I decided to contact him. I didn't have to speak to any reporter if I didn't want to, Mr. Coleshill pointed out, but the Daily Mail had offered me a flight home. I arranged to meet Ian Smith at the airport. Mr. Coleshill wasn't able to take me there, so we said our goodbyes at the house where we'd had lunch. He was reassuring and kind, just as he had been all the time since I left prison. I will always be grateful to him. I have many debts of gratitude I will never be able to repay, but he was special. I don't know how I would have managed for those first few days without him.

On the plane we sat in the first class lounge, which was virtually empty. Ian Smith explained that there was no need to talk if I didn't want to. He would even go and sit on the other side of the lounge if I wanted to sleep all the way home.

'Well,' I suggested, not wanting to seem ungrateful. 'We could always have a cup of tea together, couldn't we?'

As we sipped our tea something seemed to unlock inside me, and I poured out the story of my life to him, right from the beginning, the bad and the good things. I talked for hours about my childhood, my family, James, the arrest, Hannah, Jenny, Maria – all of it. I talked about Jesus, and what he had done for me; about Valerie, and Mary, and Linda. I shared my hopes and my fears. It all tumbled out, and Ian Smith listened patiently. Only a tiny fraction of what I said ever found its way into print. Ian Smith was kind and understanding with me, and I'm sure that my telling him everything was another necessary stage in my return to the outside world. God was guiding me step by step, and providing me with the right people to help me at each stage.

I knew that there would be crowds at London Airport. Paul McCartney was returning the same day after his arrest in Japan on drug charges. When I looked out of the plane as we landed, I saw a crowd of reporters.

'It's this plane they're waiting for, not McCartney's,' smiled Ian Smith. However, it was at least twenty minutes before I felt able to leave my seat. I was shaking with fright. It wasn't the reporters. It was the overwhelming knowledge that I was home at last. The nightmare was over.

Eventually a police superintendent came on board, a solid, friendly, unarmed London policeman.

'Are you all right, love?'

'I'm OK . . . I just can't get up . . . I can't leave the plane.'

He was very understanding. 'Look, love. Those are your friends out there. They're all on your side. But just in case, I've got 200 of my boys waiting to see you through to the airport lounge. And your Uncle George Nightingale is waiting for you round the corner.'

I stood up, suddenly calm. I went down the steps, pushed past the reporters, and made my way through the crowd.

The policeman walking by my side murmured, 'Just keep walking . . . keep walking, you'll be all right.'

And then at the end of the tarmac I saw my Uncle George, who had come to greet me and take me to my Mum and sisters. He looked beautiful, with his gleaming white hair and a broad smile on his face.

I started running towards him, forgetting the crowds,

forgetting the police and reporters. I opened my arms wide and raced across to him, crying and laughing at the same time; I half fell, half collapsed, into his arms, into his embrace, into the rest of my life.

Postscript

Several weeks after my release Lucille sent me a press cutting. Maria had been called to the Supreme Court for sentencing. The newspaper photo showed her bare-footed and bewildered outside a court cell; the court had ordered her release. She was to be sent back to Spain.

Hannah, Jenny and Chris are still in Lard Yao, serving their sentences.

Linda and Mary are still going through the court hearings at the time of writing. It will be some months before they know their sentences.

Three months after my return, my mother asked Jesus into her life. She was fifty-eight, fit, active, and very happy to have me back home after such a long absence. Several weeks after she became a Christian she fell ill, and she died within three months. I don't know why God allowed her to die, but I am so grateful to him for those months I spent nursing her. It was the best time I ever had with her.

Some time after Mum's death, I went to America. I had been invited by the Prison Fellowship, the group started by Chuck Colson, of which I had first heard in Lard Yao. Kathryn Grant had reported back to the fellowship after visiting me in Bangkok, and they had begun to pray for me with a new urgency. They were thrilled when they heard that, only weeks after Kathryn's visit, I had been released. I spent two months with the fellowship, and returned with a growing feeling that my own experiences in prison could be used by God in reaching other prisoners. In January 1981, I joined the staff of Prison Christian Fellowship, the daughter organisation in Britain, and since then have worked for this ministry to prison inmates and their families. So my own concern for other prisoners, and the prophecy Margaret Cole made to the King of Thailand about my future, have been fulfilled.

My work takes me into prisons and Borstals all over Britain. I share my prison experiences, and the love of God, with the inmates. I also go to churches and fellowship groups, encouraging them to pray for inmates, and for Christians to become more involved with the prisons.

———————

In the course of this book I have been able to say thank you to many people. There are still many more who helped and encouraged me in numerous ways during the events described, and for various reasons do not appear. Some of them I will never know about, so I am grateful to be able to take this opportunity of publicly thanking each one of them.

FREED
FOR EVER

For Trevor and Ben

Contents

Preface

In 1977 I was arrested, tried and imprisoned in Bangkok on charges of smuggling heroin. While in prison, I became a Christian. After three years I was released by Royal amnesty and was allowed to return home.

I have told the story of my arrest and imprisonment in *Freed for Life*. Many who have read that book have asked me about events since my release and about the work I now do with Prison Christian Fellowship, and that is why I have now taken the story further in this book. You don't need to have read *Freed for Life* before reading *Freed for Ever*; but as this story is a continuation, people and situations from the Far East and Bangkok women's prison appear in this book as well.

Since I returned to England, I have been helped and encouraged by many people from all walks of life. Here are just some of those I would like to thank.

First and foremost I would like to thank the many people who continue to uphold me in prayer. Without them I don't believe that this book, or the story that it contains, would have been possible.

From the early days of Prison Christian Fellowship, I would like to thank Ross Simpson, Sylvia-Mary Alison, Rev. John Harris, Tom Marriot and Tony Ralls; and more recently, Rev. Peter Timms, Peter Chadwick and Brian Stevenson. A special thank you to Christine Austen for her invaluable help in getting my programme and myself organised.

Rev. Herrick and Judy Daniels, Mona and Val Horsefield, Bob and Sheila Allison, Jim Hodson and Win ('Mother') Morgan all gave me friendship and spiritual help when I needed it most. I owe a debt of gratitude also to Chuck Colson, Kathryn Grant, Ferne Sanford, Gordon Loux, Jeanne Hurley, Peggy Morris and many more dear friends in the USA.

A big thank you to David and Tricia Porter for their hard work and late nights working on this book.

Thanks also to my wonderful family for love and understanding, through times which must have seemed so odd to them.

And last but not least, I would like to thank my dear Trevor, who married me in spite of my shortcomings.

Acknowledgements

In working with Rita on this, our second book, I have been given a great deal of help by various individuals and organisations.

Out of many who have contributed information and facts I would like to thank the following: the management of the Stirk House Hotel, Gisburn; Rev. Herrick Daniels; Mr. Ross Simpson; and Mr. and Mrs. Gilbert Kirby. Sylvia Mary Alison's *God is Building a House* (Marshalls, 1984) came to my notice very late in the project, but provides an interesting perspective on the growth of Prison Christian Fellowship in the UK. I am also grateful to Mrs. Barbara Rees for permission to use the quotation on page 179.

I have been given free access to Rita's notebooks, correspondence and other documentation. Information on matters American has been provided by Millie Thomson, Elaine Cooper and Liz Newman. Os House and staff have supplied crucial technical assistance in emergencies. The manuscript has been read in whole or in part by several people whose comments have been invaluable, including Pam Hendry and Jane Winter.

It remains to acknowledge the help and encouragement of Edward and Ann England, the wise counsels of my brother Peter Elsom, and the apparently limitless energy of my wife Tricia, who not only did an enormous amount of typing on this project but was also one of the manuscript's most discerning readers.

David Porter

1 England Again

*Suddenly, unexpectedly, astonishingly, she
was to be free. Five dizzying days and half-a-
world later, her voice came softly, almost
inaudibly . . . 'There are no words to describe
the joy and the happiness.'*

Jubilee (The newsletter of Prison Fellowship),
March 1980

I was half-asleep, half-awake. My eyelids were screwed
tight, trying to create some darkness. But the light was too
strong. It was too strong every night. You couldn't bury
your face in the pillow because after a while you had to shift
to let some air at your face. The heat was static, a forest
swelter, a moist tide lapping gently at legs and arms,
creeping even into the towel wrapped round the head
against insects and the naked light-bulb glaring
monotonously down from the insect-crawling ceiling. *Oh,
for a night with the light off!* But the light stayed on. That
was the rule.

I lay rigid and motionless. I had learned to sleep that way.
You had to. When you were sleeping with a regimented row
of others, allocated three floorboards for yourself and your
possessions, you learned quickly. Those who didn't were
bullied into conformity by grunts, obscenities, and the
occasional well-aimed kick or punch.

I shifted at last, and allowed my body to relax. It must be nearly six o'clock. Time to get up, to join the queue of others clutching their belongings in worn cardboard boxes, waiting for a turn at the dipper-bath to wash off the sweat of the night. Best catch a few extra moments' sleep. One more night got through. One more day ticked off the calendar. One day nearer 'going out', leaving Lard Yao Prison, leaving the crowded hot cells and the perpetual smell of stale fish and drying garbage. But it was never a good idea to start thinking about that day. Thinking about it could drive a girl mad.

'Rita! Rita – wake up!' Somebody was pulling at my shoulder. I grumbled complainingly, resentful at losing any precious moments of sleep. In some ludicrous corner of my memory I could smell breakfast, English breakfast. I shut the thought from my mind. But other scraps of England drifted into my half-awake thoughts. Then, as I struggled back to consciousness, from an ocean's depth of tiredness, I heard my mother's voice.

'Come on, love. Come on – you've been dreaming.'

I finally opened my eyes. The light that had been hurting them was a crisp January morning sun streaming through a neatly curtained window. Mum was holding me, rocking me gently awake. A tray of breakfast things lay on a table. Like shadows evaporating when a light shines brightly, Lard Yao and its inhabitants faded away. I was in bed, at home, in Blackburn, England. The nightmare was over.

It was a fortnight since I had arrived at London Airport on the last stage of my journey home from Bangkok. Three years in Lard Yao had burned many memories into my mind – some harrowing, some pleasant. I'd left good friends behind in prison, and other people to whom I'd been delighted to say goodbye. The same sights and sounds had dominated my life for so long; that hot courtyard, the vegetable beds bordering the prison sewer, the nursery room with its perpetual stench of rag nappies, the lines of Thai prisoners chanting Bhuddist devotions as they shuffled forward into the prison refectory – each mental image at the time as sharp as a finely focused photograph and as irremovable as a tattoo.

And yet, two weeks after the exhilarating events of my release, those memories were patchy and fading; it was often impossible to remember what some of my fellow-prisoners even looked like, try as I might. My mind was beginning to be filled with homely details such as I had not witnessed for years. It was still all a bit of a jumble, a haze of emotion and excitement. Isolated moments stood out, little flashes of sharp detail in an unconnected chain of events.

That expensive carpet, for example, in a long, well-furnished corridor in a London hotel – I hadn't the slightest idea which hotel it was. After my arrival at the airport I had been driven there with Uncle George, by representatives of the *Daily Mail*, the national newspaper which had paid for my journey back to England. I'd been bubbling with excitement, and when I'd seen the plush carpet extending down the elegant corridor, I hadn't been able to resist temptation. To the astonishment of two hotel guests who happened to be in the corridor at the time, I'd turned a cartwheel on the spot. The feel of that carpet underfoot stuck in my mind as an almost tangible memory, its impossible softness cushioning the soles of my feet, still tanned and leathery from years of eastern roads and dusty prison yards.

My crazy cartwheel took me past the door to which our small party had been heading. We retraced our steps. Uncle George pushed the door open and stood back to let me go in. Sitting in the room waiting for me were my sister June and my mother.

The last time I'd seen Mum had been in Bangkok, over two years before, when I had been sullen and angry. I had bitterly regretted many times the fact that she'd had to return home with only the memory of my rebellious, scared face watching her out of the prison office-block. Now, when I saw her again, I could only think how much older she looked, older even than she had seemed after the exhausting flight from England to Lard Yao. We clung to each other and wept – I think everybody in the room was crying. I said nothing to Mum, just repeated over and over again, 'Mum, Mum . . .' She said nothing to me. We just held each other for a long time. I was only conscious of the love that surrounded me that moment, and the fact that I was back with my family at last.

Time went by unnoticed. We must have been several hours in that room, hours which were now just a blur of happiness. I was too joyful to take in much. There was champagne, and the Press were there, and a great deal of talking was going on. I just sat on the floor, Thai-fashion (for weeks I would find it impossible to sit comfortably in a chair again), and every now and then I would reach out a hand and touch my Mum, to reassure myself that we were together again, that the long nightmare was really over.

When things had calmed down a little, Mum said, 'What do you want to do, Rita? Would you like to stay here for the night? You can, you know.'

I shook my head. 'I want to go home.'

We left the hotel in two cars. Uncle George and June went in one and I went in the other with Mum. There were journalists and photographers with us. I took in little of the journey north; it was dark anyway. I just held on to her. Once I turned to her and gave her an enormous bear-hug. She smiled gently.

'Go easy,' she chided, 'that's my sore shoulder.'

'What've you been doing?'

'I don't know – strained it, or something. It's taking its time to get better. Sign of old age.'

'Get away with you, Mum!' I laughed. She nodded at the

roadsigns flashing past the car as it raced on.

'We're not going straight home,' she said. 'You wouldn't get any peace. I haven't been there for a week. There are reporters banging at the door all day long. Ever since we heard you were coming home. We changed the phone number. You've no idea.'

I grinned at her happily. She might have been reading the Bangkok telephone directory aloud, for all I heard of what she said.

During the long journey we stopped at a motorway service station. The harshly lit dining area seemed like a scrubbed, gleaming palace. I hesitated for what seemed an age choosing between tea and coffee. It was the luxury of choice that made me linger. In the end the others chose for me. I sat absorbed in the newness of it all, playing with a paper sachet of sugar. How long since I last saw one of those?

My mother was wearing a lovely coat with a silver-fox fur collar, and as we sat at the table she took it off and put it round my shoulders. I must have looked an odd sight. I was wearing new clothes which had been sent out to Bangkok when I was released, and I probably looked quite smart. But on my feet I wore my comfortable Thai sandals that I had worn in prison. It had been so long since I had worn shoes that I couldn't go back to wearing them immediately.

'Let me try your shoes, Mum,' I said suddenly. She took them off and I slid my feet into them and stood up. The high heels felt as if someone had put bricks under my feet. It was like learning to walk in grown-up shoes all over again. I tottered a few paces and gave up. 'I'll have to work on it,' I laughed. I stared happily at the other people in the service station and put my sandals back on. After a while I kicked them off again and put them in my bag.

Back in the car I cuddled up to Mum.

The night rolled back before us as we sped north.

Suddenly, we were driving through Blackburn town centre. I stared through the windscreen, pointing out landmarks I hadn't seen for several years.

'Hey, Mum! Look at that! That's where what's-her-name used to live . . . Wow, we didn't have a Debenham's store when I left . . . Oh, look, that's changed . . . And your friend Florrie lived down that street . . .'

'You know this place better than I do,' said Mum good-humouredly.

'I want to see Ann,' I said. 'When will I see Ann?'

'She'll be there when we arrive.' Mum was solid, reassuring. It was all going to be all right.

We emerged the other side of Blackburn and finally pulled to a stop in front of an old-fashioned mansion. We must have driven almost to the Yorkshire border. We got out of the cars. I pulled Mum's coat more tightly round me. I was so dazed and light-headed that I couldn't understand what the building was.

'Is this Ann's house?'

Mum shook her head and indicated a hotel sign discreetly placed at the door. 'It's called the Stirk House Hotel.'

We went in. It was not far off midnight, a cold January night. I was wearing Mum's fur coat; my feet were bare. I must have looked weird, but I didn't care about the stares and whispers. The first person I saw was my Auntie Mary, changed since I had last seen her – her arthritis was no better, and she had put on some weight in the face – but instantly recognisable; and standing behind her, looking really beautiful, was my sister Ann. The lounge was full of people, but I had no eyes for anybody else. I went up to my Auntie Mary, kneeled down, and rested my head on her knee. Once again, I felt wrapped round by the wholeness and the love which I had not known for so long.

At the mealtable there were about twenty of us. Many of the faces I didn't know. Most were people who had been involved with my family in the campaign for my freedom.

Some had been helping Mum out by answering the phone for her or dealing with the press. Others were from the *Daily Mail*, and had been organising the details of my journey home and the arrangements at the hotels. Ian Smith of the *Mail*, who had flown to Bangkok to meet me and had escorted me back to London, was there; and so was his photographer, whom I had already met. I was introduced to lots of people and forgot their names as soon as I'd been told them. It was a cheerful, boisterous meal, and I was hardly conscious of any of it.

The other guests in the hotel were unaware of the reason for the celebrations. Auntie Mary told me later that the maitre d'hotel had stood at the door all evening, consulting his watch and frowning. Last orders for dinner had been taken at ten o'clock. As ten o'clock came and went, he had become increasingly agitated and had warned my aunt several times:

'If your party doesn't arrive soon it won't be possible to admit them.'

But during the meal he took Ann aside and confided to her, 'Now I understand who it is – it's fine, don't worry, everything is all right.'

Though it was so late when our meal was served, I enjoyed it enormously. I ordered steak, though I didn't eat much of it. I was too excited. I kept getting up from my seat and wandering round the other places, begging morsels of different food items to sample.

Afterwards we all went through to the lounge, a comfortable Lancashire lounge with polished horse-brasses on the oak-beamed fireplace, big armchairs and a little bar in one corner. Everybody was still talking, and I tried to be sociable. But I couldn't sit still for longer than two minutes at a time. I kept getting up and wandering round the room, picking up ashtrays and emptying them into the waste-paper basket. If I adjusted the curtains once I must have done so scores of times. I couldn't sit down for long and I couldn't find anything to hold my attention. I felt desperately tired, emotionally strung out and very, very happy.

The long day came to an end. I managed to get some sleep, but for much of the night I lay awake, my mind racing in a hundred different directions. What fitful dreams I had, merged into the general blur of the day's events.

2 At Stirk House

Stirk House is a privately owned 16th
century manor house updated to a luxury
hotel . . . offering 'away from it all' seclusion
giving an immediate sense of relaxation . . .

Hotel brochure

I woke up late the next day, somewhat stiff from the
unaccustomed luxury of a bed. It seemed as if I'd been
awake, on and off, most of the night, though I must have
slept for part of the time. I don't think an earthquake would
have stopped my body from insisting on *some* of the rest for
which it had been clamouring.

After the first disorientation everything came back into
sharp focus – the airport, meeting Mum, the long car
journey through the night, the joyful, disorganised time
together the previous evening. I looked around me
appreciatively. The bedroom at Stirk House was very nice,
and I was beginning to find beds bearable again – after my
release, on my way home from Bangkok I had stopped over
in Kuala Lumpur, and had had to sleep on the floor because
I wasn't used to anything else after prison.

I came downstairs into the forlorn, unoccupied
atmosphere that hotels have in the morning. From the
dining room came the sound of a vacuum cleaner whirring

away industriously, and I could see somebody laying the tables for lunch. Our celebrations of the previous night were a distant memory. I made my way to the lounge. Standing in the doorway, rubbing the sleep from my eyes, I gazed in disbelief at what I saw.

It seemed as though my whole family had packed into the room. All my aunts and uncles were there, and one by one they came and hugged me. They murmured lovely greetings – 'It's great to have you home', 'We're just so glad you're safe, Rita', 'Welcome back, love' – it was wonderful to see them. I'd heard bits of news of them all in letters that came to me in Bangkok, and you can piece together quite a good picture of how people are getting on from quite slender fragments of information. But we've always been a close family, and it had really hurt for three years knowing that I was locked away from any chance of coming home to them. I'd shed many tears at Christmas time, imagining them all enjoying the festivities at home. Now I was able to hold them, and kiss them, and tell them how much I had missed each one of them.

Ann hadn't stayed at the hotel overnight – she had gone home where John, her husband, was babysitting. Later that day she returned with the children, small strangers grown out of all recognition from the toddlers I had last seen; I wasn't sure whether they recognised me. Kathryn, now nine, stared at me curiously – I think she half-remembered who I was. Jonathan had been two when I left home and clearly had no idea who I might be. Emma, an eighteen-month old toddler, was the newly-conceived baby about whom Ann had told me when she visited me in Bangkok – I was the first to know she was pregnant. Now I was able to play with her baby.

The older children were quite unawed either by the occasion or the hotel and its grounds. My family stayed with me all day, and during a quiet lull I was relaxing cross-legged on the floor when Jonathan clambered onto my knee and delivered his verdict:

'Oh, Auntie Rita! I do like your house! I've just been in the swimming pool – it's great!'

It was a day for sandwiches and being together and walking in the countryside round the hotel. It was sheer delight to walk in the clean January sunlight, leaves crunching underfoot, hanging on to Ann with one arm and Mum with the other. I borrowed a fur coat from one of my aunts, and fur-lined boots from another. We chattered endlessly, about anything and everything. Bangkok seemed a million miles away. Over there it would be the hot season, but here everything was crisp winter green. It was as if I had been reborn into a new world of gusty skies and frosted hills. There were so many things that I had not seen for so long; the trees' bare outlines waiting for the new growth of spring, *stone* buildings, occasional walkers muffled and wrapped against the cold.

Back in the hotel, it was time for Ann and the children to go back home.

'Oh, by the way, Rita,' said Ann, 'this is yours.' She pointed to a large red sack in a corner of the lounge.

'Whatever is it?'

'It's your letters. We called at the house on our way here. They've been piling up for the last few days. They almost jammed the front door shut. The Post Office had so many the other day they sent them in the sack. Like a film star! Have a good time reading them.'

I pulled a corner of the sack open. Inside were what seemed like hundreds of envelopes, some tied in bundles.

'Wow! It's like my birthday all over again,' I grinned happily.

'Don't forget all the thank-you letters you'll have to write,' said Ann, and went to round up her children. Jonathan was reluctant to leave the fairytale palace.

'I'm hungry, Mummy,' he protested.

'Never mind, I'll get something to eat when we get home.'

'Don't do that, Mummy,' Jonathan reassured her. 'Just tell the servants to bring some more sandwiches, then we can eat now . . .'

Poor Jonathan! The staff of Stirk House had been serving afternoon tea for the past few hours, and he had watched wide-eyed as trays of cakes, sandwiches and pots of tea had appeared in seemingly limitless supply. Watching his face fall, I felt quite guilty. He must have thought that his Auntie Rita coming home meant the start of a quite different lifestyle!

Later I sat in the lounge enjoying the glowing fire, as warm as toast. June, Mum and two of my aunts were with me; I was sitting on the floor, leaning against Mum's chair. I was more comfortable that way. The sack of mail was open in front of me. I was pulling out letters and cards at random and reading them, sometimes aloud to my aunts. They were from people I didn't know, who had followed the story of my arrest and imprisonment and were now writing to welcome me home. They contained lovely messages, full of affection and kindness, some from Christians who had been praying for me, others from people who had contributed from their old-age pensions to help me while I was in prison.

'Look at this one,' I said, fishing out an orange envelope with official stamps all over it. 'It's a telegram!'

I tore it open and extracted the form inside.

'Who from?' asked Auntie Mary.

'It's from Chuck Colson in America. You know, he wrote that book I told you about. He works with prisoners in the States.' I scanned the telegram. 'He used to work for President Nixon. He was in the Watergate thing,' I added as an afterthought.

'What does he want?' said Mum.

'He wants me to telephone him reversed charges. In America. I wonder why?'

'Don't you go off on your travels again this week,' smiled Mum comfortably.

I looked at the telegram again. *Call collect*, it said, and gave the number – one of those long American telephone numbers.

We read more messages and admired the cards. We had barely got half-way through the sack when I stood up and stretched.

'I think I'll give my legs a bit of exercise,' I said. I bent down and picked the telegram up from where it lay in its bright envelope. I smoothed it out against the back of Mum's chair. Standing behind her, I stroked her head. How grey her hair was! Had it been like that before I went away?

'Do you know, Mum, I think I'll go and give Mr. Colson that phone call,' I said. She frowned.

'Now?' There was something indefinable in her voice. It sounded like fear.

'He was awfully kind to me, Mum. He sent Kathryn Grant to see me in Bangkok. That was how I found out about him. He runs Prison Fellowship over in the States.'

Mum grunted. 'Don't be long, love.'

I went upstairs to my bedroom and closed the door. I picked up the bedside telephone and asked the operator for a reversed charges connection to the number on the telegram.

It was early morning in America. Chuck Colson wasn't available, but I spoke to several of his colleagues. They were delighted to hear me; for several minutes I was greeted by one American voice after another, and there was a good deal of emotion at both ends of the telephone cable. Kathryn Grant had visited me in November when I had seventeen years of my sentence left and no prospect of release. Now I was home again, a mere four months later.

'It's the Presidential Prayer Breakfast next month,' they told me. 'Can you come over?'

'Come over?' I hadn't thought of moving outside Lancashire for the next few months, let alone England. In any case, I hadn't the slightest idea what might be so special about the President's breakfast.

'Rita, we would just love you to come to America and spend some time with us, there are so many people we want you to meet. And we want you to talk with some of our groups . . .'

'No!' I protested, laughing. 'I'm just home, you know? I'm not going anywhere, I want to be with my family!'

They were very understanding and we talked for what seemed a long time. They suggested a number of meetings and special events that they would like me to go over for, but I said no to all of them.

'Well, Rita, we understand that you need to take time to adjust. But please, do keep in touch. We'll write you. We believe that the Lord would have us share with you what we're doing. We'll keep in touch, Rita.'

For a while after replacing the receiver I continued to sit on my bed, deep in thought. It was wonderful to have felt such love and enthusiasm in the voices of those to whom I had been speaking. It was also just a little bit unsettling. Nothing could have been farther from my mind at that moment than travelling again. Oddly, it was the invitation, not the prospect of travel, that I found unnerving. I had no desire to travel again. It was a strange experience to be asked, however. It reminded me that eventually I would have to decide what I was going to do with the rest of my life. *Lord*, I said aloud, *please help me; all this is too much to handle.*

I stood up, tossed my head back, and went downstairs. Mum and my aunts were as I had left them. Mum looked up as I came into the lounge.

'How did it go?'

'Oh – fine,' I said off-handedly. I paused. 'They want me to go to America.'

My mother winced.

'I told them no,' I added hurriedly. 'I said I wanted to stay here with you.'

Mum visibly relaxed. 'Tell me about this Chuck Colson.'

I had told her a bit about him in letters, but this was different. I told her how he had been President Nixon's Special Counsel, one of his five top advisers, and had been sent to prison for his involvement in the Watergate conspiracy. He had become a Christian in the early days of the court proceedings, and after his release from prison he had had a vision of what God wanted for his life; to work among prisoners, showing them how much God loved them, building fellowships of Christians in every prison in America. That was the vision of Prison Fellowship, and that was the story that Kathryn Grant had told me when she visited me in Lard Yao in November 1979. She had brought me a copy of Chuck's new book, *Life Sentence*, which tells the story of how God brought the Fellowship into being and had made it grow.

I had read the book, fascinated. Everything that Kathryn had said struck a chord in my heart. I had been praying for some time for prisoners, not just those whom I knew in Lard Yao, but all the thousands I didn't know in prisons all over the world. Kathryn's visit showed me that God *did* care, that he had already inspired people to help those for whom I had such a burning concern.

Some of this I tried to share with Mum and the others. Of course, it led on to my own story, of how I had become a Christian in prison. It was a good time to chat; one of those relaxed, rambling sorts of conversations that you get into when you're feeling very happy and tired. I'd always been close to my aunts, and of course I wanted to share everything with Mum, so it was easy to talk to them about how I had come to believe in Jesus and what he had meant to me in prison.

I talked about my first bitterness and resentment, how I had stormed at Lucille and Margaret who had visited me faithfully for so long and talked to me about Jesus as if he might actually be a real person; and I told them about the day an elderly lady called Martha Livesey, travelling

271

through Bangkok, had called at the prison to see me and announced that she too came from Blackburn. I had broken down in tears and fled to the darkest, most secret place I could find, and there, sitting sobbing under the prison hospital hut, I had read the tract she had left me and there I had given my life to God.

I was so happy to be able to talk freely to the people I loved the most, about the things that were now most important to me. They listened to all that I said. They knew a little of it already; from letters I knew that since her visit to Bangkok, Martha Livesey had gone to see Mum and had kept in contact with her since; now I was able to tell them myself what her visit had meant to me.

I wondered afterwards what had been going through their minds as I'd talked. I'd left home a dissatisfied, restless twenty-one year old; I'd gone from a wrecked marriage to a night club in Hong Kong and from there I had burst onto the front pages of the world's newspapers accused of smuggling drugs. Now I was back, radiantly happy, talking about my new-found faith as a Christian. Did it cross their minds, as it had crossed the minds of so many, that it might just be escapism – mere wishful thinking, a prisoner's comfort? Some had already 'explained' my conversion to me rationally: 'Well, you were distressed, of course you were. And you were on your own. That made it worse. And you were cut off from everything and everybody you knew. So you turned to religion. It gave you what you needed – peace of mind, something to live for. Oh, it's not your fault . . . lots of people do the same in that situation.'

That was what Hannah, my fellow-prisoner in Lard Yao, had said to me. To her and to others before and after my release I could only reply, 'It's not just peace of mind I needed. It wasn't a psychological thing at all. I met a *person*. I met Jesus. He changed my life.'

Suddenly, as I lay stretched out on my bed, thoughts of the future swept over me. I felt myself panicking. What would I do? How would I earn my living? What was going to happen? *I can't cope, Lord!*, I cried out in my heart. *I'm so confused . . .*

I was terrified. It all seemed so difficult.

Then I realised what I had instinctively done. *I've just cried out to God*, I thought, *and he was there where I looked for him.*

Since arriving at the airport I had barely prayed or read my Bible. But that didn't mean that I had forgotten God. Quite the opposite; in the midst of all the excitement and emotion I felt myself buoyed up by a great tide of his love, secure and protected, like sailing down a rushing river in a boat you trust perfectly. In all the things that were happening I lived each moment as it came, and all the time I knew the Lord was with me.

That night as I drifted off to sleep I drowsily reminded myself of how God had cared for me in the past week. On the plane, leaving Bangkok airport, I'd been overwhelmed by an enormous conflict inside me as the joy of freedom struggled with fear of the future. In Kuala Lumpur I'd been unable to sit at table without breaking down in floods of tears. My family in England must have been wondering in what sort of state they'd find me when I came home; yet I'd sat last night at dinner with all those people, and I'd been able to order a meal and hold some sort of a conversation, just a day or two after Kuala Lumpur. It was God's perfect planning, I knew. It had been my own spontaneous decision to come home via a roundabout way, nobody had advised me to; but by doing so I had gained some control of myself by the time I met Mum and my family.

I was very aware, in that hotel bedroom, of the presence of Jesus. I began to talk to him. I told him all the things that had happened that day, and how mixed up I was. I told him about meeting my family again, about being among people who loved me; and I told him about the phone call to America and the overflowing sack of mail. One by one I handed my joys and my worries to him. I felt a deep calm spreading inside me. Whatever the future might hold, it was in his hands. It really was going to be all right.

3 Blackburn

*No-one who has not been locked away with
the prospect of being caged for 20 years can
appreciate the feeling of complete and utter
freedom and happiness.*

Interview with David Allin printed in the
Lancashire Evening Post, 24 January 1980.

And then, next day, it all started to go wrong. It seemed
unbelievable that anything could spoil the happiness and
joy which had carried me along for two days. Maybe the
strain of all the excitement was becoming too much for me.
Maybe there were suddenly just too many people to cope
with. Whatever the reason, on the third day back in
England I snapped.

It started out a bad day. In the morning I continued to
explore my sack of mail, and once again found numerous
messages of goodwill and friendship. When I ripped open
the insignificant white envelope with its scrawled name and
address it seemed no different to any of the others.

Minutes later I was still staring at it in dumb horror. It
was a typed letter, full of mistakes and mis-spellings, like
one of those ransom notes you read about. The writer
sounded as if he was eaten up with anger and vicious
hatred.

You're back home now, I read. *You're in all the newspapers. But I know what you're really like. Soon the whole world will know. You'll be back the way you used to be . . .*

I gripped the letter in both hands and shakily tore it in two. Then I put the pieces together and tore them in two again. I threw the pieces on the floor, separate from the other letters. My hands were trembling. Nearby Mum and June were talking. A dull throbbing sounded in my ears. It was my pulse. I thought I was going to faint.

'Mum . . . oh Mum . . .'

She came across to find me clenching and unclenching my fists, fighting back huge sobs. When I looked at her I collapsed into floods of tears and pointed mutely at the pieces of the letter. I threw my arms round her and wept as she fitted them together and read the words grim-faced. Then she gripped my shoulders and pushed me back.

'Now look, woman,' she said fiercely. 'Just stop that at once.'

I stared at her wetly as she gathered up handfuls of the other letters and cards.

'Just *look* at what you've got,' she demanded. 'All these people, all glad to see you home, all full of kind things to say. You got all these, and when *one* person, one sick stupid *person*, writes a stupid letter – you go to pieces.'

She flung the letters up in the air and they fluttered down again like a flock of paper birds. The effort hurt her shoulder, and she sat back holding it as she watched for my reaction. 'All these good letters,' she repeated. After a few moments I nodded miserably and wiped a sleeve across my eyes. My sobs shuddered to a stop. Mum beamed.

'That's better, love. They're not worth it, people who would write a letter like that. They're sick, they're beneath contempt.'

She's right, I thought. *What does it matter? It matters nothing*. I went on reading the letters and cards, and by the time I got to the end of them without finding any more antagonistic letters, I was nearly back to normal, with only an occasional sniff betraying the fact that I was still upset.

The episode cast a shadow over the morning, and I was subdued with other people. My nerves were jangling, and I had a hot, thundering headache. Sooner or later it was inevitable that I would explode at somebody or other, and sure enough it happened.

What made it worse was that the person who took the brunt of it was somebody who had been extraordinarily kind to me – Ian Smith, the *Daily Mail* reporter whose paper had arranged for my flight back and the hotel and everything. It was part of a contract that the *Mail* made with my family at the time of my release, by which they were now entitled to exclusive rights on my story for a period. The contract stipulated that nothing was to be printed without my family's approval. Ian had never acted like somebody who had a commercial interest in my experiences. On the flight from Thailand, via Kuala Lumpur, he had been a relaxed, tolerant companion for somebody who was almost hysterical with delight and emotionally totally erratic. In so many ways, I doubt if there could have been a better escort.

On the plane back from Kuala Lumpur, I had poured out almost my entire life story to him. He hadn't pressed me to say anything; in fact he went out of his way to say that if I wanted to sleep all the way home, that was fine. But once I'd started talking it was impossible to stop.

During that morning Ian walked into the lounge and handed me a copy of that day's *Daily Mail*.

'Well, there you are, Rita. What do you think of it?'

I took the paper from him hesitantly. There, on the front page, was a picture of me, laughing and crying at the same time, and a paragraph saying that this was Rita Nightingale who'd been released from prison and that the full story was on the centre pages. I blinked at the picture. It was disconcerting because I hadn't realised what a sight I had looked – it was taken before the Consular officials had allowed me the use of what had seemed to be the most wonderful bathroom in the world. I smiled cautiously at Ian and turned to the centre pages. My mouth fell open in shock.

It was the first time that I'd seen any major coverage of my story in the press. Friends and relatives had sent me various cuttings in Lard Yao, and when I was released I'd been shown a newspaper photo of Mum back home in Blackburn just after she'd been told the news. But it was a different experience to open up a whole newspaper and find that the centre spread was about me.

In fact Ian had hardly used anything of what I told him on the plane. He'd been very sensitive and hadn't exploited the fact that I was telling everything regardless. He'd taken a number of small parts of the story and put them together, and had checked the whole thing with Ann and obtained her permission. Ann, of course, had been getting letters from me all the time, as had the rest of my family, so she was able to make sure that the story was told in an accurate way as far as was possible. In fact, when you realise that he had been as well placed as anybody could be to exploit and sensationalise my story, his handling of the whole thing was miraculously gentle and considerate.

But that morning, I didn't think of that at all. I just stared numbly at the article. There was Maria's story, poor sick Spanish Maria who had been old enough to be my mother. She had come to Lard Yao, charged with being the accomplice of a drugs dealer; she spoke no English. Despite that, we had become very close, and when I became a Christian we began to read the Bible together, I with my English Bible, she with a Spanish one that had been sent to her by Christians in England. We used to show each other verses we'd found and look them up, each in our respective languages. In due course she went to court, and was sentenced to forty years. The news shattered her; shortly afterwards she had a nervous breakdown. Just before I left lard Yao, I had visited her in her dark, foul-smelling cell, where she had sat with her back to me, staring blankly at the wall, ignoring my voice. *Oh, Maria, love! How could I bear it, to leave Bangkok without saying goodbye?* But it had been no use. My last sight of her had been of her soiled, bent shoulders.

And now Maria's story was all over the centre pages of the *Daily Mail*, for anybody to read. Details of our friendship which I'd mentioned in letters home were reprinted in bold type. I stared at the page in blank misery. A jumble of bitter thoughts ran one after the other through my mind. Here was I, free and with my family; Maria was still in her cell, dirty and afraid. I felt dirty too. It was like a betrayal; not just that I had betrayed Maria but that Ian had betrayed me.

I rounded on him, waving the paper in his face. 'How can you do a thing like that to me?'

My voice sounded high-pitched and wobbly. I didn't care.

Ian looked taken aback. 'I'm not sure that . . .'

'You're horrible! How *could* you? You put it in a *newspaper*, about *Maria*. I hate you, I *hate* you!'

I could see I'd hurt him, but I didn't try to soften the force of what I'd said. I turned on my heel and flounced out of the room. Mum tried to stop me – I just pushed past. One or two hotel guests who'd watched the whole thing looked curious or embarrassed.

I stormed to the nearest telephone and dialled Ann's number. Her quiet voice answered.

'Rita, what's wrong?'

I blurted out my anger.

'It's horrible, it's awful, you've got to come over to the hotel. Oh Ann, it's *horrible* . . .'

I had lost control of myself. It was a real tantrum. Part of me was watching how I was behaving with a fascinated detachment, quite unable to stop it. By the time Ann and John arrived I was trembling and incoherent. John took one look at me, at my streaked and woebegone features.

'Come on,' he said. He put his arm protectively round my shoulders. 'Wash your face, I'm taking you out.'

We got into the car and he drove me into Gisburn village. By the time we got there I was already beginning to calm down. John parked the car near the old Norman church, and we went in to look around.

Multi-coloured sunlight dappled through the stained glass windows, and the noises of the village traffic were subdued as I wandered around the lovely old church. I walked to the front and stood before the altar with its great window behind, and almost without thinking I knelt.

As I knelt there I realised what the trouble was. For the past few days I'd been so conscious of God's love and care, and then in the shock of seeing the hateful letter and the newspaper I'd forgotten he was there at all. Now I just wanted to talk to him again. *Lord*, I said silently, *I don't know what's happening to me. But I know you're with me. You've got to help me to cope, because I don't understand any of this.*

John waited patiently for me at the back of the church, and after a while we left and went into the local gift shop. I felt much better, and the turmoil inside me was already subsiding. I began to enjoy myself again.

I couldn't believe all the beautiful things in that shop. I picked up one thing after another – frivolous chiffon scarves, suede-leather gifts, lots of things – and gazed at them entranced, touching and stroking them. At my side, John bought a few things, and the other people in the shop were looking at us with great interest. I was so obviously excited, he was buying things, and every now and then I hugged him for sheer happiness. After a while one of them said to John, 'Is it your anniversary?'

I giggled, and John smiled and replied mysteriously, 'No, it's not our anniversary. But it's a very special day.'

Then I felt a kindly hand on my shoulder. It was the lady who ran the shop.

'I know who you are.' She had a comfortable, reassuring voice. 'You know, we always believed you were innocent. And we're so happy you've come home.'

When we left the shop we didn't say anything as we started back to the car. Then John broke the silence. 'I reckon that's what most people think,' he remarked quietly.

It was the first time that I had talked with any of my family about the court proceedings, and it was the first time since coming home that I had had any contact with people who were not directly concerned with my case. Those few words from the lady in the shop meant more to me than I can say.

We went back to the hotel. I found Ian Smith and apologised.

'I'm really sorry. I think it's probably seeing it the first time in print.' I fumbled for the right words. 'It's not that you wrote anything bad, really it's not, it's just that for me it's still . . . still memories, you know?'

He was very kind, and said I wasn't to worry. But I felt I'd hurt him, and I felt bad about it. He could have written so much more, but he didn't. His paper had paid for the travel and the hotels – our family could never have afforded anything like it. He got the exclusive story, but I am still grateful to him for his restraint in telling it.

'I want to go home, Mum.'

It was later the same day, and I'd recovered from the upsets earlier. But now as I looked around the comfortable hotel and the countryside outside, I found myself thinking longingly of Blackburn.

We packed, and Ian Smith drove me and Mum back to Mum's house. I'd never been there, because it was a council house to which she had moved since I'd left home. I had a rough idea where it was, because she'd told me all about it in letters, but as we drove through the gathering early dusk I began to be very excited. It was dark by the time we got there, and we had to go through a complicated performance to which by now my family was well used – Ian stopped the car a little way from the house, and somebody went to see whether there were any reporters waiting at the front door. There were, and we ended up going round behind the house and creeping in secretly through the back door to escape them.

I didn't pay much attention to all that. I was so excited, I was skipping up and down, and when we were in the house I explored every nook and cranny.

'Oh, Mum, it's lovely!'

It really was. All our old treasures and knick-knacks were there, and since she'd moved house she'd bought new furniture and curtains.

At the door Ian Smith said he ought to be getting back, and after we had said our goodbyes and expressed our gratitude he left. We bolted the doors. We were alone together at last.

The house had been empty for several days, and though Mum turned the heat on it took a while for the room to warm up. June began to tidy things and put some tea things on the table. I still felt cold, and kept my coat on as I sat on the floor. *How small it is in here*, I thought; but looking round I realised that it wasn't that the room was particularly tiny. It was just that it was closed in – the door was shut, the curtains drawn. That might seem an odd reaction when you think that I had just spent three years in prison, but the cells in Lard Yao had been large dormitories, with open windows.

But it wasn't long before I got used to it, and I was much more interested in the gleaming bathroom upstairs. Soon I was revelling in the luxury of a hot bath. I'd soaked in several such since my release, and the novelty hadn't worn thin yet. For three years I'd washed by pouring water over myself from a tin dipper filled from a dripping tap, with a string of prisoners behind me grumbling for their turn. Now it seemed as though I had all the time and all the hot water in the world. I sighed blissfully, relaxed, and enjoyed myself.

4 Starting Again

For Rita it was her prayers, and the prayers of others who believed in her, that opened the gates of Lard Yao.

And as she said farewell to Thailand, she declared: 'I intend to devote the rest of my life to repaying that trust.'

Daily Express 25 January 1980

'Are you all right, love?' asked Mum curiously. I jerked myself awake, blinked and smiled vaguely.

'Oh, I'm fine, Mum – just tired, that's all.' I uncurled myself from the corner of the room where I'd been snatching a few minutes rest. It was late afternoon, I'd been home two days, and the family had thrown a party to celebrate my return. It had been a non-stop party ever since I'd got home – my aunts and uncles popped in every few hours, it seemed, to take another look at their long-lost niece; and neighbours called round to say 'Hello' and 'Welcome home'. Of course everybody who came was invited indoors for a cup of tea, and Mum's living room had seemed like Manchester Central Station at times.

It was all lots of fun, and it was lovely to see old friends and neighbours, some of whom had written to me in prison, and some whose news had been passed on to me in letters

284

from Mum. But at bedtime, when we locked the door and sat together on our own, Mum, June and I would look at each other with relief. The non-stop celebration was becoming an emotional and physical strain for my family as well as for me, and during those first few days living back with my family I was beginning to realise how bad the past years had been for them.

Watching Mum sipping her tea that afternoon, massaging her stiff shoulder and wincing with tiredness, I hoped that the excitement would die down soon.

'I'm just a *bit* tired,' I repeated, and made my way across the room to where Uncle George and Aunt Mary were in animated conversation. Mum followed me across. Uncle George beamed at me.

'Well – how's the lady in the news?'

I grimaced, and laughed. He frowned suddenly. 'You know,' he said, 'you do look washed out. Are you getting enough sleep?'

Mum agreed vigorously. 'That's what I've been saying to her, George. Look at her. Matchsticks couldn't keep those eyes open much longer.'

Uncle George peered into my eyes in mock scrutiny and nodded sagely. 'Best thing for you is bed, Rita. No, really, you ought to let us all get on with it. You disappear upstairs. You shouldn't be trying to socialise. You're wiped out.'

'Ah, come on, Uncle George!' I protested. 'I told you – I can hardly sleep at night, let alone in the afternoon. I've got to get used to sleeping properly again. I can't make it happen.'

Mum interrupted. 'That's what you say, lovey. I'm packing you off to bed. Now.'

'Best place for her,' said Uncle George.

Auntie Mary put her arm round me. 'You take it easy, love. Plenty of time for staying up late when you've got used to being home.'

'But it's only five o'clock . . .!' I grumbled, but as Mum took my arm and led me out I was quite glad to have had the matter taken out of my hands. *Come to think of it*, I decided, *I really am zonked. Maybe I will be able to sleep.*

'Auntie Rita! Auntie Rita!'
Somebody a thousand miles away was calling my name. I recognised the voices of Ann's children. So Ann had arrived. It would be nice to go down and see her. I lay in the darkened room with my eyes closed, wondering what time it was. There were still people downstairs, I could hear voices. As I was trying to decide whether to get up or not, I dozed again. I was half-aware of the children rattling the doorknob and calling my name again, and of somebody taking them away. After a while I half-woke. It was a lot quieter downstairs. Most of the visitors must have gone. I stretched and moved restlessly. The bedroom door eased open a fraction. Mum came in and drew the curtains closer together. I smiled at her drowsily and she kissed my forehead.

Before long I fell into a deep sleep, and knew nothing more until I woke up late the next morning. I had slept for over fifteen hours. 'Did I really sleep properly, Mum?' I demanded. She smiled reassuringly. 'Like a log, Rita. I popped in every now and then all through the evening, and you were fast asleep.'

Many difficulties were sorted out by that long sleep. I hadn't realised just how tired I had been. For over a week I had been surviving on nervous energy, robbing my body of rest and making up for it by sheer excitement. The practical difficulty of adjusting to sleeping in a bed again had made matters worse. I realised now that my tiredness was part of the cause of my outburst at Ian Smith, and that it lay behind my inability to do anything other than drift with events and shut the future out of my mind.

But now my body was rested, and so was my mind. I began to pick up the threads of normal life again. I read through each of the letters in the red sack again, and that gave me something definite to do in my first few days at home. Sometimes I was moved to tears, often to prayer, as I read the messages of welcome and affection.

Among the letters was one from a lady called Sylvia Mary Alison. She was the wife of a Member of Parliament. She wrote to welcome me home, saying that she had been told about me in America by Chuck Colson. She told me a little about the Prison Christian Fellowship in England, which was a group linked with the American organisation. It had begun in 1979, and now had quite a large membership.

I was interested to read about the Fellowship, and excited to know that the Lord was moving people in England as he had in America. But I didn't answer her letter then; I didn't answer any of the letters. None seemed to expect an answer and I was incapable of sitting down in one place for ten minutes, let alone the several days it would have taken to reply to each one individually. My decision not to reply to the letters in no way meant that I didn't care or appreciate the fact that so many had written. I just wasn't capable of dealing with the situation beyond thanking the Lord for every person who had taken the time to write to me, which I did.

I began to set aside time to pray again, and to read my Bible. And over the next days and weeks, I began to adjust to being an unemployed Blackburn girl, after three years of being a notorious foreign prisoner in a Thai jail.

The national Press lost interest in my story quite quickly, and because Mum had agreed that the *Daily Mail* should have exclusive rights to the story, I didn't have to talk to other daily newspapers. Soon other stories dominated the front pages, for which I was profoundly glad.

Local interest continued for much longer. Some of it was embarrassing, some hurtful, but mostly it was warm and affectionate. I had a rough time being interviewed on Radio

Blackburn shortly after I came home – the interviewer was quite hostile. But I'd expected that, and had decided to do the interview anyway because it was a way of being able to thank publicly all the people who had worked and campaigned locally for my release. The *Lancashire Evening Telegraph* had staged a magnificent campaign of articles, but also local people had helped in scores of ways – I heard of pensioners who had put hard-earned coins in collecting boxes, and other people who had worked unpaid to help publicise my case. I didn't even know who some of them were – they had never met me, nor I them. Even if I had had time to thank each of them personally I would not have been able to find them all to do so. Going on the radio was one way I could say a general 'Thank you'.

Apart from that one radio programme I turned down every request for interviews. Some time after I came home I opened the front door one day to a man who turned out to be a reporter from one of the national Sunday newspapers.

'We would be very interested in running your story,' he said. I shook my head.

'I'm sorry, I don't want to.'

The reporter grinned at me. 'It's money in your pocket,' he said, and named a figure that seemed astronomical.

'I'm not interested,' I said flatly, and wondered at myself for refusing such a handsome offer. But I found the idea offensive. Reading Ian's article had upset me, and that had been a careful, sensitive handling of what I had been through. The thought of selling a story about all the people still in prison, so that I could have lots of money to enjoy my freedom while they were still inside, made me feel slightly sick.

The reporter looked surprised. I wondered if he thought I was trying to raise his price. The idea hadn't entered my head. 'It's not the money,' I explained. He nodded sympathetically.

'Of course we'd put in about your religious experiences.'

Some chance, in that newspaper, I thought, remembering other big stories they had run in the past.

'I thought . . .'

But I said no, and eventually he left, presumably to go back to London.

'You are thoughtless,' Mum chided me. 'You didn't even invite him in for a cup of tea.'

One day Ann took me with her to Chorley, the town near Blackburn where she lived. It was market day, and we wandered round the stalls. Nobody recognised me, and I enjoyed going unnoticed. It had been raining, and we tried to avoid the drips of water trickling off the edges of the stalls onto our necks. We laughed a lot as we crammed with others into the sheltered patches in front of the counters.

I loved hearing people's voices, being surrounded by shoppers all speaking English – and not only English, but proper, Lancashire English at that! And there was so much to see, and such a choice. I suppose that now I would think it a very ordinary market much like any other, but that day it was like Aladdin's cave. There was so much on offer, and such a wide choice of goods. In a poor country, like many in the Far East, the markets that the residents use are functional and you buy what you can find. In Chorley I browsed for a long time comparing several rival fruit stalls. It was the same when we went on to a large supermarket where Ann did her weekly shopping. Freedom of choice, I was beginning to realise, is a great luxury.

'Here,' said Ann, 'would you carry these?'

She handed me two plastic carrier bags full of purchases. I took them, and she reorganised her own load of shopping and children. I was shocked to find that I could hardly carry the bags. I'd done no strenuous exercise for so long, and this was the first time I'd attempted to lift anything heavy. Up to then I'd been cosseted like royalty, with reporters carrying my bags and everything done for me. As I gritted my teeth and dragged the bags along the supermarket floor – making sure Ann didn't see, because she was heavily loaded herself – I realised that I was going to have to get back into shape.

Then Ann did turn round and see me struggling. We both began to giggle hysterically, and bystanders watched in perplexity trying to work out what was so funny about two perfectly normal carrier bags.

It was some time before I could feel entirely comfortable out of doors in Blackburn. I went shopping with June in Blackburn market one day, and there people did recognise me. As I went from stall to stall I saw people glancing at me and then openly staring. I glared back at them at first but then began to try to hide myself, turning my back on bystanders and looking distractedly at the goods on display.

'I don't like it, June. I want to go home.'

I prayed about the problem and talked it over with Mum and June. We realised that I would either have to become a paranoid recluse or just get on with my life. I decided on the latter. I learned to ignore the stares and even respond to some of the friendlier looks with an answering smile. *After all*, I reasoned, *when you think about the publicity there's been about me in Blackburn it would be stupid to expect anything else.*

In any case, there were so many new things to be tried and enjoyed. I insisted on always going upstairs on the bus, and on sitting in the front seat so that I could see everything that there was to be seen. Even at home when everybody else was out I revelled in the solitude, and paced from room to room marvelling at the peaceful quietness of Mum's house. After three years in a crowded prison I had forgotten what it was like to hear faint sounds in the distance, like a car starting up or children shouting some blocks away. In Lard Yao, there were few faint sounds.

It was like being a little girl again, when everything

seemed to be new and most things appeared highly amusing.

Going to church was a very special new experience. I'd been before, of course, on various occasions before I left home, but this was different. Now I was a Christian, I was a member of God's family, and going to church and joining in with the worship was bound to be a totally new experience. I'd occasionally allowed myself to think about it in prison, on the rare occasions when I'd permitted myself to dream of the life I'd live when I was released.

Finding a church had seemed an impossible task. When I was released I had said my last farewells in Bangkok to Jack and Gladys Martin, the missionaries who had visited Lard Yao regularly for Bible classes and had watched over my first faltering steps as a Christian. 'I don't know any Christians there,' I told them. 'I don't know which church to go to or anything like that.'

'You'll be all right,' Jack had replied. 'The Lord has his hand on your life, we know that. He is going to protect you and use you.'

Jack's words were fulfilled sooner than either of us realised. During the first week of my return home, I had a telephone call.

'Hello,' said a pleasant voice. 'I'm Bob Allinson. I and my wife Sheila live in Blackburn. We read you were back, in the *Evening Telegraph*. Welcome home.'

I had had a number of calls like that from well-wishers. 'Thanks for ringing,' I said. 'I appreciate it very much. It's great being back.' I waited to hear if Mr. Allinson had anything else to say. He had.

'I don't want to intrude,' he said, 'and I know it'll be quite strange for you for a while getting things back to normal again. But the reason I rang is to say that if you and your mother would like to come to church with Sheila and me on Sunday, we'd love to see you. And would you be free to have lunch with us afterwards?'

'That's really kind of you,' I said. I hesitated. 'I'm afraid we haven't got a car – I don't know whether we could get to you.'

'No problem,' he replied easily. 'We can pick you up.'

So on Sunday all four of us went to the Methodist church near his home. When we went in I was quite apprehensive. It felt as though everybody was staring at me – I hadn't spent much time out of doors yet, and still felt very vulnerable. Probably they weren't looking at me, but I was sure they were and I was afraid that afterwards, they would want to buttonhole me and ask me all about Bangkok. *I just want to be me*, I thought. *I don't want to be somebody 'different'.*

Bob and Sheila were ideal hosts. They didn't announce who I was or introduce me to people with a great commotion. We just went in and sat down quietly.

I gazed around with a mounting sense of joy. After two years of being a Christian almost on my own in prison, I was meeting with a group of others in church for the first time. The most lovely part of it all was the singing. I'd never been able to sing heartily with a large congregation in Lard Yao because there wasn't one. More than that, I was singing with understanding. In school assembly and in Sunday School as a child, I'd enjoyed singing hymns and had raised my voice with great enthusiasm. But I hadn't had much of an idea at all of what the words meant. Now every word had meaning. I was so excited by some of the words that I jumped up and down as I sang.

I didn't take in much of the sermon. It was a long time since I'd listened to somebody talking at length about Christianity and been obliged to sit still and keep my questions and comments to myself! So I contented myself with sitting quietly and thinking about God and talking to him, silently, thanking him for allowing me to be in church.

292

Afterwards we stood for a while in the church grounds, enjoying the winter sunshine. One or two people recognised me because they'd seen my face in the papers, and they came up to say hello, but there wasn't any sense of pressure. I was pleased that most people didn't recognise me. I suppose it was an unrealistic hope, but I wanted to put all the notoriety of the past behind me, and just be a normal person again. That ideal saw me through the first few months of my return to England, and in the Methodist church that first Sunday I was able to imagine that I was almost unknown.

Afterwards we had lunch with Bob and Sheila at their home. We talked about the service.

'It was wonderful,' I said thoughtfully. 'But I really think we ought to look for a church nearer home. Not having a car makes such a difference. It would be nice to go to a local church anyway.'

'That's fair enough,' said Bob. 'What d'you think, Sheila? St. Andrews is a good evangelical church. It might be the answer.'

Sheila nodded. 'Yes, I think you'd like it,' she smiled. Mum looked up.

'Is that the one just down the road from us? I used to know the Vicar there. Not the one that's there now, the one before him. He was a really nice man.'

We decided that next Sunday we would go to St. Andrews.

Next week Mum had a telephone call while I was out shopping.

'Mrs. Livesey rang,' she told me.

I was thrilled. I'd been longing to see her again, and had planned to visit her as soon as I could. She was living in Blackpool now.

'*Martha*! How is she? What did she say? Did she give you a message for me?'

'Slow down, love! She's coming to see you.'

'Wow! That's amazing! When?'

'She's visiting her sister here in Blackburn, and she'll call and see us.'

A few days later I was upstairs when the doorbell rang. I heard Mum opening the door and then Martha's voice greeting her. I ran downstairs. We hugged each other, and then I dragged her into the living room and we just talked and talked. It was like seeing an old friend again, though I'd seen her only one brief time in Bangkok and then had stormed out of the room in a tantrum. We had a wonderful afternoon.

I was especially glad that Martha had made contact with Mum while I was in prison. Lucille had written to her as well, and I was grateful for every chance she had to meet Christians. I didn't want Mum to think that my own experiences were simply a reaction to the things that had happened to me in prison. After I became a Christian I prayed for her all the time. Because I was so happy and had found in the Lord Jesus everything for which my heart had been longing for so many years, I took it for granted that anybody who had it all explained to them simply would also grasp the offer of salvation with both hands.

So I sent Mum the booklet which had pointed me to God – Robert Laidlaw's *The Reason Why*[1] – and told her what had happened. She wrote back, obviously very happy at the change in me, but distressed at not being able to share my new-found faith.

'I do pray,' she wrote back to me. 'And what I pray is that God will bring you home.' It was the one thing she most prayed for, and in her letters I sensed with some sadness

---

1 Many readers of *Freed for Life* have asked me how they can obtain this booklet. It is now published by Send the Light, and can be ordered through any Christian bookshop or direct from STL Books, PO Box 300, Kingstown Broadway, Carlisle CA3 OQS.

that she was making a sort of condition – that unless God brought about my release, she would not think anything of him.

Now that I had been released, Mum was happy to share with me in everything. The next Sunday we went together to St. Andrew's Church, which was our local church. Once again, I enjoyed it enormously. The congregation was quite a big one, the singing was hearty, people were as friendly as could be; and though I didn't take in much of the sermon, I could certainly see that this church took the Bible seriously and talked about Jesus as a real person. Mum enjoyed it too, because it was a local church near her home, and she saw several people she knew there; it wasn't as if it was something new and intimidating, one of the intrusive consequences of the publicity I had attracted, but part of everyday Blackburn life. Brian Robinson, the vicar, made us welcome, and because the congregation was largely made up of our neighbours I didn't feel so conspicuous as I had the Sunday before.

So the problem I had worried about in Bangkok – how I was going to fit into a church in England and find people who really knew Jesus – was dealt with gently and painlessly by the Lord, and I was very grateful.

Going to church gave me a reference point. There I found my bearings. To hear other Christians talking about Jesus, and to sing hymns of praise and worship God in the serenity and beauty of worship, was a new experience; but it only enriched what I already knew. Perhaps that was why the Lord gave me a welcoming church so soon, to give me a secure foothold in the large world outside my family and my home.

I certainly needed it. Coming to terms with living in a town again was going to take time, and there was so much that I had either forgotten or was new since I had left home. I was especially disconcerted by television. Had it been so violent when I was last in England? The killings and shootings in the plays and films seemed so lifelike, and the evening news was full of pictures of heartbreaking deprivation and harrowing grief.

In all probability I had seen many similar things before I left home. But it all seemed different now; either because I hadn't got used to TV again, or because I had changed.

One evening I was sitting in Ann's house, watching a television thriller with her family. At one point I winced and looked away. Little Jonathan turned to me and said reassuringly, 'Don't worry, Auntie Rita. It's not real. It's only pretend, it's on the TV.'

I looked back at the screen. The scene was a prison cell. A prisoner was banging his head against a stone wall, monotonously, rhythmically striking his skull against the unyielding barrier.

'It's just pretend, you see?' Jonathan repeated.

In the cell, the prisoner continued his slow head-banging. His face was expressionless, his eyes showed no pain. The prison cell bore little resemblance to the wooden huts of Lard Yao, but the look on his face was familiar and authentic. I had seen similar mute misery on the faces of hundreds of people in prison, a language of despair that demanded no fluency in the Thai language in order to be read.

It's not pretend, it isn't at all, I whispered to myself. *I've seen it. And I thought I'd left it behind.*

5 Adjusting

The euphoria was beginning to fade.

Freed for Life, chapter 24

'You know, Rita,' remarked June one evening, after I'd been home for a few weeks, 'do you realise – you've never talked about what it was like, in prison?'

'You're right,' I admitted. 'It's awful; the fact is, I can't remember one thing about the place.'

It worried and distressed me. It was true; I found it almost impossible to remember much about Lard Yao. I'd been imprisoned in the place only weeks before. In my darkest moments there, I'd surveyed the prison bitterly and thought, *this place will never leave me.* I believed – we all believed – that the sights, the sounds, the smells of that place would be engraved on our memories for ever. We used to talk about it in the dormitories, the fear that our lives would always be scarred by the nightmare memories of what we had seen and experienced in prison, and the simple, horrifying fact that we had had our freedom taken away.

How could I ever forget it? In Lard Yao, I had laughed with murderers, talked to arsonists, and known scores of women who were drug addicts, drug dealers or convicted for crimes of violence.

And yet only a few days after returning home it had all gone. It was as if the prison, every detail of which I knew so well I could have found my way round it blindfolded, had been washed from my mind. All that was left was a hazy memory of shapes and voices, shadows hard to identify or put a name to.

I was bewildered and shamed by this experience. There were good friends of mine still in Bangkok, still in prison. Who was I to forget them? It was like a betrayal. And yet I had forgotten them, for though I remembered their names I could hardly put a face to any of them.

I talked to Mum about it.

'It's awful, Mum. It's gone, it's rubbed out. I just can't remember. Oh Mum, it's horrible – to have forgotten all that so quickly!'

Though I had forgotten many of the precise details, prison still cast a long shadow over my life and that of my family. Sleep was the least of my problems; I had a few troublesome nightmares, but they were not many. Though it was months before I could feel comfortable in a chair, I slept in a bed from the first night I came back to England. After the first few nights of scant slumber and much tossing and turning, I was quite quickly back into a reasonable sleep pattern. Neither did I continue to wear Eastern clothes, but adapted back to English ones with no problems – in fact it was hardly possible to do otherwise in the depths of the English winter.

Meals were a different matter. I tried to get used to the tastes of European food once again, but it was really hard. Mum cooked all sorts of treats for me, but I was plagued by stomach upsets. My system just wasn't used to that kind of food any more.

'I've made your favourite – potato pie,' she would say, and serve me with a normal-sized helping.

'Oh, lovely!' I would reply, and try my hardest to do it

justice. Mum and June would watch me apprehensively, and sure enough, after a few mouthfuls my stomach would begin to protest and I would push the plate away.

'I'm sorry, Mum, I just can't manage any more.'

For several weeks I couldn't finish a plateful of cooked food, and I could hardly touch fried food like bacon and eggs. Mum was at her wit's end. 'What *can* you manage, then?' she demanded.

'Could you make me some pea soup? Or some spare ribs?'

Mum tried hard to devise tasty and nourishing meals for me that wouldn't upset my digestive organs. Sometimes she was successful, but often I ended up spending half the day locked in the bathroom feeling like death. In the end we devised a routine that seemed to work. During the day I ate lots of fresh salad, and then in the evening I had a very tiny helping of whatever the others were eating. Mum always took the trouble to make something special, usually a dish that we'd enjoyed when I was small.

I enjoyed helping Mum with the cooking, even though I couldn't digest much of what resulted. All the ordinary, everyday household jobs were endlessly fascinating – it was all so new and different after prison. Going for walks on the moors was lovely, but I also enjoyed just walking down to the shops, seeing all the sights and sounds which I'd taken for granted before I left home and which now seemed very precious. Life was packed with all sorts of interesting things – watching TV, chatting with Mum and June and visitors, reading newspapers. Things which are now quite mundane to me were then totally absorbing, and life was very full.

'Aren't you bored?' I was asked. 'After all, you've just come back from a hair-raising experience, and you were a seasoned globe-trotter before that. Doesn't it drive you out of your mind, sitting here in your Mum's house with nothing to do?'

'Nothing to do?' I retorted. 'Why, there's shopping, talking to people, helping Mum–'

I think some people thought I was just making the best of a bad job and was staying home to be with my family out of consideration. But it wasn't true. When you've been in prison you learn not to be bored. I could be – and still can be – contented for hours, simply lying on my bed with my own thoughts. In prison you come to value time differently to how you did outside. Forced to be indoors early in the evening, one of the skills I developed in Lard Yao was to ignore everything going on around me and be at peace. So although it was unrealistic to expect Mum and June to spend every minute of every day looking after me and making sure I was being entertained, I never felt bored at all.

As I began to immerse myself in everyday life again, I began to be able to remember the details of prison life once more. At first it was like remembering a particularly vivid bad dream, when you remember less the characters in the dream than the feelings and fears you had while it was going on. Part of it, I think, was an unconscious unwillingness to face the fact that I was at home, wearing nice clothes, eating what I wanted to, free to do as I liked, while they were still locked away. It was some time before I could summon up their faces, recall their voices, allow them to be real people in my memory again.

I finally found myself able to remember Lard Yao, paradoxically, when walking the windy hills behind Mum's house. Striding up the slope, with Blackburn spread out like a well-trodden carpet below, I found myself remembering everything. It was as if someone had unlocked the doors of my memory. Suddenly I could recall faces and voices with sharp clarity: Hannah, Maria, Jenny, Chris, Linda, Mary and all the others. As the wind whipped my face, a wonderful warm feeling took hold of me as I thought of them, probably at that very moment stabbing bright scraps of cloth in the prison sewing factory or sitting on the grass chatting in the last half hour before the guards arrived for the evening lock-up. 'Lord, it will be like this for them one day,' I cried out. Then I turned back home and wrote long letters to them.

'Look,' I wrote, 'all the things we thought about that place, they go, you know? You never think you'll be free of it, ever again. But when you go out it leaves you. You'll be free too, you're coming out, so hold on, hold on . . .'

I don't know if it was helpful or not, but I had to say it because it was so real to me.

Perhaps if somebody had written me a letter like that in prison I'd have found it very hard to respond. The one thing you don't do in prison is dream about when you'll be released. Prison is such a vivid reality, dominating the full twenty-four hours of every day. You can't get out until you are out, not even in your mind. But nevertheless, I wanted to write these things to them, and over the months I wrote them to everyone I had known in prison.

'Wow, here's a letter from Bangkok!'

It was a morning in mid-February. I picked up the fat airmail envelope with its colourful stamps and opened it, to find a letter and two newspaper clippings.

It was from Lucille, a warm, joyous letter. I had been deeply sad at having to leave her so soon after greeting her in the British Embassy in Bangkok when I was released. For over two years she had visited me in prison. When she first began to visit me with Margaret Cole, another Christian to whom I had been grieved to say goodbye, I was sullen and bitterly resentful, as I was to everyone who spoke to me. Often Lucille had queued for two hours to see me in Lard Yao only to find that I refused to talk or that I was being forbidden visiting privileges because of some real or imagined misdoings. When I met her at the Embassy it was

301

the first time I had spoken to her without an iron grille between us – the first time I had been able to hug her. It had been an all-too-brief meeting, because I was being expelled from Thailand and had to leave the country almost immediately after leaving prison.

So a letter from Lucille brought back many memories. The most wonderful and joyful memory, however, was prompted by the newspaper clippings. They were from Bangkok newspapers, both dated February 5, and both told the same story.

> In a surprise decision which overruled verdicts of the Criminal and Appeals Court, the Dika (Supreme) Court yesterday set free a Spanish woman who was earlier sentenced to 40 years in jail on a drug trafficking charge . . . The Dika Court dropped charges, deciding that she was innocent and was not connected with the trafficking of 15,995 grammes of heroin found in her possession more than two years ago.

From the clippings the face of Maria looked at me; hair cropped short, clothes crumpled, her face tired and harrassed. But it was Maria, and she had been set free.

'Whatever's the matter?' Mum asked in concern. 'Bad news?'

'No, Mum, it's good news, it's really good news . . .' I pushed the clippings into her hand. I wasn't able to say any more. Mum was moved too. She had heard all about Maria from my letters, and had followed the ups and downs of her story. I'd told her since of my anguish at leaving Maria in her cell, where she had become withdrawn and dirty, almost certainly deeply scarred mentally and emotionally. She was my mother's age, and we had been very close.

When I had pressed my face to the bars of her dark and smelly cell, trying to persuade her to recognise me so I could say goodbye, it was the one desperately unhappy aspect of my release. That was why I had been so upset by seeing her featured in the centre pages of the *Daily Mail*. Now I was seeing her story again in another newspaper, but what a different story it had become!

I looked at the clippings again. They said that the decision had been made because the Court had not been prepared to accept evidence from the two main witnesses, as they directly contradicted each other. 'Surprise decision' – yes, it certainly was. In the dormitory in Lard Yao many of us had discussed her case for nights on end, and none of us had thought there was ever going to be any chance of the verdict being quashed. I fleetingly remembered the agony of deciding which of us would have to tell her what the Court's verdict had been – we gave Hannah the task in the end, and she had found it next to impossible to make her understand. Eventually Maria's consular visitors had explained to her in her own language. At that time the official reports on the radio said that she had been given a life sentence.

'They called my release "unique", Mum, and now they've called Maria's "a surprise decision". Oh, Mum, they don't understand – it's God, do you see? He made it possible. He answered all those prayers . . . .'

I was especially anxious to find out more about Maria's whereabouts. I didn't have the address of the Spanish officials out there, so I just addressed a letter to 'The Spanish Embassy, Bangkok', asking if they could give me any information.

I didn't hear anything from them, so I wondered whether I could contact her any other way. A friend in London who knew Spanish offered to write to her for me at the address she'd given me in Lard Yao, but I decided that wouldn't be right – I wasn't sure what mental state she would be in, and I didn't want to contact her through a stranger. I wanted to see her more than anything. We were beginning to talk about going away for a family holiday in Spain, and I thought I might possibly be able to get to Madrid and somehow find her.

But all my enquiries led nowhere, and eventually I had to give up and trust the Lord that wherever Maria was, she was happy and cared for.

Money was a recurring problem, though Mum never mentioned it. She had retired while I was in prison, and though not yet at retirement age she had her widow's pension, and was living on that. Though she didn't have a job her days were always full – she visited Auntie Mary every day, for example. Her sore shoulder stopped her from doing anything strenuous, but she was active and involved in quite a number of different things locally.

I was concerned that my arrival had put a strain on the household finances. At first it was fine, because when I came home I was given several gifts of money, about £200 altogether, and I was also given the residue of some money that had been collected by public appeal while I was in Bangkok; most of it had been used to promote my case and publicise my innocence, but there was a lump sum left when I came home.

I bought myself some things I needed, and some small presents for family and friends. The rest I put aside, and out of it gave Mum some money for my upkeep each week. But I knew it wouldn't last for ever. It wouldn't be fair then to live off Mum; she had no savings and her pension wasn't enough for two to live on. June was working, and was contributing her share of the household expenses. I felt I would be doing the same. I had to do something, and one evening we had a long talk about it.

'We'd better talk to the Employment Exchange,' said Mum. 'Find out what you're entitled to. There must be something.'

304

We went to the Department of Health and Social Security in Blackburn. I was interviewed by an efficiently friendly Social Security officer.

'What attempts have you made to find employment?'

'None,' I said apologetically. 'You see I've just . . .'

'You must understand,' said the officer sharply, 'that any benefit paid to you while unemployed is only paid on the basis that you are actively looking for work.'

However, when we explained the situation to her, she was immediately understanding. 'Naturally it will take some time for you to readjust. We have discretion in these cases,' she told us, 'to make a temporary hardship grant. It means that you will receive a single lump sum payment to cover your present needs.' She flipped through a file of notes. 'Now, presumably you will be in a position to start looking for work in due course.'

I nodded.

'I'm afraid that you are not eligible for Unemployment Benefit, as you were last working outside this country. But you are eligible for Supplementary Benefit.'

She put a form in front of me. 'Will you fill that in, please. You'll be notified in due course.'

Afterwards I wondered again what I ought to do about looking for a job. I considered resuming my nursing training, but wasn't sure how to go about it. Also I had a dominent idea in my mind that somehow, somewhere, I would be working with prisoners. *After what I've been through, there has to be some way I can help people who are like I was*, I reflected. Perhaps the Probation Service? I didn't want to be a 'do-gooder', but involved in some practical way. Various possibilities sounded interesting, but I was determined to think hard about them. I wasn't going to rush headlong into things. That was how I'd got into trouble last time.

When the notification came through from the

Department of Social Security I found that I had been awarded Supplementary Benefit of £17 a week. Out of it I was able to give Mum money for my keep, though she was always reluctant to accept it.

It was strange to have a regular income again. I'd come back to an England which had a grave unemployment problem, and I knew that when I began to look for work I would find it difficult. A working knowledge of the Thai language and the ability to dance and chat with visitors to night clubs were not very impressive qualifications when job-hunting in Lancashire! But now at least I had a small income.

In Lard Yao I had sometimes wondered what it would be like to have a salary again, and what my attitude should be to money as a Christian. When I had been home a few weeks, Brian, the vicar at St. Andrew's, preached a sermon about how Christians should handle their money. He spoke about giving. It was a very direct sermon.

'When you give away a few pennies that you didn't need anyway, it's not *my* problem,' he said. 'But what does God think about it? Is that the sort of giving that he talks about in the Bible?'

Sitting with my Mum I remembered the Bible passages I'd read, about how we ought to give freely to God because he has given so freely to us. All that we have comes from him. All that we have belongs to him. It's a privilege, said Brian, to be able to give out of what God has given us.

That's what I must do, I decided, as the sermon came to an end. From that Sunday on, I put part of my weekly income into the collection at St. Andrew's.

As I grew more in the Christian life and read more books and met more Christians I found out about 'tithing', and it made a lot of sense to me. But I'd already acquired the habit of giving one tenth of my income to God. It wasn't an intellectual decision reached after careful consideration of the relevant Bible texts. It was a spontaneous response to what God had done for me in those weeks after coming home. I don't think I was ever so blessed in my life as when I first came back to England. I wanted to share it. In the middle of such happiness and joy, giving seemed the most natural thing in the world. And I can certainly testify to the fact that I've never been poor, I've never starved, and God has given me far more than I have ever given back to him. I would recommend any Christian to consider what the Bible says about tithing. It could open up a whole new dimension of the Christian life!

6 Shadows

*To some it may have seemed odd that I could
stand up before total strangers and proclaim
my faith, while with my own family I was
sometimes faltering, always reticent. I didn't
understand it myself. I like to think it was
the guidance of the Spirit urging boldness at
one point and caution at another. More
likely, as a new Christian I was just making
the bucketful of mistakes which all excited
freshmen believers do.*

Charles W. Colson, *Born Again* (1977),
chapter 14

Mum's sore shoulder wasn't getting any better, despite
several visits to the doctor. One day when it seemed to be
bothering her more than usual, I couldn't stand watching
her in pain any more.

'Mum, whatever's the matter with your arm? You look
really uncomfortable.'

She shook her head and wriggled her shoulder
experimentally. 'It's such a nuisance, Rita. It's been like it
for ages. I've had this ache for twelve months or more.' She
winced and cradled her shoulder in a brief twinge of pain.

Suddenly I was really concerned. 'Twelve months? You

should see a doctor, Mum. Get it sorted out. You shouldn't be in pain for that long, it isn't right.'

Mum shrugged. 'I did – months ago. They gave me some painkillers. They didn't work all that well, so they gave me some other ones. If they've tried me on one kind they've tried me on a dozen. They say now they think it's arthritis and want me to have physiotherapy.' She frowned fretfully. '*More* running around. I've got to get it X-rayed first. As if I'd got time for all that.'

Outside some kids were playing. Distant screams and laughter floated through the window. For a minute or two Mum sat nursing her shoulder, and I sat watching her. There wasn't much I could do. I reached out a hand to rub her back, but Mum got to her feet and smiled. 'I'll make us a cup of tea, Rita.'

'Let me, Mum,' I said. She shook her head.

'Exercise, that's what this arm of mine needs. That's what they told me.' She went through to the kitchen. 'Fat lot of good it does,' she added.

I began to pray about Mum's shoulder. I added it to a list of things I was praying about. After the first week or so of disorientation I had got back into a routine of regularly reading the Bible and talking to God, thinking through the next few days with him and asking him for his help, and bringing various matters to him that I wanted to specially talk to him about.

I found it helpful to read my Bible at the same time each day, just as I'd done in prison. Sometimes it wasn't possible to do so, and I don't believe at all that it's catastrophic if a Christian can't always read a certain amount of the Bible at a set time each day (though it can be very helpful, especially when you're just starting out in the Christian life). We're told to feed on God's Word and let it be a light to us, but deciding how we're going to make it part of our lives is an individual choice.

For myself, I always read the Bible in bed in the morning, before I got up. Mum was a much earlier riser than I was and she'd usually been up and about for a while. She used to bring me a cup of tea in bed. Gwen Abbott, who had regularly sent me a series of Bible notes called *Every Day with Jesus* when I was in Lard Yao, continued to send them to me in Blackburn after I got home, and I found it very helpful to have a guide to what I was reading to make me think, and explain the difficult bits or the parts that had to do with life in first-century Palestine.

In prison, I'd been sent a Christian book and discovered to my delight that Mum had also been sent the same book. In our letters, we discovered that we'd both been reading it – it was a devotional booklet, arranged in passages for each day – and we began to quote it to each other, often just mentioning the date. It was a little like Maria and myself reading our respective Bibles, pointing out the chapter and verse numbers to each other so we could look them up and read them. 'Remember Tuesday's words?' Mum might write to me, and I'd know exactly what she meant. It had been lovely to think of us both getting excited about the same things and underlining the same words, but it was even better now I was home and we could sit together in the same room with the book.

In fact, when I first got home, I had no books. I'd had a copy of *Daily Light* in Bangkok which Lucille had given me, but that and my Bible had been left by accident in an Embassy car and I only got them back after several months had passed. So I borrowed Mum's Bible and her copy of the other book. I was thrilled to see that she had been reading it and marking the bits she'd enjoyed.

I found praying strange at first. For so long I'd prayed for one thing in particular, and that was my release. Now it had happened. It wasn't exactly an anti-climax, but I found it hard to adjust to laying my daily life before the Lord without that single, over-riding plea to crown all my other thanks and requests. I found it easy to read a bit of the Bible and enjoy the good things I found there, and then leap out of bed and get dressed and rush off to do exciting things. Then later on in the day I would think, *Oh, I didn't have my prayer-time this morning, I didn't talk to God.* Then I'd excuse myself by saying how busy I was and how exciting everything was that day. But often I would find myself thinking, *But he's never too busy to speak to you . . .* So that evening I'd try to make time to talk to him longer.

The Lord was really gentle with me in those first weeks. I've heard many Christians say that if they don't have a proper prayer-time first thing in the day then nothing goes right, and they know that something's badly wrong. But God was very good to me. He let me have my bubbly time and settle down at my own pace, and he gently reminded me when I had neglected to talk to him, and when I prayed to him it was as if I'd never wandered away.

The transition from prison to home was a difficult one spiritually, because in so many ways I had had extraordinary experiences as a Christian, and yet I was ignorant of so much. I had lived a solitary, lonely life in Lard Yao, with only a few Christians to help me. Now I had to take my part in the family of God's people, as part of a local church congregation. The prospect was thrilling but a little frightening as well.

Looking back on my prison experiences I sometimes thought of them as almost a honeymoon time, when my relationship with God was uniquely intimate and revolved around very special demonstrations of his goodness to me. Each new book of the Bible I read was like a new jewel I'd discovered, and every aspect of the Christian faith gleamed as if it was brand-new and I the first who had ever encountered it. I'm sure God would like us to be like that all the time, and I'm sure he forgives us when we're not. In my case, I simply found it all too easy to stop depending on him. That was how I'd got into tantrums at the Stirk House Hotel, but at least there I had some sort of excuse because I was exhausted and over-excited. Now, back in a more everyday routine, I was alarmed to find myself showing signs of spiritual laziness. When I'd prayed to God for my daily bread in prison, it had been a prayer of real need. Money from the Social Security was just as much a gift of God, but I found it hard to see it in quite the same way.

Fortunately I didn't have to sort out all these problems on my own. I had the church to help me, and as the weeks went by I came to value that church more and more as I realised how much I'd missed in Lard Yao.

To begin with we just went on Sundays, usually the morning service and sometimes the evening one as well. At first I felt that that was enough. It was all so new and exciting, and I wanted to take things slowly. But St. Andrew's was a welcoming church, which didn't let bystanders remain on the fringe of things for very long, and we were soon drawn into the life of the church.

In a strange way I resented becoming so involved. I felt that I wanted to set my own pace, to feel my way back into things; and I didn't want others pulling me along faster than I cared for. I wanted to be with my family, not pushed into other situations. I went to church to worship God, I told myself, not to get tangled up in telling everybody where I'd been and what had happened to me.

But then, as I began to go to the Thursday night Bible studies, I realised I'd been silly. On Sunday everybody had been very friendly and we'd really enjoyed being there, but it had been a formal service with people disappearing after church to make sure their lunch wasn't burning in the oven. Thursday nights were quite different, a time of relaxed fellowship where we began to get to know people properly and study the Bible together as fellow-Christians. In Lard Yao I'd led Bible studies, but there I'd been the 'mature

312

Christian', helping other people to understand. Now I was part of a small group, with some who were much older in the faith than I was and some who were much younger. We learned together, and talked about what we were learning, and for the first time I began to understand what 'Christian fellowship' really meant.

Mum often came to the Thursday evening meetings with me, and she enjoyed it just as much as I did. I didn't say very much, and I appreciated the fact that the group didn't push me in any way. They knew my situation, and as time went by I frequently asked the group to pray for me as different things were happening and various decisions had to be made. But they never pushed me to give talks at the church or give my testimony.

The group was sometimes led by the vicar and sometimes by the curate, Herrick Daniels, a West Indian. Later it met in Herrick's house, and we got to know each other very well. He became a very special person in my life, and he helped me in scores of ways. I came to value his advice very much indeed. Mum liked him, too, and he was a great help to her.

I'd always known, since I became a Christian, that studying the Bible was important. But it took on a new meaning in that group, as we shared our experiences and read the Bible together.

The Bible study at St. Andrew's wasn't the only regular commitment I had to a Christian group. My other involvement came about as the result of a surprise visit from somebody I didn't know.

As my memories of people I'd known in prison came flooding back, so did my desire, first experienced in Lard Yao, to find a way to do something with my freedom which would help prisoners not just in Bangkok but world-wide. I began to pray that God would show me how this might happen. In prison I'd made a commitment to help other people in prisons once I myself was free. The newspapers had picked it up. I'd shared the hope with people in my family and in church. But how could I actually *do* it?

Several weeks after I came home I was sitting on my own one evening when there was a knock on the door.

'Hello, I'm Mary Thomas.'

I asked my visitor in, wondering who she was.

'I came to ask you whether you would be interested in coming to a prayer meeting. It's to pray for people in prison.'

I was immediately interested, and readily agreed to go. 'Yes, I'd love to come!'

The prayer meeting was at Preston, which is near Blackburn. It was held in a Baptist church where twenty or so people from different backgrounds had gathered to pray for different aspects of the prison work. Mary introduced me to the group with the minimum of fuss, and we began to pray. Individual prisoners were prayed for by name, and obviously the group had prayed for them before and knew a good deal about each of them. *It was groups like this that prayed for me when I was in Lard Yao,* I realised.

I began to pray aloud with them, talking about people I knew in Bangkok, for prisoners and for the Christians involved in visiting there, like Jack and Gladys Martin. It was a very poignant experience. I'd prayed at St. Andrews for my friends in prison; but there I was, in the middle of this group which had been praying for *me* while I was in Bangkok.

Afterwards we had coffee and biscuits, and I browsed among some leaflets at the back of the room and found some Prison Christian Fellowship literature. It was then that I realised that this was one of the regional prayer groups of the Fellowship. I was excited, and asked lots of questions, and took away with me a form to fill in and send to the London office for further details. I had an immediate reply, saying that the Fellowship had been wanting to make contact with me, having been in touch with the American

314

Fellowship – I remembered Sylvia Mary Alison's letter which I'd never answered. I became a regular member of the monthly prayer group and it was a way of keeping my commitment to prisoners while I waited for the Lord to show me the next step. I'd discovered how good it was to join in with the life of the church, and how important it was to be part of a fellowship of Christian believers, to share with them and learn from them. But there was another aspect of living as a Christian. Just as I couldn't expect to hide in my family and avoid committing myself to sharing in the life of the church, so I couldn't expect to take refuge in numbers and just be a Christian at church. If Christianity was truly a total change in my life, then that change must affect my life at home with my family.

From my first arrival home I had found it easy to talk about my new faith. I've always been an outgoing sort of person anyway, and I was so full of gratitude and excitement that it all flowed readily as I talked with my family.

I've never felt that I should preach to my relatives. We've not been the sort of family that talks very deeply about our religious beliefs anyway. But becoming a Christian was part of what had happened while I was away, so I was able to talk about it a great deal as I chatted about my experiences abroad generally. I talked a lot about what it meant to me to have given my life to Jesus, just as I'd written a lot about it in my letters from prison. But I didn't feel it right to argue with other people, whoever they were, and demand that they should become Christians there and then. I tried to share Jesus with them naturally and I prayed for them continually.

When I was a little girl, before my tenth birthday, I often went with Ann to stay with my Auntie Margaret and her husband (June was then too small to be away from home overnight). I remember that every night Auntie Margaret prayed with us, and that was something we never did at home. As I grew up she was always within reach, never saying much about Christianity; a gentle, caring aunt whom we all loved – as indeed all our aunts were loved. But I had a special relationship with her, because she was my Godmother, and I always thought of her as different.

Auntie Margaret listened quietly as I talked about what had happened to me in prison, occasionally asking the sort of questions that mean that the person asking them really understands what you're talking about. One day, after I'd been home for a while, she and I were talking together when she told me that many years ago she too had become a Christian.

'But it's always been for me a very private matter,' she said. 'I've never talked much about what it means to me.' She smiled. 'I'm really thrilled for you, Rita. I'm going to talk a bit more about what I believe from now on.'

I was so happy for her; and I had another wonderful surprise to come.

My Auntie Mary was another much-loved aunt. When I was in prison and Ann and June flew out to visit me, they brought bad news about her. She was seriously ill, so ill that John (Ann's husband) had advised them to tell me that she had already died; she wasn't expected to live for more than a few days, and it would have been better for me to hear it from them than by a letter after they had gone. In the end they told me the facts, that she was dreadfully ill and wasn't expected to recover. I had been heartbroken, not just because she was my Auntie but because I desperately wanted to talk to her about Jesus before she died.

So I prayed unceasingly for her and I know that many other people did; and not long after I heard that she had made a miraculous recovery. When I came home, it was wonderful to see her again, and she was a frequent visitor at home in Blackburn just as she had always been. One day she too told me that she had made a commitment to God many years ago. For her it was a joyful surprise to find her wayward, worldly niece coming home a Christian. For my part, it was lovely to come home to find two Christian aunts, though it was several months before they were able to share their faith with me fully.

There is no doubt that God blessed me by giving me the family he did. I know of many Christians living in homes where Christianity is ridiculed and where they suffer appalling hostility. Some who have become Christians in prison return to bitter criticism and contempt. I came home from Lard Yao to find nothing but love and understanding, and I was overwhelmed.

I hope that my family saw a dramatic change in my life, but I had been away from home for quite a long time, even before my arrest; so I don't know whether they ascribed any changes in lifestyle to that or to the fact that I was now a Christian. I went to church regularly, of course, and there was always a Bible lying around the house, but in other ways our family life wasn't altered.

I think that I feared that all the publicity, which had made a good deal of reference to my conversion, might make people think that I was going to come home as a Bible-thumping ranter, intent on bludgeoning everyone within reach into becoming Christians. I so much wanted my family and friends to share my new faith that I deliberately kept a low profile, saying what I could when I could, and praying very much that the Lord would not let me fail when opportunities came (as they often did) to explain, simply and clearly, exactly what it was that God had done in my life.

That was why I had reacted against the journalist who had promised to write about my 'religious experience'. I didn't want to be seen as a fanatic, somebody whose faith shone as the pinnacle and crown of her life – a 'religious' person. I desperately wanted my Christian beliefs to be seen as part and parcel of my whole life, not a separate commodity to be cultivated on its own and thrust before people willy-nilly. I believed in evangelism, I still believe in it; sharing my faith is vitally important to me. But I walked with care for the first few months of my return, and the Lord blessed me with the knowledge that others really understood what he had done for me.

Though we didn't pray at mealtimes as a family, we did pray together. The first time we did so was when I was sitting with Mum and Auntie Mary and Auntie Margaret discussing a family problem. It was something we were all concerned about and we didn't know what to do for the best. We'd been going over various alternatives and none had seemed helpful.

We sat staring at the teapot for a while, thinking. Then I plucked up my courage.

'Why don't we pray about it? I'll pray for all of us, if you like.' So I prayed, and it wasn't so terrifying as I'd thought.

After that first time it became much easier, and we prayed together quite often. It was never a forced or formal act, but flowed naturally from the situation we were in at the time.

I prayed with Mum, too, on my own; but that was less relaxed.

'I don't know, Rita, I haven't got faith like you.'

'What do you mean, Mum?'

'Uh – well, I'm not good enough to be a Christian.'

'Oh, Mum, that's not what it's about at all. Being a Christian hasn't got anything to do with whether you're good enough to be one. It's because of what Jesus has done for us. He did all that's needed.'

Such conversations were quite frequent in the first weeks of my return and they were frustrating in the extreme. I used to agonise for hours afterwards. How could she miss the point like that.?

'I did ask Jesus into my life once, Rita; I really did. But it doesn't seem real to me, somehow. I don't feel it. I'm not good enough, that's what it is . . .'

For a few weeks I tried to argue her out of it, and took every chance of explaining why she was wrong and what the Bible said, but I began to realise that I was only building up resentment and making Mum feel guilty. So I stopped that, and I just handed over the whole problem to the Lord. I went to church with her and talked with her about what we'd heard when I could. I tried very hard to stand back and let the Holy Spirit do what he wished in Mum's life. It was difficult to let go. I wouldn't have let go at all, had I not known that the Lord Jesus knew all about the situation.

7 Living Forwards

*I'm praying for guidance and he's giving it
to me. He's not going to let me down
now – he's guided me this far.*

Jubilee, March 1980

The slightly built man in the immaculate suit beamed at
Mum. Mum repeated what she'd just said. He turned to
Ann, his face wrinkling with amusement.

'Please, what is Momma saying?'

Mum giggled, Ann attempted to translate, but Mr. Goehr
smiled at Mum and said genially, 'No, I understand. But
Momma must talk a little slower. Then it will be fine.'

She slowed down for him, and measured her words
carefully, but after a few sentences she was back in full flow
and Mr. Goehr had to bring Ann in as translator. When a
Blackburn resident gets into his or her vocal stride it can be
a problem for those from other parts of the country to keep
up; and Mr. Goehr, whose English was impeccable and
precise, was no exception.

We were having a wonderful time. Mr. Goehr was a
distinguished consultant on international law who had done
a tremendous amount of work on my behalf while I was in
prison. He would take no payment for this, and our family

320

were deeply grateful to him. A few days after I arrived home a crate of champagne had arrived at Mum's house with a message of congratulations from him.

Mr. Goehr's card had a message promising that he would be in touch with us in due course, but it was an unexpected surprise when his invitation arrived six weeks later: he invited us to have lunch with him in London.

Mum, Ann and her baby Emma, and I went down to London on the train and met Mr. Goehr at his office. It was an emotional meeting for Mum and Ann, because he'd been very supportive and had encouraged them while all the anxiety and waiting was going on. I thought he looked quite like I remembered my father; a dapper, pleasant-looking man with greying hair, very distinguished and with a lovely kind expression in his eyes. After the greetings he and his assistant took us to a very grand restaurant, and we lunched on oysters, smoked salmon and other delicacies.

Before we said goodbye he took me on one side and talked to me on my own, and I had an opportunity to tell him how much we appreciated what he'd done. But truth to tell, I never will know all he did, just as I will never know more than a fraction of the efforts that many people made in securing my release. I do know that he made a special effort to protect Mum from a lot of the legal paperwork and similar worries, and so I have a special gratitude for him. There wasn't time to say much to him then, but I was so glad to have met him after knowing so much about him.

We walked down Piccadilly and on to the Foreign Office. The London theatres were closed, because it was lunchtime, and the neon signs were lifeless skeletons in the spring sunshine. Here and there were the entrances to night clubs, with gaudy signs and garishly coloured photographs pinned on boards outside. Although the red London buses and the English shopfronts made the scene familiar and known, I couldn't help remembering the Hong Kong clubs, the faded plush entrance of the Kokasai where I'd been a hostess and all my problems had started. It seemed a remote, distant world.

Into my mind came the memory of a disco I'd been to with June a few weeks earlier in Blackburn, and the terrible sadness I'd felt as I watched the dancers strutting up and down, men predatory for women, women predatory for men, and all the other things I'd seen every night in Hong Kong. In that northern disco I had realised, probably for the first time, what it means when the Bible talks about people being lost without God. *People are looking, looking for what they don't find, and they never will find it. I know, because I looked for it all over the world.*

I broke out of my reverie as we walked into Whitehall and the massive edifice of the Foreign Office. Mr. Southworth, who'd been so kind to me in Bangkok, knew we were coming, and he welcomed us and introduced us to some of the people who'd been involved in my case. As a special treat we were allowed a glimpse of an enormous pile of folders, all of which apparently were to do with my arrest and imprisonment. I knew that my arrest had caused a great deal of work in official quarters; to see the documentation was very impressive.

On the train home we enthused over Mr. Goehr's hospitality and reminisced about the long struggle for my release. Ann, who had been the family spokesman to the press and whose husband John had also been involved in keeping public interest in my plight going, told me several parts of the story I didn't know, having been isolated in Bangkok. All in all, it was a day which reinforced as nothing else could, my gratitude to so many people who had refused to let my problems be ignored.

At Easter we went on a family holiday to Spain, where we relaxed and enjoyed the break from what had been, all in all, an exhausting few months. We lazed on the beach and went for walks around historic parts of the resort, ate at

322

exotic restaurants and had a lovely time. Mum in particular looked as if she really could do with a rest. The doctor had put her on a different course of tablets, and she was having heat treatment for her shoulder. She looked grey and tired, and the holiday seemed to do her good. Looking at her sometimes I caught myself thinking, *It doesn't seem fair, she's had to go through such a lot – and now this on top.*

I tried to find out where Maria was, and made a few enquiries in local government offices, but had no success. By the time we left Spain I'd heard nothing, and I have heard nothing from her since. I pray for her regularly, and I hope that one day we will meet up again.

When we got home we all felt better for the break. We got back into the routine of church and local events, and somehow, having been abroad again and back in a short time, I felt much more at home in Blackburn – I'd lost the feeling of 'just got back from Thailand' and replaced it with the feeling of 'just been away from home for a couple of weeks'. The local people still occasionally stared in the street, but I didn't mind.

By now Mum had been put on a course of physiotherapy for her arm and shoulder which were still giving her a lot of pain. But we still went to church together, and by now Mum wasn't just 'Rita's mum', tagging along after me, but a member of the group in her own right. She didn't say much at the Thursday Bible studies – neither did I – but she listened very carefully to all that went on, and from time to time I had the opportunity to discuss things with her and sometimes answer questions she had.

Then one Thursday night we came home from the Bible study and Mum was rather quiet. I flopped into an armchair and Mum came into the lounge after me. Without any fuss she remarked, 'I really asked Jesus into my life tonight.'

She was abrupt, matter-of-fact; I stared at her, not quite taking in what she'd said.

'I asked him into my life, Rita.' She gazed at me and I at her. She blinked. 'Share with me again, Rita. Tell me what it means, me making that decision. Go over it with me.'

With my heart bursting with love and thanks to the Lord Jesus I showed her what the Bible says about becoming a Christian. I carefully explained, in a way that I had not done with Mum for weeks, how it wasn't a matter of her *doing* anything, but of God loving her so much that he sent his Son, Jesus, to die for her. 'All you have to do is to believe, Mum – have faith that he loves us, and ask him to save you.'

There was a moment's silence and then Mum looked at me bright-eyed. 'That's what I did, Rita. I did that tonight. It's real, I know it's right.'

The joy of knowing that Mum had become a Christian lit up my life. It was a time when I was very aware of God working. Several things were happening which made me realise that the Lord was very specially directing my life step-by-step.

I went to London for a few days to visit Gwen Abbott. It was hard to leave Mum. She was very distressed when we said goodbye.

'You're going away again, Rita.'

'Mum, it's only London – only a few days. I'll ring you every night. I promise.'

As the train started on its journey south I was haunted by the picture of Mum's set, wan face, smiling bravely as her slight figure receded into the distance and merged into the formless mass of people on the station platform.

While I was in London I had a telephone call.

'My name's Ross Simpson,' said a friendly voice. 'I'm ringing on behalf of Prison Christian Fellowship.'

'Oh!' I said. I dimly recalled the name from Prison Christian Fellowship literature. I wondered what could be his reason for calling.

'Mr. Colson is in London at the moment,' he explained,

324

'and he has said that he would very much like to meet you. Would you be free to meet him over dinner?'

'Of course! When?'

I was delighted. Chuck Colson represented for me somebody who had actually chosen to work among prisoners and had founded an organisation to make this possible, and I admired him tremendously.

'We would love you to meet us at Gilbert Kirby's house. He is the principal of London Bible College and is entertaining Mr. Colson and some of the staff there on April 21. Can you come?'

'I'll certainly be there,' I promised.

Gilbert Kirby and his wife Connie lived in a large, comfortable modern house attached to the College in North London. About ten people had been invited, but the dining room was big, so we were able to relax and enjoy a delicious meal, talking all the time. When I arrived I was welcomed by Mr. Kirby – I hadn't expected the principal of a Bible College to be such a friendly, homely person – and introduced to Ross Simpson and John Harris. John was six feet tall, with distinguished grey hair and spectacles. He greeted me in a jolly, booming voice that fitted his height. I liked him on sight, as I did Ross, another very tall man who was most excited because that day his wife had had a baby. Both men were relaxed and amusing to be with. Chuck Colson wasn't there yet as he was coming from a meeting elsewhere. So I had a chance to sit with John and Ross and get to know them.

They were full of enthusiasm for the way that God was blessing the work of Prison Christian Fellowship, and told me many encouraging things. I was moved that people had prayed for so long for prisoners, and had a vision of working with them. I was so absorbed in talking with John and Ross that by the time Chuck Colson appeared I'd relaxed enough to forget my shyness.

He arrived with Gordon and Beth Loux, his associates in

Prison Fellowship USA. I was surprised how tall he was. Prison Fellowship seemed to attract large men! He had the most extraordinary face, expressive eyes that looked straight at you, and mobile, well-used features which seemed to reflect every changing mood and thought. Talking to Chuck you get the feeling that he holds nothing back. Meeting him for the first time, I felt completely at ease with him.

His wife Patty, who I'd met in her husband's books, was lovely. She hugged me and sat down with me, and we were soon in animated conversation. I suppose I had thought that the wife of somebody so important as Chuck Colson would have been remote and inaccessible, but neither of them were like that.

'I'm sure glad to meet you, after all this time,' said Chuck warmly. 'People ask me about you wherever I go, all over.'

He talked to me about Kathryn Grant's visit to me in Bangkok, how she had reported back that it was a terribly sad situation and a bleak prospect for the future, but that I was happy and contented in the Lord. And then I'd been suddenly released. When I made my telephone call to the Fellowship offices from the Stirk House Hotel, they'd been praying for me at a staff prayer meeting minutes before.

'You should come to the States,' Chuck remarked. 'See the work at first hand, how we do things. We'd love to have you come over.'

I shook my head. 'It's not the right time just now,' I answered regretfully. 'My mum's not very well, and anyway I still feel as if I've only just got back. I oughtn't to go away at present.'

Chuck nodded sympathetically.

'But,' I added impulsively, 'I am really interested in the work. I don't want to lose touch.'

'We won't lose touch,' promised Chuck.

During the evening many things were talked about, and for much of the time I listened entranced, not contributing anything because I wasn't familiar with the situations they were talking about. The picture that emerged was of a group of people in several different parts of the world who shared Chuck's vision of Christians taking the message of the gospel into prisons, sharing the good news in seminars and small groups, and inspiring local Christians to meet together and pray for prisoners, giving them help and support in whatever ways presented themselves.

I learned that John Harris and Ross Simpson had been associated with Prison Christian Fellowship in England since its earliest days, when Sylvia Mary Alison had invited them to join a prayer group which was looking to God for guidance about the formation of the work. John's base was now the London office, and Ross, who was a senior probation officer, was an unpaid worker who travelled around the country visiting local groups and encouraging the work there. It wasn't a very grand organisation, and the staff were few. The Fellowship's priorities, just like those of the American organisation, were to concentrate its resources on building up a network of praying, caring Christians and on getting its representatives into the prisons to share the gospel with prisoners.

I was able to talk with Chuck for a long time, and he told me how widespread had been the concern and prayer for my release. I learned that there had been groups of people formed for the particular purpose of praying for me.

'One day you must come to America,' he reminded me. 'There are so many people who would love to meet you. You have a lot of friends there.'

Afterwards I wondered when it would happen. I'd been in touch by letter with the American Fellowship staff since my return, and Kathryn had raised the question of a visit. I really wanted to go, and I'd been praying about it.

But it was entirely the wrong time. Mum was looking tired and washed out, and the treatment on her shoulder didn't seem to be helping her at all. There was no way I was going to travel abroad until Mum was better. It would have been unfair to leave her. So I wrote to Kathryn, explaining that I couldn't think about going to America just yet, but that I wanted to go later on; then I put the matter out of my mind and concentrated on my family.

8 Mum

*Months of raised hopes and shattered dreams
had failed to daunt the courageous woman
who witnessed her daughter's distress, first-
hand during a visit to Thailand. During the
months of waiting, Lily's spirit never
faltered. She'd have done battle with the
whole government if it could have brought
Rita home earlier.*

The Guardian, 5 February 1981

The next few weeks were a lovely time of sharing Mum's
happiness as she began to rest in the security of her new-
found faith in Jesus. Our churchgoing was transformed,
and Herrick Daniels in particular spent a lot of time with
her. Mum was very quiet about what had happened – she
wasn't somebody who went around speaking her feelings to
everybody – but you could see in her face that something
had happened.

Sadly, her joy had to compete with her pain. Even with
heat treatment and exercise, she didn't improve.

I found myself very confused about it. *Lord, what are you
doing?* I prayed. *Mum's given her life to you. She loves you.
Why isn't it for her like it was for me? Why don't you take
away her pain?* I prayed earnestly and often, and talked to

friends about it, and was given wise counsel, but none of it really answered my questions. I sat with her, reading the Bible with her, praying with her; all the time looking at her when her attention was distracted, looking uneasily at the worn face and the awkward positions she was having to adopt in order not to put her shoulder under stress.

Then one day she stayed in bed. It was the May Bank Holiday, and we were all going to Blackpool for a day out. I went into Mum's bedroom to see what the matter was. She was lying in bed, staring bleakly at the wall.

'Why, Mum whatever's wrong? You look dreadful!'

'I'm ill, Rita,' she said wearily. 'I'm not so well at all.'

I felt her brow. She seemed very unwell indeed. I plumped up her pillows and tried to make her more comfortable.

'I won't go to Blackpool, Mum. I'll stay home and look after you.'

'Oh, don't do that, you go on to Blackpool,' Mum said weakly. 'I feel too weak to be bothered with anyone.'

I thought for a minute. Maybe Mum was right. She'd been overdoing it and her shoulder had been really sore recently. A day on her own might give her some needed rest.

'Well, what I'll do,' I told her, 'is to take the phone off the hook. Then you won't have to get out of bed to answer it every five minutes.' I tidied her bed. 'Have you got everything you need? Can I get you anything from downstairs?'

'I'll be all right,' she replied. 'I just need to rest, put my arm up for a bit. Don't worry. You go. I'll be fine.'

June and I went to Blackpool and had quite a good day, and got back that evening. When we went up to tell Mum all about it her bed was empty.

I looked at the empty bed, and at June. A strange cold fear was taking hold of my insides. 'What on earth has happened?'

330

'Ring Ann,' said June. 'She might know.'

Ann told us what had happened. She had tried to call Mum on the phone and had found it off the hook, so she had come over to find out what was going on. Mum had got much worse since we had gone, and was by then really sick and in pain. Ann rang John, her husband, who is a doctor. John came immediately and arranged for Mum to be admitted to the hospital in Wigan where he worked.

Two days later the results of her tests came through. Mum had a huge tumor in her neck. It was almost attached to her lung, and it was entwined with the nerves of her shoulder. That was what had caused the pain. Every time she moved her arm her nerves must have shrieked in agony. The biopsy had determined that the growth was malignant. All the painkillers and arthritis treatment had been useless.

The news hardly registered. It was too much to take in. I was angry that Mum's symptoms had not been recognised earlier, but I scarcely took in the fact that Mum was seriously, possibly, terminally, ill. The staff at Wigan gave us the facts straightforwardly. The tumor was inoperable. But the reality only began to sink in a week or so later, when she was transferred to Christies, a big cancer hospital in Manchester.

She was put on a course of anti-cancer drugs there, and was also given radium therapy. She experienced dreadful side-effects. The drugs made her vomit terribly.

The doctors didn't hold out any hope. 'It could take a long time,' they told us. 'We can try to control her pain as much as possible.'

I was numbed with grief and shock. Again, I went to God with my questions. *Please don't let her die*, I sobbed, and gazed at Mum each time I arrived in her ward half-expecting to find her healed. But nothing happened. She was getting worse. The staff at the hospital were very kind to us, and we appreciated how Mum was being looked after. But when they spoke to us you could tell that they were choosing their words carefully, phrasing their words so as not to accidentally offer a hope of recovery.

She was allowed home from Christies and we persuaded her to stay at Ann's house, where John could keep an eye on her progress. Back at home the house was empty and cheerless without her, and the sight of her possessions where they'd been left was almost unbearably painful. June and I had been closer than ever as sisters since I came home. Now we became even closer as we watched Mum's illness taking its course.

We set up a camp bed next to Mum's in Ann's house and we all took turns sleeping beside her. The hospital had given us a supply of pain-killing drugs, but the quantities were strictly controlled, and we were only allowed to give Mum a certain amount. After a while there was nothing you could do for the pain, once that day's ration of drugs had been used up.

I sometimes sat by her bedside reading the Bible to her all night, as she grunted in pain and tried not to shout out as each wave of nausea hit her. *God*, I cried out silently, *why is this happening to us?* In that sickroom I reached out for some sign of God's presence, but only silence came back. Yet I watched in awe as Mum's pain seemed to subside a little as I read to her.

One Sunday at church, one of her friends came up to me.

'I thought your Mum might enjoy this,' he said. He handed me a small flat package.

'Oh, thank you!' I peeped inside the wrapping. It was a cassette of gospel songs by a singer called Len Magee. 'I'll give it to her tonight,' I promised. 'That's very kind of you.' I had reservations, because Mum wasn't really into that kind of thing.

But she loved it. Those songs meant such a lot to her, and I would often arrive at Ann's and find her in the sun lounge listening to them. They were really special to her. I have never been able to listen to them without tears since, because they were so much loved by my Mum in those few weeks.

I knew in my head that God was in control but in my heart I couldn't cope. How can you explain pain? I saw Mum in such distress over those weeks, as the pain-killers wore off and there were no more for her that night. You can't just grit your teeth and say, 'Praise the Lord'. It doesn't always work. It's not that you've lost faith. It's not that your faith has disappeared. It's just that there are times in the Christian life when it's very, very hard and you just have to battle on knowing that God is there even if you can't sense it.

As the days grew into weeks and Mum made no improvement, I slumped into a black spiritual depression. I refused to read my Bible. I refused to pray. I was so angry inside that I often went to bed saying to God, *If you're going to do this to Mum, I'm not even going to speak to you.*

In others' company, I said all the right things. I went to church, to the Thursday meetings and the Preston group meetings. Outwardly, I was the mature Christian undergoing stress. Inside I was being torn apart. It got to the point where I was attacking God in my heart, accusing him of not wanting the best for her—*If you do, why don't you do it?*

But when things were at their blackest I would suddenly find a picture coming into my mind unbidden, a memory of my mother coming into our lounge that Thursday night and telling me that she had given her heart to Jesus. It was as if, through the sadness and the despair, God was saying, *Look, be patient. I am in control. Don't despair. Look what has happened in your Mum's life already.*

July came, and Mum was much worse. Before they knew that I was going to be released, Mum and Ann had booked a holiday at Pontin's Holiday Camp at Blackpool. When I came home they added me to the reservation and the children as well, so it was going to be a real family holiday.

One day in early July, Ann said, 'Of course we'll cancel the holiday.'

We were with Mum, and I agreed but she was adamant. 'You can't cancel it. The children haven't had a holiday for two years. They're looking forward to it so much. It's only a week, after all. You go.'

'Oh, Mum,' I said. 'We can't possibly go. You're ill, and we don't want to leave you.'

'I'll be all right. I'd rather go into hospital. There's no reason for you not to go on that holiday.'

She was so determined, it was making her over-excited. We let the matter drop and later we discussed it together as a family. We decided to follow her wishes, but we didn't want her to go into a hospital. Instead we arranged for her to be admitted into a hospice for the week in Cheadle Hulme near Manchester. It was a lovely place, where the staff were as kind and sympathetic as anybody could wish. They were so understanding.

'Does she know that she is probably going to die from her illness?' Ann and I were asked in a preliminary interview. We explained that we had never spelt it out to her. It just hadn't seemed right.

'We do prefer that she knows,' said the matron gently. But she didn't press the point, and that was good, because we couldn't bring ourselves to break it to Mum. We reasoned that she must have known anyway; she knew about the biopsy, and the pain she was having must have indicated to her how serious her illness was. To spell it out in words seemed like pronouncing the death sentence. So we left it unsaid.

We travelled down from Blackpool twice during that week to see her. She had other visitors too; Herrick went to see her, and so did Jim Hodson, a friend from the Preston

334

prayer group, and several others. Each time I visited Mum I made some excuse to go into the little chapel attached to the hospice and there I raged at God. I shouted my anger and my grief at him and I accused him of cruelty, as all my sorrow at what he was having to do boiled over into rage.

On the Saturday morning we came back home, and went to Auntie Mary's. She opened the door. Her face was very sad.

'The hospice rang. They want you to go there as quickly as you can.'

Mum was conscious, but suffering terribly. The staff had given her massive doses of pain-killer but the pain was defeating them. At intervals a nurse or doctor would appear and administer further drugs. They spoke to us gently and sympathetically. 'She's very poorly,' we were told.

We had arrived there shortly after lunch. We sat at her bedside. After an hour or so I could control myself no longer, and got up quietly. I made my way to the chapel. Pulling open the door, I crept inside. It was empty and curiously cold after the summer afternoon sunlight. I made my way up the aisle and knelt.

There in that deserted chapel I hurled abuse at God. I stormed at him for what was happening. Part of it was grief because my Mum was dying, part selfish fury that such a thing should be happening to me after all I had been through. *I don't want Mum to die. It isn't fair*, I screamed silently. *I don't believe you're even there*, I raged.

It was like lancing an abscess. As the angry, strident thought took shape my rebellion ended. I knew that I simply did not believe the statement I had just made. He *was* there. I knew it was so. After all the sorrows and my Mum's sufferings, I still knew that God had not gone away.

I remained in the chapel a while longer, praying. Then I went back to Mum's ward. We sat there together for several hours. Memories and emotions were filling our minds. We didn't say very much, and there were long silences. The pain made it hard for Mum to say much.

At about eleven o'clock I looked at her and I knew that she was dying. I looked at my sisters. 'Let's pray,' I said suddenly. I prayed aloud. I thanked God for her and for her life.

A little while after that, Mum died.

'I'll tell Sister,' I said. The three of us looked at each other silently. The sadness in Ann and June's faces must have mirrored my own, but in my heart I had an incredible feeling of peace.

I found the Sister. 'My mother's died,' I said.

She looked shocked. 'We didn't expect that,' she said. 'Not now. Your mother could well have lived on for weeks, perhaps months, in that pain. We thought she would have to suffer much longer.'

Mum died in the late evening of July 26, six months to the very day after I stepped from the aeroplane at Heathrow Airport the previous January.

Our neighbours were very kind. Lancashire people are like that. Mum had been much loved in Blackburn, and had many friends. When I was in prison she had as many letters of encouragement as I had, and numerous telephone calls and visitors. Now that she had died we realised more than ever before how many people had been fond of her.

People took the news of her death in different ways. One night not long afterwards I was out for a stroll. It was dark. As I walked past a street lamp, a passer-by saw me and stopped.

'Hello Rita, love.'

I peered at his face in the gloom. I recognised him. He had known our family for years. He had been a regular at the pub my family used to run. We stood talking for a while. He said how sorry he was about Mum, and I told him a little bit about her last few weeks – happy things,

things which I had been cheered up by; things she'd said and done.

He sighed thoughtfully. 'I don't know, love, I don't understand how anybody can say they believe in God after a thing like that.' His troubled voice was genuinely sympathetic. 'When I think of your Dad dying, and then all that's happened to you, and what your Mum suffered while you were in prison . . . and now you're back home she has to go and die. It don't seem right; not right at all.' He sounded angry and upset at the monstrous injustice of it.

I wasn't angry with him. I had felt like that not long before. I knew he meant to be kind. Standing at his side in the pool of yellow light I tried to think what to say to him. I scanned the dark horizon. Above the houses, the moors were indigo smudges against an inky sky. I took a deep breath.

'Well, I do believe in God. I don't understand a lot of what's gone on – but I do believe that he is there and he is real.'

He was taken aback. I hadn't gone out of my way to seek publicity about my new-found faith, and though the newspapers had talked about it quite a bit at the time of my release many local people didn't know that I had become a Christian.

He said goodbye, and I said that I appreciated his sympathy, and that was quite true. Then I went on my way home. I felt sad inside. I remembered my bitter anger at God, the rebellion of the past few weeks. After all the good things God had done for me and for Mum, I'd been capable of turning round and telling him he didn't exist.

But I was also at peace. I had no answers to the questions that Mum's death had raised. Perhaps I never shall have. But looking back, when my rebellion was ended, I could see his hand in everything. He really had been in charge.

Where will you go, I asked myself, *if not to him?* I'd seen both sides, I'd tried my own way and I'd walked in his.

There was no real choice that needed to be made. It really was true. God *was* there, whatever my sadnesses and perplexities.

9 Going On

In sure and certain hope of the Resurrection
to eternal life, through our Lord Jesus
Christ.

Book of Common Prayer.

We went through the formalities of bereavement almost without thinking. John put a note in the 'Deaths' column of the local newspaper. The next night there was a short article about Mum, which we appreciated.

The vicar called to discuss Mum's funeral. He was a great support at a time when we needed help and advice on all sorts of practical details.

'Herrick knew your Mum best, I think,' he said thoughtfully. 'He visited her more than I did, so I think it would be best if he led the service. I'll get him to come round to see you as soon as possible.'

Herrick was sympathetic and direct. 'Rita, you do believe that your Mum was a Christian?'

We both knew what he was talking about. I didn't get involved in theological definitions, I just told him what Mum had said to me shortly before she died.

'I think she really was a Christian,' said Herrick, when I'd finished.

'I know she was. And I know where she is now. The Lord has really comforted me with that,' I said.

In the end Brian and Herrick took the service together, because they both wanted to be involved. Many of the people there were people we'd come to know since I'd arrived back and had been going to the church regularly, but I didn't take notice who was there and who wasn't.

Herrick spoke of the first time he called round to have a cup of tea with Mum; what sort of a person she was; the way she bore up while I was in prison and her courage in her illness. It was a lovely time because both Brian and Herrick not only said wonderful things about Mum but also spoke plainly about the Christian hope, and how Mum had died as a Christian; but it was also a very sad time in all the ways that funerals always are whether you are a Christian or not. I looked at the grief on my sisters' faces, and there was a heavy emptiness in my own heart side by side with the peace which I had felt at the time of her dying and which had not gone away. Mum was no longer with us, and six months had been all too short a time. It would be wrong to say that it was a radiantly happy time for anybody. That's not what the peace of God means.

At the reception afterwards I moved round mechanically, exchanging words with people, shaking hands, being hugged by relatives, but not aware of very much. As a family we survived it all as best we could, and everybody was very kind. We had arranged a meal for visitors, but I couldn't eat a thing. For several days I was unable to eat anything at all. I was already underweight because I had been eating very sparingly since coming home. Now my family became concerned.

'You'll make yourself ill,' they said.

Ill, I thought, *what does that mean? What does anything mean?*

But the emptiness I experienced after Mum died was very different to the black anger I had had during her illness. It was the product of exhaustion and watching somebody through a long illness. We all felt the same, and I think that anybody who has been through a similar experience will know that awful sense of meaninglessness that descends on life just after the person you have cared for for so long finally dies.

It must have been hard for June, as we settled back into domestic life after the funeral. She'd seen Mum upset for so many years by my travelling, and waiting longingly for me to come home. My own attitude wasn't as helpful as it could have been. I found it hard to forget the privileged status I'd had as a foreign prisoner in Lard Yao, and sometimes I think I really irritated her. For her own part, she had been brought up almost as an only child, as Ann and I had left home when she was quite young; so she too felt a bit threatened. I didn't help, being sometimes unable to resist the temptation to criticise when she was doing housework or cooking. I'd forgotten the social graces. In my own mind I was being kind to June, trying to help her to do things more effectively, showing her where she was wrong. In practice I was probably unbearably arrogant.

But we came through that phase, and grew very close to each other again. In a strange way such difficult times can make a relationship stronger than before.

Early in August I telephoned Kathryn Grant in America and told her what had happened. As we talked, I decided that I would try to visit America later that year.

'Give me some time to help sort things out here,' I asked. 'Then I'll come.'

It wasn't a return of the travel bug. That had left me for good. It was a combination of factors – a desire to get away for a break after Mum's illness, a desire to meet my American friends again, and above all an overwhelming curiosity to find out what Prison Fellowship in America was like. I knew bits about it, and I'd read Chuck Colson's books. The Preston group had told me about the work in

England, and how it related to the American situation. But I wanted to go over there to see for myself, because I had such a strong inner conviction that God was going to make it possible for me to work with prisoners and share the gospel with them.

I had a bruising reminder of my own prison record when I was invited into prison in the north of England. I met the Governor at a Christian businessmen's dinner, and he said that he felt a visit from me would be helpful. I was tremendously excited about this, and prayed very hard about it both on my own and at church and with the Preston group. I was advised that the most effective way of gaining admittance was by obtaining a visiting order to see a particular inmate, and this I did. But when I arrived at the prison gates with my form duly completed, I was refused permission to go in.

My first impulse was to argue with the prison officers there and then, and demand to be allowed inside. I contemplated waving my piece of paper at them and insisting on my rights. But I thought better of it, and I had a strong suspicion that my Bangkok prison record lay at the bottom of the whole matter.

So I went home and prayed about it. I was upset, of course, and I just asked the Lord to show me what he wanted me to do. If he did want me to have some sort of a role in caring for prisoners and telling them about him, how could I possibly begin to do so when I'd been told I couldn't even set foot inside the prison?

As I prayed I felt the presence of God in my room, a comforting reality that soothed my distress. Over the next few days and weeks I asked him, *Well, what do you want me to do with my life?* And I began to recognise him saying to me: *What I want is for you to be you, and share what I've done in your life.*

I was dubious about that. To me, speaking in public was

the same as preaching, and I didn't feel that I could possibly be a preacher. But the Lord showed me that the mental picture I had of a preacher was different to somebody simply sharing their own story with a group of people. I began to look forward to whatever the next step was.

In the end I first spoke formally to a public meeting as the result of some astute plotting by Martha Livesey. I was staying with her one weekend, and she took me to various services and meetings.

We arrived at one meeting room which was at the top of a long flight of stairs. As we came in I saw rows of people listening to a lady at the front who was leading the meeting. When she saw us she beamed.

'Praise the Lord,' she said. 'Our speaker has arrived.'

I realised immediately that she was talking about me, not Martha, and I turned tail and ran from the room, heading for the stairs. Martha was after me in seconds and took my arm. 'It'll be all right,' she murmured.

What had happened was that Martha had promised the group beforehand that I would share with them the story of how I became a Christian, but she hadn't told me – because she'd accurately predicted what my reaction would be. I'd never spoken in public from a platform, though of course I'd taken part in lots of informal group discussions and prayer meetings.

Martha knew what she was doing. She didn't throw me in off the deep end and let me fend for myself. She'd arranged for the two of us to be on the platform, she asking questions and me answering. It wasn't long before I found myself telling the congregation the story of what had happened to me in prison, and though I was petrified, I was able to speak clearly and simply.

I had had many invitations to speak since my return, and until then had refused all of them. After the meeting that Martha had 'arranged', I decided that I should start accepting at least a few invitations. I didn't eat for twenty-four hours before the first of them, and was feeling physically sick as I rose to my feet. But as I began to talk a certainty came upon me that I had found what God wanted me to do for him.

Looking back many months afterwards, I realised that the Lord had been telling me that I had to come to terms with speaking in public before I could think of visiting prisons.

I received a large number of invitations to speak, and still more and more arrived. I was reluctant to accept them all, because I saw that it would be possible to become simply a speaker at church meetings, with a ministry of just giving my testimony, being a travelling evangelist. I felt that the Lord was pointing me in a different direction. *This isn't what I have for you. I have another plan.*

But I accepted quite a few of them, and told of my prison experience, and what it was like to receive Christian visitors and know that Christians were praying for me. I urged my hearers to consider the biblical challenge to remember those in prison.

Sometimes I had difficult moments. On one occasion I was given hospitality before speaking at a church, and was confronted at the mealtable by a lady who seemed to have something on her mind.

'Every week, when I was a young woman, I got my pay packet,' she announced.

I waited, munching politely.

'Of course I wasn't saved then, I didn't know the Lord. Well, each week I set aside some money to buy myself something nice. First of all I bought myself a powder compact.'

I nodded approvingly.

'Then the week after that, I bought a lipstick. The next week . . .'

As the catalogue of cosmetics went on I wondered exactly what the point of this story was going to be.

344

'Then I was saved. It was wonderful. Praise the Lord!'

She told me how it happened, and who had led her to the Lord. 'Then,' she said triumphantly, 'my friend who led me to Christ, and I, we opened my handbag, and we took out all the paint and perfumes – and we threw it down the drain together!'

I was suddenly aware of my own, rather discreet, makeup. I licked my painted lips nervously. 'Huh – are you talking about me? My lipstick?'

She smiled gently at me. 'Well, do you think now, that . . . that makeup is . . .'

I shook my head firmly, and prayed not to lose my temper in front of my host and hostess. 'I'm sorry,' I said, 'but I am sure that for you it is wrong, that it would be a real problem for you to paint your fingernails or use powder. But for me, I don't have a problem with it. Please, leave me alone.'

I was still a young Christian and I had a lot to learn, but it seemed that some Christians were more intent on pointing out what I was doing wrong than on being loving and caring and discussing things in a helpful way. After an article appeared about me in *Today* magazine, with an accompanying photograph of me wearing jeans, I received a letter from one shocked reader quoting Scripture at me and telling me about Jezebel who was thrown to the dogs.

It's true that at that time my clothes were rather more flamboyant and my makeup more noticeable than they have since become. I had much to learn in this area as in many others, and really needed the help of other Christians. But I have to say that sadly, the criticism that some Christians provided me with didn't help me to grow at all. As I considered their comments I felt that many of them had a mental picture of an ideal Christian, to which all young believers should conform. *I don't want to be a stereotype*, I reacted. *I want to be like Jesus.*

Later, I saw exactly the same prejudices standing in the way of some people in the churches accepting prisoners as fellow-believers. Because they wore leather clothes, or because they still had parts of their old life which they were finding it hard to shake off, prisoners often found stiff handshakes and forced smiles the nearest they could get to real fellowship with some Christians.

When I now think back on the setbacks I suffered as a Christian in my early days of being with other believers, it makes me resolve to be extra careful that I do not in my turn hold back some young Christian through my own insensitivity. One such setback it took me days to recover from, was to do with the lady who was organising a big service some way from my home. I was by then fairly well-known as a speaker, and the advertising had drawn in a large congregation. There were posters all round the church which announced the meeting, and other churches in the neighbourhood had been invited. I spoke for three quarters of an hour, and at the end the lady announced that a collection would be taken up. I watched the money piling up; it took quite a while for the plates to go round the hall.

At the end of the meeting I was drinking a cup of tea in a room behind the hall, and the lady organiser was counting up the collection.

'Now, my dear,' she said. 'What are your travel expenses for tonight?'

I told her. She methodically counted out the exact sum in loose change and handed it to me, and put the rest away without further comment.

I was devastated. Not because I wanted money for myself, but because I had hoped that after my talk the money collected would at least in part be given to work among prisoners. Perhaps it was used in that way; possibly, the next day a cheque had been sent as a gift to some prison work. But nobody ever told me, and I never found out what happened to the money generously given on that morning.

Many Christians I met couldn't understand why, with a knowledge of the Thai language, I wasn't going to be a missionary in Thailand. I had to explain that being a missionary was, I believed, a matter of God's call, and I felt God calling me elsewhere.

In fact I couldn't have gone back to Thailand, even had I wanted to. I was *persona non grata* there, and my passport was endorsed. But more than that, I never had wanted to return, which was why I had reacted angrily when, not long after my homecoming, I had heard of a news report about me on television. It was announced that I had 'been refused permission to go back to Thailand'. I was upset to think that people would imagine that, having just left Thailand, I was planning to go back. What would my family think? I had made no such application.

The end of summer saw the return of the national Sunday press. This time they had increased the fee offered by a couple of thousand pounds.

'Have you decided about your story?'

'Story?' I queried, to the journalist at my door.

'Are you interested in doing anything yet? The money's good. I'd think it would come in handy.'

'No, thanks. I don't want to publish.'

The journalist became affable. 'Look, you know we won't be printing anything that hasn't been in print before. It's been over all the papers, you won't be betraying any secrets. You're on Supplementary Benefit, aren't you? Well, then.'

Talking with other Christians later about my refusal to take up the offer – which did indeed come with a great deal of money attached – I had various reactions. Some said I should take the money. It was true, they said; everybody had read the Rita story in the *Daily Mail* and the *Lancashire Evening Telegraph*. Why worry about it being recast? You could give the money to the Lord, use it in his work.

But I pointed out that all the previous press coverage had

been written without my participation, and I have never had the opportunity to tell my own story. I was going to be careful when and how I did that, I said. And did the Lord need money from that source? What was important, after all?

The prospect of capitalising on my release while my friends were still in Lard Yao didn't attract me at all; but if it had, I would have been pulled back to reality by the letter which arrived during August. It was from Linda. She, like Mary her companion, was a black American, very beautiful and extrovert, who had arrived in Lard Yao shortly before I was released. They had joined a prayer group which I and some others had started, and over the time I knew them I had become very fond of them. Both were Christians, and we prayed together about their trials, which were still moving slowly forward, stage by stage, when I left Bangkok.

Linda's letter told me that the day for sentencing had finally come. At the Bangkok courtroom, she and Mary had been sentenced to twenty years each.

I knew how they felt. I too had been given twenty years. But even though they had been expecting the sentence just as I had been expecting mine, it was a crushing blow for them. When I wrote back it was one of the most difficult letters I have ever had to write.

So Summer came to an end, in sorrow for friends in trouble and still with the dull grief of Mum's death in my heart. When Kathryn wrote to me, with a long list of things that Prison Fellowship would like to organise for me to be involved in when I went to the USA, I made up my mind. I wrote to her and asked when she would like me to arrive.

10 Problems Solved

*. . . We really rejoice, Rita, and feel that
everything is right for you to come. Now we
are going to join in prayer that the visa will
all work out.*

Letter from Kathryn Grant, 25 August
1980

Kathryn's reply was reassuring and calm.

'You need to be in the United States for two months with
all that we have planned,' she explained. She outlined the
results of discussions she had had with Chuck Colson and
Gordon Loux. They had put together quite a programme
which included, 'a period of spiritual study, the dedication
of our new building, and the opportunity to attend one of
our seminars'.

As I read on, I began to be excited by the prospect of
going. It wasn't the travel I was looking forward to. It was
the people I would be meeting. Kathryn's letter continued:

> In October we have ten women prisoners here for
> our seminar. On November 13 there will be a
> meeting and a large gathering of persons who were
> part of the prayer support for you. You will have
> an opportunity to share with them . . .

349

I was also greatly encouraged by the fact that the staff of Prison Fellowship in the States were praying for me continuously. As I read on I felt the need of those prayers, because the mechanics of getting me into America seemed to be quite complicated:

> In order to enter the United States, because of a prison record, you will have to file a paper with the American Embassy in London called 'Waiver of Ineligibility'. The enclosed letter should be sufficient for you to receive the waiver and your visa.

Now I knew I was finally going to America, I obtained the required form for a visa application. I filled it in without any problems until I came to a section which asked for details of any criminal convictions, drugs offences or prison records. I didn't see any alternative to telling the truth, so I carefully wrote a brief account in the small space provided – my handwriting isn't tiny at the best of times, and there was only space to give the barest outline of events. I sent the form off enclosing the letter that Prison Fellowship had provided, and waited for my visa to arrive.

My application was refused. The letter from the USA Embassy was not unfriendly, but it was absolutely firm. Because of my previous conviction it would not be possible to grant my application.

Lord – what's happening? I prayed. *Please, show me what to do.* It had all seemed so straightforward. Kathryn had even sent me a letter for the Embassy. I had thought there might be some difficulties, but I hadn't dreamed that there would be a flat refusal.

As I prayed, I heard no words and saw no miraculous signs. But inside me there grew a real assurance that God wanted me to go to America for this trip, and that it *would* happen. I also felt that this problem would need hard work on my part. I couldn't just sit back tranquilly and wait for the Lord to work miracles.

I formulated a plan of action. Kathryn had said that ideally I should plan to be in America from mid-September to mid-November. I wrote to her and explained that this would not now be possible. But I also told her that I was sure that this was not the end of the matter. Before, when I'd only just got back to England and then later when Mum was ill, I'd known that it wasn't right to go. Now, I was just as convinced that it *was* right for me to go. All my contact with Prison Fellowship in England, all my telephone calls and letters from America, all my own prayers and thoughts about the future had reinforced my belief, going back to my time in Lard Yao, that somehow my future would be involved with the needs of prisoners. I wanted to go to America because I wanted to find out more about Prison Fellowship and I wanted to spend more time with its full-time workers in the USA. Would it be possible, I said to Kathryn, to come later on – perhaps October, if things were sorted out by then?

As well as writing to Kathryn I telephoned Ross Simpson.

'Read the Embassy letter to me, Rita,' he said.

I read out the letter with its matter-of-fact sentences – regretting that because of the facts I had given it was not possible at this time to grant a visa for entrance into the United States . . . I read on, to the last paragraph, where the writer had added that if I wish to discuss the matter further it would be necessary to attend at the Embassy in person and speak to one of the immigration staff.

'That's what I'm going to do, Ross.' I made up my mind there and then. 'I'll come down on the bus. I'll go and talk to them.'

'Well, all right, Rita. Maybe that's the best thing to do now. Only—'

He hesitated. 'Rita, don't build your hopes up. There's a

lot of red tape involved, and you're not long out of prison.'

'I'll telephone you before I come down,' I promised.

'And I'll see what I can find out in the meantime,' he said.

Before I left Blackburn a telegram arrived from Kathryn. It was brief and emphatic. 'Yes, yes, come.' I rang Ross to say I would be in London the next day. I boarded the bus for London in a very determined state of mind.

London's Victoria coach station was busy with passengers and dozens of vehicles. As the coach pulled in I looked for Ross in the crowds. He was waiting for me as I climbed down. He looked worried.

'Rita, I rang the Embassy this morning. I'm sorry, it's bad news.'

'What did they say?'

'There's no way they're going to give you that visa. Even if you can talk them into giving you that Waiver of Ineligibility, there's a time limit, you have to have been out of prison a certain length of time. I'm afraid you don't qualify, Rita.'

We walked to where his car was parked. I was thinking hard. At the car I squared my shoulders.

'I've got to go, Ross. I've got to go to the Embassy.'

'Sure?'

'I just feel so strongly that I have to go and get the visa.'

Ross smiled. 'All right, Rita. I'll take you round there. Get in.'

Before we said goodbye we prayed together and put the whole problem into the hands of the Lord.

The Embassy in Grosvenor Square was packed with a throng of people. I handed in my letter and explained to the reception officer why I had come. I was instructed to join a long queue of bored-looking people.

I waited for ages, supposing that if I'd got there first thing in the morning, it wouldn't have been so bad, but my coach got in to London at midday and by the time Ross dropped me off at the Embassy the queues were enormous.

In my pocket I had my New Testament, and I squatted on the floor, shifting forward as the queue moved, feeling perfectly at peace as I read. Being in the middle of such a crowd of people could have intimidated me, but didn't. This and all the discouragement I had met with over the visa seemed irrelevant by comparison with the deep sense of peace that I had.

Eventually it was my turn. I was taken into an office where a friendly American official rose from his seat as I entered and shook my hand.

'Miss Nightingale!' he smiled. He scanned the papers in front of him. 'Sit down.' I perched on my chair and looked at him expectantly.

'Now don't worry, Miss Nightingale. I'm familiar with your story. Personally, I myself was a US consul in Turkey. So I believe I can understand something of where you've been. Now, tell me why you want to go to America.'

He was very kind and listened to me carefully as I explained about Prison Fellowship. 'You see, I want to go over there because I think perhaps I can be involved, eventually, in some way.'

As I talked he was scribbling notes on the sheets of paper in front of him. When I'd finished, he smiled at me. 'Fine, I've got the picture. Now I have to make some phone calls.'

He was gone perhaps ten minutes. I sat in the interview room reading my New Testament. It wasn't even enough time to begin worrying. Suddenly he was back.

'Well, Miss Nightingale, you'll have your visa in twenty-four hours.'

I almost hugged him, I was so delighted.

Back at home a letter from Kathryn was waiting for me.

> By now you should have our telegram . . . we want you here so very much, and believe that God works

his own time out. We will plan for your coming as
soon after October 20 as is convenient for
you – then you would return by Christmas to
England.

Kathryn's final paragraph contained wonderful news.

This week Margaret Cole called from
California – she is so in hopes of seeing you. I will
be writing her with your schedule. What a blessing
it was to talk to her . . .

Margaret! With Lucille, she had been so faithful in talking
to me about the Lord when I was in prison. She had visited
me, prayed for me, and rejoiced with me when I became a
Christian. She was only in Bangkok for a part of my time in
prison, but before she left she wrote to the King of
Thailand and offered to serve the remainder of my sentence
for me. The reason that she gave for this astonishing act of
love was that, as she explained to the King, she was nearing
the end of her life and mine had hardly started.

'I believe she has a work to do for God,' she had written,
'among prisoners in many prisons.'

How excited she must have been to know that I was in
touch with Prison Fellowship and was going to America to
see the work at first hand!

And how I praised God, that his timing was indeed
perfect. Not only was I going to America, my visa sorted
out, I was going to see Margaret again.

When within days I also received a letter from Jack and
Gladys Martin, saying that they too would be in America
while I was there – 'We're having a short furlough' – it
seemed as though there was nothing God could possibly do
to make the visit more wonderful.

11 Embarking

We are praying now for wisdom to our
loving Father in putting [your programme]
together in the way best for you, that he can
use for his glory.

Letter from Kathryn Grant, September
1980

I wrote back to Kathryn exuberantly. I had sorted out my
diary, re-arranged what could be re-arranged and cancelled
the rest. The travel agent had given me all the details of
flights and connections, and I planned to arrive in America
on 23 October.

It was over a month before I was due to arrive there, but
the time sped by. In a number of ways God confirmed that
this was the right thing for me to do next. One problem, for
example, was money. Prison Fellowship in America were
paying for my travel and hospitality, but I realised that just
being in a foreign country again would mean that I would
have to have some spending money. (In fact, when I got
there, I found that everybody was so kind and generous to
me that I hardly needed to spend anything). I'd been
receiving Supplementary Benefit for the past few months,
but it was only intended to cover essentials, and there
wasn't much money to spare. I certainly hadn't any spare
cash saved up.

Though I knew this was a difficulty, I didn't worry very much about it. I prayed about it, and the Lord gave me the assurance that it would not be a problem. I didn't advertise the fact that I needed money. Then, shortly before I was due to leave, several gifts of money arrived, totalling about £200. One cheque was for £100; it came in a letter which said, 'We felt that the Lord was telling us to give this money to you.'

In the middle of my preparations I managed to get some other things done. Early in October I went to the Birmingham BBC studios where I recorded a short television broadcast. I had been invited to take part in a series called *The Light of Experience*. Though I welcomed the opportunity to share with hundreds of thousands of people what the Lord had done for me in Lard Yao, I was very nervous. I found it disconcerting to be seated in front of a camera, telling my story to an unseen audience. I'd never done anything like it at all, and my first broadcasting attempt was consequently, despite the help of the producer and studio staff, rather stilted when it was finally released in 1981.

By now I was doing quite a lot of public speaking, and when Tony Ralls, a Prison Fellowship worker in Exeter, invited me to spend a few days in his area I was delighted to accept. Tony had himself been in jail, and since leaving prison he and his wife have developed an extensive ministry with Prison Fellowship.

1980 was turning out a good year for them. With the support of a chain of intercessory prayer-groups – the 'Lydia' groups – they established links between prison chaplains and Prison Fellowship, and links had also been established with Christian businessmen in the locality, the Christian Police Association, and Probation Officers.

In addition, many people in the area were beginning to develop their own ministries in fellowship with Tony and his team; one family, for example, had opened their home to ex-visitors, another had committed themselves to regular prison visiting, and numerous individuals were praying regularly and sacrificially for prisoners by name.

Tony and the members of the fellowship in Exeter and the nearby areas were faithfully putting into practice the biblical command which had inspired Chuck Colson at the very beginning of Prison Fellowship – 'Think constantly of those in prison as if you were prisoners at their side' (Hebrews 13:3).

I was very much looking forward to going down there, and I enjoyed my brief visit very much. I spoke to a group in Exeter and stayed overnight with Tony and his family, returning to Blackburn the next day. Before leaving for Devon I'd visited Martha in Blackpool, so it had been a wonderful week.

The following week Ross had invited me to a conference of Christian Probation Officers in Wales, and I attended it with him the weekend before I was due to leave for America. It was a challenging experience to hear a group of Christians, professionally involved in dealing with problem youngsters, talking together about the relevance of their faith to what they were doing.

Looking back a month or two later I realised that both experiences had been invaluable preludes to my first trip to the United States. The Exeter trip, besides enabling me to see at first hand Prison Fellowship work in the south-west of England, gave me the chance to spend some time with one of the work's pioneers. The conference in Wales showed me that there was more to Christian work among young people than simply preaching the gospel and giving my testimony.

I began to understand something of the importance of a biblical understanding of the whole of life, where the transforming power of Christ reaches into and changes every corner of one's daily existence, not just the 'religious' bits but work, leisure, relationships – everything.

So it was with a sense of having been specifically prepared by the Lord in all sorts of ways that I arrived at London airport to catch the 11.45 flight to Washington.

The flight was comfortable and without incident. I had been to Spain with Mum and June since getting back from Thailand, so it wasn't the first time I had been in a plane since then. But Spain was almost a local journey by comparison with the transatlantic flight; and inevitably, as I gazed at the sun gleaming off the cloudbanks far below the plane, I remembered other long plane journeys.

I remembered the flight to Australia, when I had left home as a teenage bride with my husband to start a new life; the flight from Australia to the Far East less than a year later, my marriage a disaster; the flight back to England for my twenty-first birthday, full of good intentions of settling down, helping my Mum in the pub she ran; the flight back to Australia, part-financed by Mum, both of us aware that my wanderlust had got the better of those good intentions; and then the flight to Hong Kong where I had become a night-club hostess, lived the glamorous good life, acquired a rich and handsome Chinese boy friend and ended up being arrested at Bangkok with three-and-a-half kilos of heroin which had been planted in my baggage.

And then there had been my last long flight, back to England from Kuala Lumpur, having been released from prison in Bangkok by a miraculous royal amnesty. On all the other flights but the last I had been a restless, dissatisfied wanderer, not even knowing what it was I was travelling to fir... On the plane back from Kuala Lumpur I was a radiant'y happy, joyful Christian, giving thanks to God for his deliverance and all the amazing things that had happened.

Eventually the plane began its preparations for the final airport approach, and it was time to strap ourselves into our seats and adjust our watches to US time. We would arrive in Washington at 10.45 am – an hour before we had left London!

We dropped through the clouds into a bright American morning. Washington lay beneath, stretched out like an architect's model in muted greys and greens. The city disappeared from view behind us as the plane entered its runway approach. As the ground rose to meet us, all I could see for miles around was a thick pine forest. It seemed a very beautiful place to have an airport.

At disembarkation I didn't anticipate any problems. All my papers were in order. I had my visa in my passport, and before the plane landed I checked to make sure that I had all the documents I would need.

I looked again at my disembarkation card, which had given me a temporary headache: filling it out, I had had to think for a while about two questions: one asked what my job was, and the other asked what my income was. I had no job, and I was not coming to America to find one; so after some deliberation I left that section blank. I pondered even longer over the question about income, and in the end I wrote that my income was Social Security in England, but that Prison Fellowship was paying for my trip.

The plane taxied to a stop, the steps were wheeled into place, and I joined the stream of people through the immigration procedures. In the crowd of people at the exit barrier I saw Kathryn, who was waving enthusiastically. I waved back excitedly.

At the passport check a crisply uniformed woman officer glanced at my papers, looked at me, and then looked at my embarkation card again. Her face was suddenly grim.

'How do you intend to live?'

I blinked. 'What do you mean?'

She looked over my shoulder at the long queue behind me. Her manner was abrupt and unfriendly. 'Over there, please.'

She nodded towards a part of the immigration hall where

a number of individual desks were arranged, most of them occupied by people being interviewed. The officer closed her booth and escorted me over to the desk. I glanced across at Kathryn apologetically. She shrugged and made a face. A few bystanders in the queue behind me watched us curiously.

'Now,' demanded the officer. 'How do you propose to live?'

'I don't understand,' I said uneasily.

'Who is supporting you? Is a man supporting you? What are your available means?'

'Well–I've got some money–'

'How much?'

I showed her. She scribbled the amount on a pad, laid the pen down, and waited expectantly for me to proceed. Her face betrayed nothing.

'There's nobody supporting me,' I said. 'I'm here as the guest of Prison Fellowship. Look, it says here.'

I didn't see the point of the questions, and I didn't know why I was being asked them. Later I realised that they were standard 'feelers' designed to trap illegal immigrants and smugglers. But then, I was becoming alarmed. Why on earth were they asking me all these things?

'Into that room, please.' The officer pointed me towards a small interview room. I trailed after her. There were a few other passengers in the room. Nobody was talking to anybody else. As I entered, porters brought my baggage in and dumped it on the table.

It's all happening again. Oh, God, it's all happening again, I cried silently. I began to tremble. Behind me, a male officer entered. I half caught his words. I didn't hear whether it was a greeting, a statement or a question. I just picked up two words–'arrest' and 'imprisonment'.

He was slightly friendlier than the other officer, but his tone was accusing.

'So when were you in prison, Ma'am?' he asked.

360

'Uh – 1977. I was released in January.'

He seemed extremely surprised, whispered to the woman officer, and left the room. I thought he knew who I was and what my prison record was, and that that was why they were cross-examining me. But watching his reaction I wasn't so sure. Maybe it had been a trick question to find out whether I *had* been in prison.

When he came back he said, 'Well, do you want to tell us about these drugs?'

I was tired and angry by this time. 'What drugs? What are you talking about?'

He took one of my bags and weighed it experimentally in his hand. 'Do you mind if . . .?'

'Look,' I said tightly. 'You can do whatever you want. You can rip the whole lot apart if you want to. I don't care. I'm going to sit over here.'

I stalked across to a bench and sat down, watching them angrily. Then I closed my eyes. *Lord Jesus*, I prayed, *help me. I wasn't expecting this. I don't know what to do.*

I looked up. They appeared to have decided against searching my bags. My briefcase was opened and examined item by item. I was asked to identify each item.

The Prison Fellowship leaflet, in which my story was featured, was taken from my case and put before me.

'What's this?'

'It's just something about Thailand . . .' I replied wearily. Saying 'Thailand' made something snap inside me. I blurted out, 'It just reminds me, you know? I thought there was only one place in the whole *world* where that sort of hassle could happen. But you brought that all back to me. All of it . . .'

I was tearful and upset by now. I was thinking of Kathryn waiting for me at the other end of the arrivals hall. She would have been waiting for over half an hour by now. 'Look,' I pleaded, 'there's someone waiting for me outside. Can you send a message to say I'm delayed?'

'Sooner we're through, sooner you're with your friend, Ma'am.' The reply was firm but slightly less unfriendly. They finally finished going through my briefcase.

'How long is your visa for?'

'Two months.'

'Well, we'll just have to stamp it, Ma'am.'

The words 'Not to exceed two months' were added to my hard-won visa.

'OK Ma'am, you can go now.'

Within minutes I was being hugged by Kathryn and being taken out of the airport, away from the officials, the questions and the panic.

Talking about it all afterwards, my hosts thought that the problem was not the fact that I had a prison record, but that by filling in the disembarkation card as I had, I had aroused the officials' suspicions. They had held me back to see whether my incomplete replies meant that I was attempting to enter the country illegally, and were probably quite taken aback to find out what my history actually was.

I had assumed that because my visa had been granted and my name was presumably on a computer somewhere, it was all sorted out. I hadn't realised that getting a visa and actually entering the country are two quite different things.

Looking back, I felt that it could have been worse. After all, the last time I had had an experience like that in an airport, I had gone from the airport into police custody. Relaxing with my new American friends, I began to put the incident behind me.

'Wow, though,' I said to Chuck Colson later, 'they didn't half give me a hard time.'

He grinned at me sympathetically. 'Rita, I still get that. They do that to me even if I'm just going to Canada. It's having a prison record, you see.'

Somehow that made me feel a lot better.

362

12 Washington DC

*My greatest joy was a week spent early in
my visit with a group of ten women released
through Prison Fellowship from their various
institutions to complete an intensive two-week
discipleship course in Washington, DC.*

Prison Christian Fellowship (UK),
Regional and Development News, Spring
1981

With Kathryn Grant at the airport was Vivien Nielson,
with whom I was to stay. I was given a wonderful welcome.
I quickly forgot the worries in the immigration offices, and
was soon relaxing in Vivien's beautiful home.

I knew very little about Prison Fellowship, though I had
corresponded with Kathryn and the others in America, and
seen first-hand the work that was beginning in Britain. Any
worries that I might have had about my inexperience were
quickly forgotten – I had no time to think about it!

The first function which I was to attend was already in
progress when I arrived in Washington. The 'Prison
Fellowship Twenty-Sixth Graduating Class' had commenced
on 19 October and was due to end on November 1. This was
the seminar which Kathryn had told me of in her letters, and
which was to be one of the main events of my visit.

'We have ten women and girls,' explained Kathryn over dinner, 'all of whom have been released from prison for the period of the seminar. They are staying in the home of a Prison Fellowship associate who has loaned the house for this fortnight.' She riffled through a sheaf of papers. 'Look – this is the schedule for the seminar.'

I took the paper and shook my head in disbelief. 'You mean they're allowed out of prison – just like that? That's incredible!'

Kathryn nodded 'There are chaperons with them, but really the prisoners are on ten days parole leave.'

'I can't imagine that happening in England,' I said impulsively. 'It's a wonderful idea.'

'We're praying it will happen in England, one day – soon,' said Vivien. 'You've no idea how great it is, to hear how they share all that God is doing in their prisons. And it's a time of really intensive Christian training for them.'

I looked at the timetable in front of me. It certainly was packed. 'Where is Ligonier Valley?' I asked.

'It's a Christian study centre,' explained Kathryn. 'The first week, the women go there for a period of residential study. Now they're back in Washington, and you'll be meeting them very soon!'

We talked for a while about the seminar, and chatted about all the things that had happened since my release. I was enjoying the evening tremendously, but was having difficulty keeping my eyes open. While it was still quite early, Vivien smiled at me apologetically.

'There'll be lots of time to talk, Rita. We're so glad you're here at last. But now you should get some sleep. Don't feel you have to be up early tomorrow!'

One of the attractive things about the seminar programme was the very thorough hospitality programme which Prison Fellowship had arranged for the seminar participants. A 'family sponsorship' scheme made sure that each of the women was entertained in somebody's home several times during the fortnight. On the first Saturday, two days after my arrival, Vivien entertained one of the girls from the seminar for lunch and supper. It was a memorable day. I really liked Alie, I enjoyed being with Vivien, and we went to the Air and Space Museum in Washington, which was well worth seeing – I've always been an enthusiastic sightseer when abroad.

Alie was very fashionably dressed, and it was difficult to imagine her in prison, much less doing prison chores and being part of that grey, shapeless prison population. She was attractive, smart and fun to be with.

The next day I went to church with my hosts, and afterwards there was a buffet reception for the seminar participants. It was quite crowded and I didn't identify who they were until somebody pointed them out to me. I suppose I was expecting them to look alike in some way, to be a recognisable group; to be wearing identical clothes or identical expressions. But it was quite different. The prisoners looked gorgeous – beautiful clothes, smart high-heeled shoes, very well made up. Most of them were black. They were radiant.

The other amazing thing about the prisoners, besides their stunning looks, was their singing. During the time I got to know them they sang a great deal, and there was no mistaking them as a group then. I never heard singing like it.

We all – Prison Fellowship staff, associates, seminar participants and others involved – stood up one by one and introduced ourselves. We said who we were and where we'd come from. When it came to my turn I got up hesitantly and said, 'My name's Rita Nightingale, I only just arrived in Washington, I'm spending two months with Prison Fellowship staff here.' I was feeling very new and rather overawed by the situation, not least by the attractive, radiant women and girls who were the focus of the whole event. We all chatted afterwards; people were welcoming and interested – many of them said they had prayed for me while I was in prison – but I was awkward and shy, and had to rack my brains for things to say. Chuck Colson made his way through the throng of people and welcomed me. It was lovely to see him again. As the evening progressed, I began to feel more at home and to enjoy the warmth of hospitality surrounding me.

I was still feeling overawed the night before I was due to give my first formal talk to the group. A series of different speakers each talking about something they were involved in or expert in was a major feature of the seminar, and I was to speak about my experiences in Hong Kong and Lard Yao.

That night I lay in bed feeling terrible fear. What could I possibly have to say to these smart, amusing women, with their vibrant personalities, laughter and marvellous singing voices? I'd held my own with Alie with no problems, but that had been different. Alie was just one person, and at Vivien's house there had been more of 'us' than of her. But tomorrow I was to talk to the whole group. *I should never have come*, I thought wretchedly. I wasn't a prisoner any more. I'd begun to forget all sorts of things. Would I even be able to relate to prisoners?

I prayed about it, telling the Lord how frightened I was, and began to feel more at peace. Inside me I had an assurance that it would be all right, that it wouldn't be a fiasco.

Next morning I still had that feeling of peace deep inside me, but I was still nervous as I thought about the meeting. Kathryn drove me to Prison Fellowship headquarters, where the session was to be held. I was shown into a conference room, where the women and girls were sitting in an informal semicircle. My doubts began to return. Did I really have anything in common, anything worth communicating, to this group? I felt a few moments of total insecurity and self-doubt. Then into my mind came the thought, unprompted, *Of course you have something to share. They are prisoners. So were you.*

We went to the front of the room. Kathryn introduced me to the group. Then she smiled at me and nodded. I rose to my feet shakily. The circle of women gazed at me expectantly. There was no clue in their faces as to what they might be thinking about me.

'Hello,' I said. The circle of faces smiled back at me. I cleared my throat and started again. 'Hello. I just want to share with you today what the Lord did for me in my life while I was in prison . . .'

As I spoke I began to relax. My doubts left me. After all, I had spoken to small groups, in fellowships and churches. I'd given my testimony quite a few times. In a way I had become well-practised in summarising my story and testifying to what the Lord had done in my life.

'I thought I was the smart one,' I told the group. 'I thought I knew it all. But I was the mug.'

It was the same story I had told many times already, in small prayer groups in Lancashire, in churches wider afield, seated under the hot studio lights in front of the cameras, recording *The Light of Experience* for British television.

But this time it was different.

As I spoke on, I felt myself gripped by what I was saying. I was aware of someone guiding my mind and my voice, telling me what to remember and how to say it. I wasn't just narrating the story, I was *sharing* it in a way I had never done before. I poured out the story both of my spiritual crises and becoming a Christian, and of what I had been through in prison as a woman. 'I swore, I screamed, I was bitter and angry,' I recalled, and saw answering nods of recognition as I said it.

Suddenly there was nothing I wanted to hold back from

these women. I wanted to share with them everything that the Holy Spirit brought to my mind. I told them about my ambitiousness, my restless search for happiness that had taken me halfway round the world, my fascination for the glamour and night life of Hong Kong which had led me step by step further and further into trouble. And I shared my experiences in Lard Yao prison. But it wasn't particularly easy to speak, because I was finding it extremely emotional. Part of the time, my throat tensed as if I were about to burst into tears, and I had to struggle to finish.

I finished, pulled myself together and looked round at the women and girls.

Over half of them were in tears. I stood there, breathless, with an extraordinary sense of individual love for each person in that room. There was silence for about a minute. I wasn't sure what to do.

Then one of the women, a big, very beautiful black girl in her twenties, got up and came over to me, tears streaming down her face. She put her arms round me and gripped me tightly.

'I know,' she said; 'Oh, I *know* . . .'

Afterwards we all hugged each other, and wept and laughed together for what seemed a long time. There was such an overpowering feeling of fellowship that it seemed impossible that I had ever felt shy of these people.

It was the first time that I'd had contact with prisoners since I had left Lard Yao.

From the point of view of my American visit as a whole, that session was a very small part of the whole thing, and it happened right at the beginning. But for me personally it would be no exaggeration to say that it was a turning point in my life. I now *knew*, without a shadow of doubt, that I wanted to work with prisoners.

It was such a terrible situation to which they were soon to

be returning. I knew something of American prisons from reading Chuck Colson's books and talking with various people. I had my own experiences of prison. I knew the daily ridicule they would receive from their fellow inmates, the cynicism and hostility, the accusations of false piety and of being 'wardens' pets'. So I could see how important it was that they should have had this special time of fellowship, study and training in discipleship.

But at the same time I could see how important it was for them to be reminded and encouraged in their role as ambassadors of Jesus in their prisons. Hundreds of prisoners would watch these women as they lived their daily lives, and by their example would see the power and the grace of God. We could never reach those hundreds in the normal ways open to us. But they could – and would – be in contact with them, sometimes for years.

God opened my eyes that week to the limitless power of a ministry among prisoners, if that ministry is truly consecrated to him. I became gripped with the excitement of the vision of Prison Fellowship, which had begun out of the ruins of a disgraced Presidential Counsel's life, and was now bringing hope and new life to hundreds. I wanted to be part of it. I wanted to commit my life to it, for as long as God wanted me to be involved.

For the week of the seminar I was scheduled to stay in the home of Gordon and Beth Loux, of the Prison Fellowship staff. But when it was time for me to move there from Vivien's home, I plucked up my courage to suggest a change in the arranged plan. I asked to be allowed to move into the house where the prisoners and their chaperons were staying. I wanted to spend as much time as possible with them. Arrangements were made for me to do this.

During that week I was with them wherever they went and whatever they were doing. It was an exhilarating time. They had been released from prison to attend the seminar, so there was all the excitement and relaxation of a holiday – I could well identify with that, because I could imagine what it would have meant to me to be let out of Lard Yao for a fortnight to live in a lovely home in suburban Washington! But there was also the thrill of fellowship in such very special circumstances – for some of the girls it was the first time they had ever met with other Christians outside prison. There was a sense that every moment of every day was precious, because the time was so short.

On the last Sunday the seminar came to an end with a Dedication Service at Falls Church in Washington. I was invited to speak at it. I will never forget that service, because it drew together so many of the new and exciting things I had been experiencing. In the morning I had attended another service where Fred Rhodes had been preaching. He was the person whom Chuck Colson, five years earlier, had invited to be his personal administrator when, after his release from prison, his paperwork was beginning to increase beyond one man's ability to handle. Invitations to speak and letters on many different topics were arriving at the Colson household from all sorts of places, and to add to the problem Chuck was trying at that time to finish writing *Born Again*, his account of his Watergate involvement and surrender to Jesus Christ. Fred Rhodes had restored order to Chuck's desk and brought a wealth of varied and distinguished experience to bear on his administrative problems. He had been Chuck's first colleague in the prison ministry and was deeply involved in the founding of Prison Fellowship.

As I listened to him that morning it was good to be able to fit a face to the name I had come to know well. It was to Fred Rhodes that Jack and Gladys Martin had written when I was in Lard Yao, and he had circulated my request for prayer throughout the United States and in other countries. In fact he had been in Bangkok shortly before my release, and had applied to visit me but had been refused.

The Dedication Service in the afternoon was led by a number of those who had led sessions in the seminar or had been involved in its organisation. The members of the seminar were introduced one by one and presented with certificates, stating that they had attended and completed the programme. Then they took turns to speak about what the seminar had meant to them. Woman after woman testified to the deepening of their faith, a renewed commitment to Jesus. They spoke movingly of where they had come from and what it was like to be a Christian in prison; and they talked about going back there, and what their hopes and fears were. It was a sober time, but also an inspiring one.

When it was my turn to speak, Kathryn introduced me to the large congregation. When I rose to face them I was a little nervous, but I was no longer talking to strangers. Sitting in front of me were the women and girls I had come to know and love in such a special way in one short week.

13 Learning

I've had a pretty full schedule, but I've been receiving so much from the Christians around me.

Letter to the congregation of St. Andrew's, Blackburn: published in the December 1980 parish magazine.

That night I made my belated arrival at the home of Gordon and Beth Loux. It was a lovely family home, and Gordon and Beth welcomed me warmly. Gordon controlled the day-to-day operation of the Washington office. I stayed with them for a week, much of which I spent in the office observing what was going on and the various activities of the Fellowship.

Until then I had been unclear about how the various parts of Prison Fellowship fitted together, and how the prayer group in Preston and Sylvia Mary in London fitted into the overall situation. Now I learned that there were two linked organisations: Prison Fellowship USA was the movement originally spearheaded by Chuck Colson as the result of God's guidance to him in prison; and Prison Fellowship International brought together people and fellowships all over the world, and had come into being largely because of the many people around the world who had read Chuck's books and wanted to be involved. Chuck Colson was Chairman of the International and the USA Fellowships; Gordon Loux was President and Kathryn Grant Vice-President of Prison Fellowship International.

The organisation in England – Prison Christian Fellowship – was part of the Prison International Fellowship, by whom I had been invited to America. Sylvia Mary Alison was its Chairman, and the English representative on the International Council.

It sounds complicated, but it seemed to work well. The offices of Prison Fellowship USA and Prison Fellowship International were at that time in the same building, so I had an excellent opportunity to gain an overview of what was happening. I was taken aback to discover what a huge ministry Prison Fellowship, in all its aspects, had. Seminars were continually taking place, many of them inside prisons. Each entailed an enormous amount of paperwork – initial negotiations with prison authorities, whether requesting permission for individuals to be allowed 'furlough' to attend an out-of-prison seminar, or for an in-prison seminar to be held and prisoners to be allowed to attend. In some cases there was considerable resistance, in others Prison Fellowship was well-known and its visits encouraged. Each seminar was carefully planned and prayed over.

Then there was follow-up – the Fellowship maintained large files of prisoners and ex-prisoners with whom they were in touch. Sometimes a correspondent would need counselling, sometimes there were practical problems in which it was possible to lend a helping hand. Occasionally an ex-prisoner could be put in touch with a Christian employer prepared to offer a job – just as in Britain, a prison record makes it virtually impossible to get a good job in America, but the Fellowship, which is based on trust between Christians, has made it possible for many ex-prisoners to begin a new life.

Besides the needs of the prisoners the work among the

supporters and prayer-partners was a major part of the daily activities. The quarterly newsletter, *Jubilee* (the first issue of which after my release had featured my story, so that the hundreds in America who had prayed for me could know how my release had happened), gave an indication of the numbers of people involved.

There were Prison Fellowship organisations, I discovered, in Australia, Canada, England and New Zealand as well as America. Most operated like the English organisation, centering the work on small groups of praying Christians who worked and prayed to arouse the Christian community in their locality to the needs of prisoners. Groups like these had prayed for me when I was a prisoner, in 'prayer chains' in Australia and America.

Much of my time in the office was spent writing letters to prisoners all over the world, many of whom had written to Prison Fellowship International since my release expressing their good wishes and asking to be put in contact with me.

It was a long time since I'd worked in an office, and I enjoyed the friendliness. It wasn't a grand suite designed to impress the visitor with the wealth and prestige of the owner. It was efficient and pleasant, and it looked out to green fields in which horses grazed. It had one striking feature. The room had originally been divided by a system of screens into one or two smaller offices. You could see how, as the operation had grown in size, further subdivisions had taken place, and yet more. At the time I saw it, the Prison Fellowship International office was composed of the smallest cubicles I'd ever seen. Everybody tolerated the situation with great good humour, and it was a dramatic visible sign that God was blessing the work and making it grow!

After my week in the office, November was a whirlwind of visits and events. For the next fortnight I travelled. From 2nd-7th November I was in California, where I had a hectic programme, mainly speaking to churches. It was hard work but I was buoyed up the whole time by the warmth of the welcome I received from everybody I spoke to, many of whom had prayed for me while I was in prison.

When I returned to Washington I worked in the office again, and amongst the letters I wrote was one to my home church, St. Andrews. I listed the schedule I had for the remainder of my visit, and asked for prayer as I undertook the various commitments.

> I'd appreciate your prayers very much. God is leading me into a deeper understanding and commitment. I may not like some aspects of it, but I praise him that he is using me. Pray that I will have the courage of my convictions.

My schedule was, I reported, as follows:

14-20	November:	The Study Centre for Discipleship Training.
21-24	November:	Denver, Colorado; fellowship and sharing with various churches.
1-3	December:	Visiting prison in West Virginia. Meeting some of the women I met at the Washington Seminar and speaking in the prison chapel.
4	December:	Speaking at a church in Washington.
7	December:	Speaking at a very large church in Virginia.
10-12	December:	In New York, seeing publishers for a book. Special prayer for me.
21	December:	Speak at a women's luncheon.
23	December:	Fly home.

In between these dates I was usually in the office, writing

letters and getting to know more and more about the work of the Fellowship.

The 'Study Centre for Discipleship Training' was the Ligonier Valley Study Centre, where the women from the seminar had been for the week before I met them in Washington. Now it was my turn to go, for Prison Fellowship had arranged for me to study there for a week.

Ligonier is a beautiful brick-and-timber house in a property in the Laurel Highlands near Pittsburgh. A variety of courses of study are offered, and I had been registered for the general study programme.

The other students were on long courses, and I was registered for just one week. It would have been easy to treat it as a holiday – the atmosphere was very friendly, I enjoyed meeting the other students, and the countryside around was very tempting. But before very long I was enthralled by what was going on.

It wasn't just that it was a lovely place to be, that the people were very nice, and that it was in many ways more of a retreat than a training session. I think I could have spent the week relaxing and doing nothing if I had wanted to. But I sat in on two lectures and listened to a number of taped talks.

It was a revelation. I'd never heard concentrated biblical teaching before; subjects like the holiness of God were opened up in a way that thrilled me, and I drank it all in. I sat up half the night in the audio laboratory with headphones over my ears, and I was struck dumb by it all; sometimes I was in tears as I listened. I was seeing things I'd never seen before – it was so real and so simple at the same time. As I listened to 'RC' (as R. C. Sproul is called by all his students), I began to understand what the apostle Paul meant when he talked about 'the unsearchable riches of Christ'. You could study things like that for a lifetime and barely scratch the surface, yet under a hospital hut in a

Bangkok prison I had understood all I needed to know that God loved me and that I belonged to him. As I became gripped by the excitement of it, I hungered to know more and more. I didn't see how any Christian could fail to be excited by finding out what a great God we have. The word 'theology' is such a dull label for what it represents!

Ligonier marked the beginning of a desire to study, and was a very special time when I seemed to be able to absorb all sorts of teaching that I'd previously not been ready for. It was a privileged period. While the excitement hasn't faded since then it hasn't always been possible to keep going at the same pace, and while there have been times when I've been gripped by study and the 'deep' things of the Christian faith, there have been many more when I've just read my Bible and prayed and been content to feed on the things I've already learned. The picture of feeding is quite helpful, in fact; after you've eaten a large and satisfying meal you don't go out and eat another immediately!

But learning wasn't an intellectual exercise that served just to stimulate my mind. I discovered very quickly that when you learn any real truth about the Lord, your life changes because of it. One night I was listening to a tape by somebody who had been a prisoner of war in Korea. It was a tape on the subject of forgiveness – something I thought I knew a bit about, after my experiences in Lard Yao. But I was jolted awake by what the man said.

Imprisonment had confused his mind, he explained. He had seen himself and his companions acting irrationally and completely out of character. 'Prison does that to you', he went on. 'It messes up your mind. We're not all of us in prison in the way I was,' he added. 'But in a sense we are. And because we've all had our minds messed up by being imprisoned in this fallen world, we've got to change. We've got to see things differently.'

I remembered my own feelings as I had sat under the hospital hut in prison, just after my own meeting with God,

377

looking out across the dusty yard at the anonymous figures in the distance. *The whole world's in prison*, I had realised, *and I've just been shown the way out.* I really understood what the man on the tape was saying. I remembered my painful exercises in forgiveness, as I had struggled, with the help of my few Christian friends who had access to the prison, to learn to forgive. It had been a bruising, daily process, laying aside real and imaginary hurts and coming to Jesus again and again seeking his help in learning to love the people I had hated.

The Lord brought me out of prison with a mind that had been changed, but the change was not complete; now in Ligonier I realised that I still had bitterness in my heart, a bitterness largely directed at Hannah; Hannah, the prisoner who had taken me under her wing when I arrived in Lard Yao and with whom I had had a stormy friendship which had eventually shrivelled into frigid antagonism. When I had left prison I'd found it impossible to say goodbye to her, my emotions were so mixed up. I'd taken refuge in the fact that I was leaving and she wasn't, so I could forget her. And I had, but now I found myself remembering her again; the good times, the bad times, the laughs, the arguments. *She can't hurt me any more*, I reflected. *When she did hurt me, it was prison that made her like that.*

I wrote a long letter to Hannah. 'I'm sorry,' I wrote. 'I know you didn't like me, for many reasons; but I know that you did like me in some ways as well. And I know that that place did things to both of us . . .' I apologised for not having written to her before. 'And we left on such a bad note,' I added. 'But I hope we can somehow put that all behind us. I hope you'll feel able to write to me.'

She replied immediately, and we began exchanging letters every month. And that was one very practical working-out in my life of the things that the Lord was teaching me. Whoever said that doctrine and Bible Study are boring!

378

For the rest of my time in America I travelled a good deal, speaking in public and seeing many aspects of Prison Fellowship at first hand.

One disappointment was that it seemed to be impossible to fit in a visit to Jack and Gladys Martin. They were on furlough in Louisiana. Early on in my visit I discussed with Kathryn how I might possibly visit them.

But America is a large country. After looking at the distances involved we both regretfully came to the conclusion that it wouldn't be possible to fit such a trip into my already crowded schedule. The cost would be so high that it wouldn't be right to take it from Fellowship funds – most of which had been donated by people specifically intending their gift to be used in work among prisoners.

It was a blow, but I completely understood that it wasn't possible. I know that Kathryn tried several ways of solving the problem and contacted a number of people who might have been able to help, but nothing worked out. She was as disappointed as I was, because she knew how much I would have loved to have seen them again.

We prayed about it several times, asking the Lord whether there might be some way in which I could go to Louisiana after all. Then we left it in his hands.

'We've allocated you eight-and-a-half minutes,' said the efficient organiser. I swallowed apprehensively, and clutched my piece of paper.

Kathryn and I were at a huge Baptist convention in Washington. She had warned me in advance that I would be speaking for that length of time, and I'd sat up late and worked out what I was going to say and how best to fit it into the time given me. Then I'd carefully written it all out in the form of notes.

When it was my turn to speak I stood at the lectern and gazed at hundreds and hundreds of people in rows that seemed to stretch away into the distance. I froze. *Lord, I can't do it*, I pleaded. My tongue seemed like a block of wood; I couldn't open my mouth.

Then as if by instinct I dropped the piece of paper with my notes on it. As it fluttered to the floor I found I could open my mouth again. I spoke for eight-and-a-half minutes and said what I wanted to say.

I learned a valuable lesson from that experience – apart from the fact that it was the only time I ever tried to speak from notes (though I know others find it helpful to do so, I just can't do it). The Lord taught me that any gift I might have as a speaker and communicator was given to me by him. It was sobering to discover that speaking in public wasn't something that I could do in my own strength, but it was encouraging too. God was in control, and I could trust him.

He had more for me in that convention, too. One of the main speakers was a man who worked at the Baptist Radio headquarters in Texas. He introduced himself to me and gave me an exciting invitation. 'Would you come down to Dallas to do some radio work for us? Of course we'll pay all your expenses.'

Jack and Gladys! I thought, and immediately turned to Kathryn, my eyes sparkling. 'Kathryn – is that anywhere near Louisiana?'

'Not far away!' she smiled.

I only had to be in Dallas for one day and night, and then I made the short journey to Louisiana.

I spent two days with Jack and Gladys. We walked endlessly, laughed a lot and wept a little and thanked the Lord together for the way in which he had made it possible for us to be together for that time.

Meeting Margaret Cole was easier. I had special links with her church in Los Angeles. The minister Wilbur Wacker and his wife Shirley had been in Bangkok during my imprisonment and had visited me in Lard Yao. So I was special to them as they were to me, and the church had been praying for me ever since. When they knew I was coming to America, the minister had contacted Prison Fellowship and arranged for me to visit the church.

I arrived at Los Angeles airport, and Margaret met me. I shrieked with delight when I saw her and gave her an enormous hug. She was wearing a gorgeous flamboyant pink dress, and her face was wreathed in smiles.

She led me to a huge car, talking enthusiastically, and we threaded our way through the Los Angeles traffic. I gasped involuntarily several times as it seemed that she would never be able to steer the vehicle between the elusive gaps in the unending flow of cars and trucks, but she wove in and out expertly, chatting nonchalantly as she drove.

We talked for hours, making up for all the frustration there had been in Bangkok when we had only had brief, noisy visiting sessions in which to talk and the all-too-short farewell party on my last day in Thailand. When we had caught up with each other's news, she told me all about her ministry in America and I told her what I was doing in Prison Christian Fellowship.

When later I spoke at her church I felt completely at home. I knew that I was speaking to people who had prayed for me a long time. It was a joy to be with them and to be able to tell them, as I was able to tell so many during my American visit, what it had meant to know that at every hour of the day and night somebody, somewhere in the world, was praying for me, that I would be released, and that until that day the Lord would be close to me and give me peace.

Of all the things I said from platforms in America, that was the thing I said most often. I wanted to thank people, to remind and encourage them, to tell them that praying for prisoners does make a difference.

In my travels and in Washington, I got to know many of the Prison Fellowship staff well. One with whom I established a special friendship was Ferne Sanford, Resource Officer of Prison Fellowship International. I was scheduled to stay with her after my time with Beth and Gordon Loux. She had been involved in Christian work in Africa, and was now living in a 'hospitality house' attached to one of the churches. We struck up an immediate friendship, and when I left we said goodbye with real sadness, and a promise from Ferne to visit me when she came to England later in the year. She was somebody very special whom the Lord provided for me at that time. I was able to relax with her, have fun and unwind after the hectic round of each day's new experiences.

There was much to see. I saw small groups which had only just been formed, in areas where Prison Fellowship was just beginning its work. I spoke to established groups and church congregations, school classes and groups meeting in people's homes. Everywhere I went I was made welcome.

As I came to the end of my visit I reflected on what I had learned and I certainly had a lot to think about. Nothing had prepared me, for instance, for the standard of living enjoyed by many Americans. I had met more wealthy Christians during my stay than I had thought existed, and for a time it bothered me. But as I got to know them I found most of them incredibly generous. Many of them shared their prosperity freely, making no distinctions about whom they helped and why. I was given many lovely presents, including a wardrobe of clothes and a splendid leather wallet stuffed with money. But I also saw many examples of generosity where the people who benefited weren't people like myself on a speaking tour. I know what the Bible means when it says that riches cause many problems – sometimes I think they cause more problems than they cure! – but I also know that I experienced the presence of the Holy Spirit in wealthy Christian homes in America as clearly as I have felt his presence in prison cells and ordinary homes in England.

But apart from the culture-shock, I had been revitalised. 'I was losing touch,' I wrote to my friends at St. Andrew's. 'But God showed me a "mountain top", a vision of what is possible in England.'

For indeed my thoughts were turning back to England, where I had so many friends who were working and praying to build a similar ministry among prisoners to that which I had seen in Washington and in my other travels.

America had been a whole new world, full of exciting and unimagined experiences. Now I was looking forward to going home. I was beginning to feel that this was the work I was meant to do. Somehow, in England, I knew that there would be an opportunity to commit myself to it.

14 Starting Work

We are not promised guidance far ahead, nor are we assured that we shall always know how God is going to work; but we are promised that, as and when we need to make decisions, God will overrule and guide.

Oliver Barclay, *Guidance* (1966), chapter 1

I arrived back in England very early on the morning of Christmas Eve. Ross Simpson met me at Heathrow Airport, before I flew on to Manchester and home. I came in out of the murky cold and dark into the bright lights of the reception lounge and there he was, looking tall and familiar. He hugged me and manoeuvred me through the crowds thronging the complex. We found a coffee bar and talked for ages. I had lots to tell him. Ross listened carefully and sympathetically, punctuating my narrative with 'Praise the Lord!' whenever I stopped for breath. It was one of Ross' favourite expressions, but always sounded fresh and meaningful when he used it. It certainly echoed my feelings then.

It was quite a time before I slowed down and sipped my coffee, by then almost cold. 'It was wonderful, Ross. I've come back with such a vision for prisoners. It's changed my life.'

384

Ross smiled at me thoughtfully.

'I'm so glad you had a good trip, Rita. Praise the Lord. We were praying for you all the time.' He hesitated. 'Rita, we've been thinking and praying for some time about this, and now we feel that the Lord is definitely leading us to invite you to work with us full-time. We'd like you to consider becoming a member of Prison Christian Fellowship staff here in Britain.'

I was speechless. It was a completely unexpected invitation. While in America I'd felt God telling me very directly that I was somehow to work with prisoners, but I hadn't yet worked out how I was going to go about it.

Ross smiled at my excitement. 'You must realise, Rita, we couldn't pay you a large salary. Not what you'd probably be able to get somewhere else. Prison Christian Fellowship isn't a rich organisation. We would pay you more of a retainer.'

I found my voice again. 'I don't think that would be a problem . . .'.

'We do feel very strongly that you should be a part of what God is doing in the Fellowship,' he added. 'We feel that it's important. Will you pray about it?'

'Oh, yes, I'll certainly pray about it . . .' I promised, my head whirling. Ross beamed.

'Pray about it and have a good think about what it would mean, the changes you'd have to cope with. You know how we work. You'd be travelling a lot, speaking – let us know when you've decided.'

I said I would. 'Praise the Lord!' said Ross. But I think I had already made up my mind. I knew an answer to prayer when I saw one.

I went home to Blackburn and Christmas with June and Ann. I gave them the presents I'd bought for them in America and told them all about my trip, and we had a lovely Christmas, even though there was sadness as well because it was our first Christmas without Mum. I enjoyed being in church at Christmas time. For the first time I was celebrating the birth of somebody I knew personally, in a congregation of his friends.

I told my family a little of what Ross had said at the airport, but I didn't go into details. For most of the holiday I hugged the secret to myself, and whenever I could I talked to God about it, half-afraid that I would suddenly receive a dramatic assurance that this was not the way he wanted me to go. I was open to whatever he wanted me to do. But I did hope that working with Prison Fellowship was what he wanted!

But as I prayed and read my Bible, the conviction grew stronger and stronger in my heart that God had clearly shown me exactly what his plan for my next step was. Looking back I remembered my growing concern in Lard Yao, not just for the prisoners there, but for prisoners all over the world. How thrilled I had been when I had first found out about Prison Fellowship, when Kathryn Grant had visited me in prison and left me Chuck Colson's book!

I remembered the letters that had awaited me when I arrived home, Chuck's telegram, the letter from Sylvia Mary, the increasing opportunities to be involved in local activities of the Fellowship. At the time it had sometimes seemed a random sequence of events. But looking back, it was as if a straight line connected my arrival at Lard Yao, a confused and bitter prisoner, and the conversation I had had with Ross at London Airport on Christmas Eve four years later.

So, shortly after Christmas, I found myself back in London, sitting with Ross, John Harris and Sylvia Mary, at Sylvia Mary's house.

'As Ross has explained to you, Rita, we will pay you a retainer.' Sylvia carefully explained the terms under which I would be employed. 'You'll have holidays, time off, and so on. We will fix your retainer to cover all your living expenses—rent, that sort of thing. Then we will also pay any expenses that the work involves—train fares, petrol, meals on the way. You'll have to keep good records!'

There were quite a few details to be sorted out, the kind that have to be dealt with when you start any new job. But it wasn't all paperwork and business. There was a wonderful sense of embarking on a new venture, a new stage of God's work.

'We believe that God has raised you up for a purpose,' said Sylvia Mary gently. 'We are very sure of God's leading in this.'

It was a sobering and joyous thought. But it wasn't earthshaking or mind-blowing. God has a plan for all of us. He hears us when we ask him for guidance. He answers prayer. So why should we be surprised, when he makes his plans known? My chief feeling at that time was gratitude to him for making it so clear to me, so soon. I know that sometimes he chooses to wait before answering prayer. He waited two years before he opened the gates of Lard Yao in answer to my prayers and those of thousands who were praying for me—and I can see many reasons why I can thank him for waiting. But when I prayed about joining the staff of the Fellowship, he gave me my answer very quickly, so that I never had any doubts at all.

'What do we do now?' I asked them. 'What's the next step?'

'Well,' said Mary, 'firstly we need to know what you need to live on.'

The retainer which was finally settled on was rather more than the £17 I had been receiving from the State Supplementary Benefit scheme. Many Christian organisations are unable to pay salaries equivalent to those paid in secular firms for similar work, and those who choose to work for them do so knowing that they will never become rich! But I was not poor working for Prison Christian Fellowship, and never have been.

That settled, the next question was: what exactly should I be doing in my day-to-day work for the Fellowship? That too we decided to allow to shape itself as we asked the Lord for his help in planning this new development.

To begin with I travelled round some of the local regions of Prison Christian Fellowship with Ross. We went to Durham, Bedford and Liverpool, and Ross explained that this would help me to get to know how the Fellowship operated nationally and also would give opportunities for me to speak to local groups.

'But what do you want me to *do*?' I asked Ross.

'Just share with people. Share your testimony, tell people what God has done in your life. Tell them about what it's like in prison, and the needs there are there.'

By now I knew quite a lot about Prison Christian Fellowship. I was fired with enthusiasm by the fact that in America it wasn't an enormous operation run from an impressive headquarters. I'd caught the vision of a movement that was made up of individuals in local groups, ordinary Christians involved in local prisons by praying and visiting. This was what the Fellowship in England was engaged in building up, and this was what I was to be involved in.

In those early days the pattern of meetings was quickly established. Ross would begin by explaining how Prison Christian Fellowship began in Britain, and about the American organisation and Chuck Colson's original vision. Then I would share my own experiences, which illustrated the prisoner's point of view. I talked about what it was like, as a prisoner, to be visited by Christians – about Lucille's faithful visits, about Margaret and Martha Livesey. The thing about Lucille, I pointed out, was that she wasn't an expert, she'd had no training in prison visiting. She was a very ordinary person without special qualifications. And yet you don't need qualifications. You need love. God put it into Lucille's heart to minister to me in a special way, and though she had to put up with antagonism and bitterness for a long time, eventually God honoured her commitment and I became a Christian.

I shared these and similar experiences with the groups that I visited with Ross. I wanted to encourage Christians, especially those who already had a longing for an opportunity to share the gospel with prisoners.

For some time I went to one meeting a week, or sometimes two in the same area on consecutive days. At the same time I remained a member of the Preston prayer group, and each month I shared with them what I'd been doing and the people I'd met. They prayed for me regularly and I was very grateful, because I knew that it made such a difference, just as the prayers of the congregation at St. Andrews made a difference.

Though at first I only had a couple of engagements a week, it meant that I had to be away from home more and more. A local Methodist minister, Albert Greasley, helped me with the correspondence and the invitations which were beginning to come in as word spread that I was now on the staff. Groups who had prayed for me, or who had read my story in the newspapers since my release, wrote to ask if I could go and speak to them, and because mine was still a comparatively recent front-page story, it meant that people who weren't Christians or who weren't previously involved in the group would be willing to come along. So it wasn't long before I had a programme of my own to follow instead of accompanying Ross on his rounds.

John Harris organised the London office. At first I found myself telephoning him frequently. 'John, please – tell me what I'm supposed to be doing!'

I never had a formally-stated job specification; few people in Prison Christian Fellowship did. It took me some time to get used to the fact that I wasn't full-time with the Fellowship in the same way that one might be a full-time school teacher or shop assistant. I was a representative, retained to help Prison Christian Fellowship by speaking to groups and individuals, presenting the Fellowship's work to local churches, and being available in whatever capacities might be helpful in the work. I reported regularly on what I had been doing, to Ross and to John, but nobody kept an hour-by-hour check on my activities.

Many of the speaking invitations I received when I first started work were sent to me personally, because people knew who I was from the newspapers and the various broadcasts, but not many knew that I was with the Fellowship. We resolved this by deciding that the gifts of money which were often given to me after I had spoken at a meeting would be passed direct to the London office and used for the Fellowship's work, and from the London office I would receive my monthly retainer and my travelling expenses. It was a good arrangement which worked well.

Ross Simpson became a trusted friend and advisor, and I benefited from his experience as a speaker and as a representative of Prison Christian Fellowship.

I had never worked with anybody like him before. He was an open, warm-hearted man who tended to include the Lord in conversations with other people. 'Thank you, Lord!' he would say, or 'Praise the Lord!', when something worked out well. He never said it in a particularly 'holy' way; it was as if he was addressing somebody as much in the same room as I was but who happened to be invisible. Working with Ross I learned an enormous amount about talking to groups, dealing with questions, and ministering to people's needs. I also found my faith reinforced as Ross constantly praised and thanked the Lord.

In January I heard that Chris, the cheerful Dutch blonde with whom I'd been friends in Lard Yao, had been released. In her letter to me she gave me her telephone number in Holland, and I telephoned her as soon as she got back. We had a crazy conversation, just like the ones I'd had with people just after I'd got back to England, and we promised each other we'd meet up as soon as we could.

For the present I had enough to come to grips with in England. Apart from anything else I was beginning to feel a little bit guilty about June. I wondered whether it might seem that I was going to get wrapped up in my new interests and leave her more and more on her own. June had her own life, of course, with an interesting job and lots of friends, but we'd become very close since Mum died, and I didn't want her to feel that I'd only been passing the time until something exciting came along. But I need not have worried, because June was marvellous. She didn't resent my frequent absences and increasingly unpredictable timetable; she was happy for me that I had found something I really wanted to do, because we'd discussed the future together and my need for a job.

Though my week now revolved around my speaking engagements, I didn't spend all my time working. I went out with June quite often, and had friends in church and outside. There wasn't time to have a hectic social life, but neither did I have my nose to the grindstone all the time.

One evening late in January I went with June to the twenty-first birthday party of one of her friends from work. I was tired and a bit depressed; one of the reasons I'd gone out that evening was to cheer myself up.

We arrived early and were sitting waiting for the others to arrive when a male voice behind me said, 'Hello, Rita!' It was the kind of enthusiastic greeting that you would normally expect from a long-lost relative.

I looked round. The speaker was a good-looking man about my own age. I didn't recognise him. 'Hello,' I said reluctantly.

'Don't you remember me? I went to school with you. You remember me.'

I looked at him sceptically. 'Come off it,' I said severely.

'You don't know me from school. You know me from the newspaper.' I was still sensitive about the fact that people started at me when I went out of the house, and I had become expert at fending off men who thought that because I had worked in a Hong Kong night club I might be easier to charm than other girls.

He looked disconcerted. 'No, really, I went to school with you. We went to St. Wilfrid's together.' June watched in amusement.

'Oh yes?' I challenged, still unconvinced. 'Well then, what's your name?'

'Trevor Carroll,' he replied.

I gulped. 'You were in the football team.'

He sat down. 'Of course I was.'

We began chatting. After a while other people arrived and the party got under way. Trevor said, 'Would you like an evening out some time?'

'I'd love it,' I replied. I'd enjoyed being with him.

'I work nights so I'm not always free in the evening, but what about Saturday?'

My face fell. I was away that weekend on a visit for the Fellowship. 'I can't make it.'

'How about Friday?'

'Oh – I'm afraid I'm due in Liverpool on Friday . . .'

I think anyone else might have given up at that point, but Trevor persisted. 'The following Monday?'

'I'm free that night,' I grinned.

Trevor was fun, and I had a really enjoyable time with him that Monday. What I liked about him especially was that even on that first date he didn't try to press me for details of my Thailand experience. He just didn't mention it. I'd been asked out several times since I returned from Lard Yao, but the conversation had invariably turned to prison, and that had spoiled things. I wanted to feel that I was worth talking to on my own account, not just because I had been in the newspapers.

I began seeing him from time to time, though there wasn't much opportunity for regular meetings while I was working away from home increasingly and Trevor worked his night shifts. But we met when we could. I found myself liking him more and more, and began to wonder where it might lead. I started to pray about him, asking the Lord to guide me in that part of my life just as he had in all the others.

15 Into Prisons

*We are pleased to inform you that Rita
Nightingale has agreed to undertake ministry
on behalf of PCF and is available for the
following: 1. Public/Church meetings;
2. Prison visits; 3. Seminar work.*

Prison Christian Fellowship, *Regional and
Development News* (Spring 1981)

From my first days in Prison Christian Fellowship, I
prayed before every meeting I attended and every talk I
gave. As my workload grew I found that I had to pray about
which invitations I was going to accept and which decline.
It was becoming physically impossible to accept them all,
for reasons of time if for no other. As each invitation was
forwarded to me by Albert Greasley it had to be talked over
with Ross. What group was it? What part of the country
was it in – did it fit in with my movements at that time?
What were the needs of the group in question? Then we
would pray about it together and make a decision on
whether I should accept or decline.

My 1981 diary shows an increasing number of speaking
engagements in all parts of the country. In addition, my
personal mail was increasing. In January, for example, I
received a letter from an American prisoner who had been

on Death Row for three years. He had seen my photograph and an accompanying article in the Prison Fellowship Newsletter. I received many letters from America, from prisoners who had read my story or had heard tapes.

The meetings I attended in those early months were of several different kinds. One of the most important tasks I had was helping to encourage the growth of the small Prison Christian Fellowship 'core groups' which Sylvia Mary described in the Spring 1981 newsletter:

> Most exciting to me has been the gathering together in 13 different areas, covering 29 prisons, of the body of Christ to pray for prison and prisoners in those areas and to help prisoners in practical ways. These areas have been set up by Ross Simpson, our Regional Director, and John Harris, our Administrator, initially . . . The first principle is that a small core group, brothers and sisters in Christ, meet to pray together and to take on the responsibility for collecting together the Christians in that area.

After my American visit, and particularly after the week I spent with the girls on the discipleship course, I came back inspired with the vision of how it might be in England. The small regional groups were considered very important by us all. We knew the power of prayer, we'd proved it in our own lives. We knew that if the Lord so chose he could take the groups and build a mighty network of praying Christians, and use them to reach into prisons and transform the lives of prisoners.

Prisoners, of course, were the focus of the Fellowship's work, and almost as soon as I joined the staff I began to visit prisons with Ross. There was not now a problem of access, and I made my first prison visit – to a women's prison in the North of England – in January.

I'm not sure what I was expecting, though I was aware that the frequent cosy television and film portrayal of prison as a jolly rogue's club was a glamourisation. Beyond that I had nothing to prepare me in advance.

We went in through a heavily-secured gate, and were taken into a dreary stone corridor with iron walkways which clanged when people walked along them. Every hundred yards or so there was a rusty stain down the wall where the iron pipes that ran the length of the walls had leaked. There was a feeling of dampness in the air, and though there were radiators, I shivered.

I was shocked by what I saw. After Lard Yao I'd had high hopes of British prisons – for a while it had seemed I might be transferred to one – but I'd reckoned without the overcrowding. The best and most enlightened governors often struggle unsuccessfully with the problem. It is a matter of simple mathematics; a prison can hold only a certain number of inmates comfortably. Buildings that are used by a lot of people suffer, and so do the people. In many chamber-pots are still used because of the queues for bathroom facilities in the morning. Though I usually visit the prisons later in the day and there's no noticeable trace left by then, I have been told that there's a characteristic and unpleasant smell that hangs around the corridors of such prisons first thing in the morning.

A prison officer took charge of us. 'Follow me,' she said politely, and led us to the room where the meeting was to be held. Her face was virtually expressionless; most of the staff in that prison were severe and unbending, and their aloofness contributed substantially to the frigid atmosphere. The room she took us to was in the basement. It was a stone-walled, fairly large interview room. Guards with immobile faces stood at the door and watched us incuriously.

The scenes inside the prison did not arouse in me any vivid memories of Lard Yao. One reason, I suppose, is that prisons in the West are very different. When I go into an English prison there's very little that I see there to physically remind me of Lard Yao. But a stronger reason is that whenever I am in a prison talking to the prisoners, when I get into conversation with individuals and small groups, I don't think about whether it's a good one or a bad one. Of course I'm aware that I'm in a cell or a prison meeting room, but I know from my own experience that when you're a prisoner who's become a Christian, what hurts is not the environment but the sight of your visitors leaving. It's the lack of freedom, not the colour of paintwork that hurts.

If you are a believer serving a prison sentence, you feel wonderful when Christian visitors come in from outside. You have a great time sharing with them and praying with them. You are on a spiritual 'high'. Then your visitors leave, and you go back to your cell and they go to wherever they choose, and you slump.

That's why I always try to encourage people who are in prison. I know how they are going to feel after I've gone. 'Yes, I really know how you're rejoicing now, it's great, the Lord is blessing us as we meet here together; but after we've gone and you're on your own, *hold on* to this. Because this is reality, not the other. God is giving us the joy of his presence now, but he won't take that from you when we go.'

I made many prison visits and got to know prisoners in different parts of the country. Sometimes we spoke to large groups, sometimes to three or four. As a result my mail continued to increase. Prisoners wrote regularly.

In work with prisoners, keeping up with one's correspondence is a major task. For most people serving sentences, visiting time is all too short and letters are a very real window onto the outside world. Some prisoners have broken marriages or have been disowned by their families, and when a sympathetic visitor writes to them, the reply fills page after page of prison notepaper.

The sight of the ruled sheets, with the sender's name and institution written at the top among the censor's stamps and the official reference numbers, moved me profoundly. There are not many more obvious symbols of the loss of freedom that prison entails. In their letters as in daily life, the inmates are regimented and organised. 'Prisoners should only write below this line' is printed firmly across the top of the sheet. Below, the handwriting often sprawls and slants as if struggling to escape the cramped ruled lines on which regulations insist the letter be written.

All the letters had to be read and prayed over. Answers could never be superficial. Clearly some of the prisoners were writing merely to pass away a half hour, raising clever theological points and challenging me to provide an answer. But the apparently sarcastic jibe about evolution or the authority of the Bible might conceal a real hunger to know. Somebody was waiting anxiously to receive your response to the fear expressed or the spiritual problem raised. It might well be of crucial importance to the prisoner who had written.

Some of the letters were heartbreakingly sad.

> I sit and wonder sometimes [wrote one prisoner]
> what life is really like without prison and how good
> it would be to live a good and holy life without
> ever doing wrong again . . .

I answered them all with much prayer.

As the year progressed I became increasingly involved in my new work. I continued to see Trevor, and we enjoyed each other's company more and more. Also I still wrote to Hannah and the girls in Lard Yao and to my friends in America, and I telephoned Chris in Holland quite often.

In March, June and I went to Holland to visit her. It was a madcap week. We enjoyed sightseeing in Amsterdam, but for most of the time Chris and I were reminiscing about prison, shrieking with laughter as we recalled some escapade or other, and talking endlessly about the people we'd known there and the things we'd done.

'You know,' June said to us in some amazement, 'anybody would think you'd been on holiday in Bangkok all that time, the way you go on about it.'

Chris looked at me, and we burst out laughing. It was true; we'd laughed and giggled about most of our reminiscences, and if one shouted a Thai word to the other it was a cue for instant merriment. June must have thought we'd had an incredible time together.

We hadn't, of course. It's just that you remember the good times. There were lots of bright moments in Lard Yao, and funny things did happen. But that wasn't what prison was about. If I were able to remember the bad times with such clarity, I doubt if I would sleep at nights.

After five days we said goodbye with regret, and June and I returned home.

A month later, I got down from the coach at Victoria coach station in London and looked around the crowds. I had arranged to meet somebody there. We were going to discuss writing a book together.

Although I had resolutely refused to sell my story to the newspapers, a book seemed a very different matter. When people heard me speaking about what had happened to me in prison, they often asked me whether I had written a book. I could see that having control of how the story was written would be a different matter from allowing the possibility of newspaper distortion and sensationalism. I had read Chuck Colson's two books *Born Again* and *Life Sentence*, and I knew the power of such books. Thousands who had never heard Chuck speak had had their lives changed by his writings. If God wanted me to write a book, I knew that God would use it.

399

Meetings with publishers had been part of my itinerary when I was in America.

'I don't know whether I *could* write a book,' I had admitted to Chuck Colson. 'I've never done anything like that at all.'

He explained to me that many successful books had been produced by somebody with a story to tell working with somebody who had the ability to write – it was called 'ghost writing'. A number of the most widely-read Christian books of recent years had in fact been written by one husband-and-wife team of ghost writers, John and Elizabeth Sherrill.

I remembered seeing their names on the title pages of books I'd read since I became a Christian. They'd collaborated with Corrie ten Boom on *The Hiding Place*, with Brother Andrew on *God's Smuggler*, and with several more authors I'd read. They'd also given Chuck Colson a tremendous amount of help with *Born Again*, and as publishers had been closely involved with *Life Sentence*. 'Find somebody you can work with, and you'll find you will be able to produce a book,' advised Chuck.

He arranged meetings with several publishers. They were much more approachable than I had expected, and I enjoyed the discussions. It was agreed that a ghost writer would be a good idea, and several names were suggested.

In the end, however, I came to the decision that I wanted to work with an English writer. 'It's not that I think the American writers couldn't do it, it's not that at all,' I explained. 'But I'm English, you know? That's where my roots are. I'd really like to find somebody in England, if I could.'

Chuck, who had put in a good deal of work on my behalf setting up the meetings, was understanding. 'Well,' he said, 'make sure you get good advice when you get home.' He reached for an address book. 'Contact Edward England. He's a literary agent. I've known him for years. He'll look after you.'

Back in Blackburn, I received a letter from Edward

England. Chuck had telephoned him and told him he had discussed a possible book with me. Edward arranged for me to meet David Porter, a Christian freelance writer who had written several books, and in April I arrived at Victoria coach station to meet him.

We liked each other immediately, and decided very quickly that we would be able to work with each other. Edward arranged for us to meet a publisher and the formalities were rapidly dealt with. Over the next few months we met several times, either in Blackburn or at David's cottage in Hampshire, and armed with a tape recorder and notebook David set about the task of setting down my story.

It was a strange experience. I was having to think about things that I hadn't thought about for a long time. There were tearful times and hilarious times, as I relived the sad moments and the good ones. Slowly we put together a first draft, often working late into the night to make the most of a few days snatched from crowded schedules. As the story took shape, I, David and his wife Tricia became good friends.

The work of Prison Christian Fellowship during my first year expanded in a number of directions. The Trustees launched a number of new activities. Courses for voluntary helpers were started, designed to give a basic grounding in work with prisoners and an orientation for those who, all over the country, were contemplating offering themselves as volunteers in various ways. 'Breakthrough '81' was a project that linked many of the prisons and borstals in the South of England, and, like all the Fellowship's activities, relied heavily on committed prayer support. 'Springboard' was the title given to a study series intended to give discipleship training to prisoners, and was a first step in planning seminars out of prison, such as I had attended in Washington, and which the Fellowship was praying might happen in England before long.

When I look through my 1981 diary I find that I was involved with many of these and other exciting projects. It was a time of growth for the Fellowship and for me as well. The Lord looked after me throughout, providing me with the fellowship and support of my church, plentiful help and counsel from my colleagues, Trevor's friendship, a great deal of spiritual satisfaction from what I was doing and a fortnight's summer holiday in Spain with June, when I lazed on the beach, contemplated the cloudless sky, and forgot all about work and travelling around the country.

16 Shepherds

*'New lives for old' has been our theme, and
it is being proved true day by day here as
men find for themselves the power of the
Risen Lord.*

Strangeways Prison prayer letter, May
1984

In the pub a man was gazing at me, his mouth open. His
head was framed in the hatch that separated the two bars.
We'd come in for a meal. All round, people were chatting,
coming and going, ordering food and drinks. In the hubbub
the man continued to stare at me, oblivious to what was
going on.

I nudged Trevor. 'It's because I'm so gorgeous,' I
laughed. We both turned deliberately to face the man and
stared back. I waited for him to blush and turn away. He
continued his openmouthed, unvarying gaze.

Trevor crossed the room and confronted him. 'What are
you looking at? What's so interesting?'

The man transferred his gaze to Trevor for a moment and
then looked back at me. He didn't say a word.

We moved out of his line of sight. I sighed.'It still
happens a lot, Trevor. Even now. People remember I was
the one in the papers. Sorry.'

I did enjoy being with Trevor, with or without publicity. He was a quiet person, unruffled by the fact that I was liable to disappear at a moment's notice and ring up from Dartmoor or Glasgow to tell him I'd just spent the evening in the local prison. He wasn't part of Prison Christian Fellowship, and he didn't go to St. Andrew's. He was somebody outside the new and exciting life I was leading, and because of that I could relax when I was with him in a way that was otherwise very difficult.

As I began to realise that he was becoming fond of me, and I was growing closer to him, I prayed about our relationship. Trevor wasn't the sort of person to talk much about religion. He had his own beliefs and he thought deeply, but he disliked over-enthusiasm in any shape or form. We talked about Christianity a great deal, even in the process of me telling him what I'd been doing between our dates. Trevor believed very strongly in a personal God, and he had a churchgoing background. The fact that he didn't shout about his beliefs didn't mean that he had none.

I knew all the arguments about having non-Christian boyfriends, and I could see their validity; but to me Trevor wasn't a non-Christian. He gave me a lot of strength, and some of that strength was spiritual strength. We prayed together and shared my vision for prisoners, and all that was an important part of our relationship. On the other hand, I had real doubts. I wasn't sure whether it would be right to move forward in the relationship. Trevor was unique, he wasn't like any Christian I knew. I wanted to be sure, and I wanted us both to be sure. So I continued to pray.

I was really beginning to enjoy the variety in the work I was doing. One day I might be speaking to a tiny group, a few interested people who'd come together to discuss the starting of a Prison Christian Fellowship prayer group in a remote part of the country; a few days later, I might be speaking to a crowd of several hundred. I was speaking to audiences of all ages, from children's groups to old age pensioners. I spoke at organisations like the Christian Police Association and groups of Christian lawyers.

Sometimes I caught myself thinking, *What am I doing here?* I had very little in common with the members of many of the groups I spoke to, though they were usually very kind to me. Apart from Christ, I had absolutely nothing in common with some of them. Yet God had put me in those situations to share something of what he had done in my life.

The size of a group has never bothered me. In a prison situation I would rather talk to a small group than a large one. I thank God for every opportunity I get to be with prisoners, but there is a difference between talking *at* a group, say in a ten-minute spot in a Sunday morning chapel service, and talking *with* a group. In a chaplain's hour or a discussion group the conversation is two-way. The people in the group haven't come to prison because they wanted to, but they've come to the group because they're Christians, and that gives you a tremendous basis for sharing. You can ask them questions, you can be interrupted, you can change the direction of what you're saying as you begin to get to know the needs of the different members of the group. You can't do that in a formal service, where you just have to pray that the Lord will prepare you with something that will be helpful to the listeners.

Something that I learned very rapidly from working with Ross and John was the fact that the prison chaplain is a key factor in the work of the Fellowship. Today links have been established with many of them. His is a very exposed role. He is in the prison to help people to find Christ.

I've been saddened in my travels when I have asked church groups, 'How many of you ever pray for your local prison chaplain?' Even in churches which have prisons in their locality, it's rare to find believers taking on the burden of supporting the chaplains in prayer. If you have no time or opportunity to help prisoners in any other way – pray for the chaplains! God has put them in the prisons to reveal him to those who are locked inside.

The chaplain is invariably overworked. He has administrative duties which would take up a large part of anybody's working week, and then he has a pastoral duty to the prisoners to whom he ministers. As well as being available for spiritual counselling, in many prisons he has the task of interviewing every prisoner on arrival and discovering any domestic problems that need to be taken care of over a period of time.

It's the kind of job that you never get on top of, because the scope is limitless. The Sunday service, which is the aspect of prison religious life of which the public is usually most aware (through television and film portrayals of prison life), is only a small part of his responsibilities, and an effective prison chaplain will find he has to earmark precious time even to prepare for that.

The policy of Prison Christian Fellowship has always been to work through the chaplains, who are approached for permission to enter the prison. In my own case, for example, I was from the start invited into prisons either because the chaplain himself had heard of me and invited me himself, or because Prison Christian Fellowship had written to say that I would be in the region at a certain time and would be able to visit the prison if required.

In some prisons, I discovered, the chaplain organises several activities each week. There are Bible studies, chaplain's hour, discussion groups, and other opportunities for prisoners who want to find out about Christianity. Some inmates are Christians already, having got into trouble since their conversion or having become Christians in prison. In either case, the ministry within prisons is vitally important.

And in prisons all over the country (and all over the world) Prison Christian Fellowship is seeing that ministry growing and expanding as the Lord brings men into the prison service who long to bring prisoners to him, and as he brings to maturity the patient work of chaplains who have struggled for years and, until recently, seen little fruit of their labours.

The Holy Spirit is on the move in the prisons!

Strangeways Prison is a good example. It was one of the first prisons that I visited. I had heard a lot about it because it had some television attention. Like many British prisons, it has a severe overcrowding problem. That means that the chaplain's workload is much heavier, because more people need individual attention.

Yet God is doing wonderful things in that prison. Noel Proctor, a chaplain there, has seen miraculous things happen. Lives have been changed, apparently insuperable problems have been swept away, hardened criminals have become radiant, caring Christians. There are no riots at Strangeways. So many people are becoming Christians that the chapel is filled three times over on Sundays.

Noel is adamant that the credit does not belong to him. He points to his team of colleagues in the prison, and to the great numbers of people outside who pray regularly and specifically for the needs of Strangeways. The local branch of Prison Christian Fellowship prays, and also circulates a prayerletter to 2,000 praying Christians. The Holy Spirit has honoured these prayers and has used the labours of the Christian team in the prison. The results have been astonishing.

That's a good illustration of the vision for Prison Christian Fellowship. Local Christians, praying for their local prison situation; and beyond that, becoming a fellowship such that when prisoners are released they can be told. 'Look, here is a group of Christians who are from all sorts of backgrounds and who know where you've been. You can link up with them and continue to grow in your Christian faith, while you decide what to do next.'

So I continued in the work of helping local groups and visiting in prisons. Ross and John were always available for help and a shoulder to cry on. There were times when I felt bitterly discouraged, and sometimes people were insensitive and even unkind. At those times I knew I could count on the wisdom and support of Ross, John, Herrick Daniels, Tom Marriot (another Prison Christian Fellowship worker with whom I had made good friends), Tony Ralls in Devon, Trevor, and a number of others.

I was finding it difficult to adjust to becoming a full-time speaker. I was now speaking much more than the one or two meetings a week that I had been allocated when I began. I'd never envisaged that happening, and it gave me some problems.

There were aspects of speaking in public that thrilled me. For example, I never tired of telling my own story, because it was always new to the people I was sharing it with, and it was a way of telling people who God could do for them. Essentially, what happened to me in Thailand happens to everyone who becomes a Christian. We're all the same inside. We are all conscious of an emptiness within ourselves, we try to fill the gap. The void in my own life had nothing to do with prison. It was there before I was arrested. When I had fine clothes, an exotic job, a handsome boyfriend who lavished gifts and money on me – I used to cry myself to sleep at night. Prison wasn't the problem. Prison was where I found out how the problem had been solved for me, two thousand years ago.

I was sometimes in situations, like in America, where I would be speaking at two or three meetings in a single day, and each time giving basically the same message. I had to remind myself: *Don't let it become automatic.* But it didn't, because I prayed that the Holy Spirit would reveal to me what each audience needed, and I would adjust my talk to be relevant. Usually I spoke for about half my time about Lard Yao and the rest about Prison Fellowship, but I varied it each time. If I thought that a number of the audiences were not Christians I'd emphasise Lard Yao and give a gospel address, and so on.

Problems arose in certain situations, like the occasion where I spoke to a very large audience, and it was like talking to a mattress. Nothing came back, no warmth, no response, nothing.

As I spoke I began to resent these people. Speaking is something that is very emotional for me. I'm talking about crises in my life, giving a large part of myself to the audience; and it hurts to sense no answering sympathy.

I finished my talk and afterwards stood at the door, and people shook hands as they went out. Most of them made some sort of polite comment. When a large lady approached and extended her hand I expected her to do the same. By that time I was feeling very depressed and just wanted to leave.

'Oh, Rita!' she said enthusiastically, grasping my hand and squeezing it. 'That was such a *lovely* story!'

I was so upset that I almost smacked her hand away. 'It *isn't* a story,' I retorted, and then retrieved my polite smile and shook hands properly. Inwardly I was fuming. *What's the point of talking to these people? You can lay it on the line what Christian commitment is, and it rolls right over their heads.*

When I got home I complained to God. *Lord, I'm not doing any more of this stuff. You saw what happened tonight. I'm sticking with the prisoners, who need to hear about you.*

Almost there and then, I felt an overpowering conviction that I had been totally in the wrong. *Who are you, to decide what has gone in and what hasn't? This is what I want you to do, and I want you to do it whether you get any encouragement or not.*

I went to Ross and told him about it, and he was very

supportive, but I had learned an important lesson from the experience. If you do a lot of speaking in public you quite often find an audience that seems to be taking in nothing of what you're saying. But I have discovered that it's often in just such meetings that God is really dealing with somebody, or that the meeting marked a breakthrough in the life of some present.

17 Discouragements and Encouragements

I feel deeply that I must change my life for the better . . . please can you send me some Scripture leaflets.

Letter from a prisoner.

By Spring 1982, Albert Greasley, who had taken on the work of keeping my diary even though he had other commitments, was no longer able to devote the necessary time to the task because of other pressures. I was very grateful to him for what he had done, and it didn't mean that I was left without help because a few months later Christine Austin joined the London office staff of Prison Christian Fellowship.

Christine and her husband Brian had been involved with work among young people for several years, and were already supporters of Prison Christian Fellowship. Among other responsibilities, she took over the organisation of my appointments, and I was able to channel invitations through her.

I continued to work in the two main areas of speaking to Fellowship groups and other Christian gatherings, and of going into prisons to share with the prisoners. It was very humbling to see the hand of God working in all sorts of situations.

My correspondence files contain many evidences of God at work in the prisons. 'I have a very nice church visitor,' wrote one man, ' – now a personal friend, who comes in to see me every fortnight, and we do discuss a lot about belief and faith . . .' Another writes, 'I try my best, though sometimes I fail. What saves me is the fact that occasionally I get brief "flashes of light" (metaphorically speaking) in which I feel the Lord's hands upon me and on those occasions my faith is like the hardest granite.'

Many of the Christian men and women have been coming to Bible studies and sharing groups for as long as I have been working in prisons. We've seen wonderful instances of people growing incredibly strong in the Lord, and developing real gifts of leadership and understanding. We've seen prisoners converted by the testimony of other prisoners. We've had amazing encouragements.

But there are disappointments as well. I think, for example, of a man who used to come to a group in a prison which I visited regularly. Over a number of meetings I and other members of Prison Christian Fellowship came to know him well. He was just coming to the end of a major sentence when I first met him, and I was sure his commitment to Christ was genuine.

Eighteen months after he left prison he had found a home with a Christian family, he had a job, and he sometimes gave his testimony in public and spoke of how the Lord had changed his life. Then he suddenly disappeared. He left the house in which he lived, and gave no indication of where he was going. We lost touch with him completely, and the follow up group that was involved with him could do nothing but pray.

Much later, we heard of him again. He was back in prison in the South of England.

How do you cope with a disappointment like that? You can write the man off, say that his conversion was a sham; and there's no doubt that some Christians who observed the whole sequence of events have assumed that this was so. Or you can simply accept that discouragement is part of the Christian life, that often things do not turn out as we would have expected. And you start back at the beginning, going to him where he is and seeking to share the love of Christ with him all over again.

Many times, in such situations, I remembered my Mum. How many questions I asked when she became ill, and how many of them remained unanswered! Yet I knew the Lord was in control. And in the same way I was able to pray for that man. I may never know the end of the story. But God does.

Yet nothing can destroy what God is building in the prisons, and so many times, we are privileged to see God revealing part of what he is doing. There are tremendous encouragements as well as disappointments. One of the most wonderful visits I have made with Prison Fellowship was to Northern Ireland.

When I arrived in Ulster with Ross Simpson in October 1982 it was the first time I had ever visited the province. We flew across one damp and misty day, and we were due to go to the notorious H-Blocks to meet with a small group of Christian prisoners. Soon several of us were packed into a small van driving down a tarmac road towards the main prison block, through drizzling rain and a succession of checkpoints.

The sight of armed men, uniforms, and the grey prison blocks rearing dismally ahead filled me with a dread that verged on panic. It was like a black-and-white film of the Second World War, with that same colourless hopelessness that ruled out the possibility that any normal life existed outside. It would not have surprised me to have seen such a

413

a place in the Soviet Union, but it was a shock to see it in Britain. *What am I going to say to these men?*, I thought. *What have I got to offer them?*

In a way that's a good reaction. I experience it almost every time I speak in public, and it's helpful to me, because it reminds me that what is important isn't so much what I have to say but what the Lord is going to say through me. But that day it was an almost totally depressing feeling, as if a dull black cloud was hovering over my head as I went into the building.

We went down long bare corridors with cells leading off them, and all around us we could hear shouted conversation and the other sounds of prison life. We were shown into a tiny room, and Ross and I sat and waited with a couple of people from Prison Fellowship Northern Ireland (which is a separately chartered group – with which the London-based organisation works very closely – within Prison Fellowship International).

One by one the men filed in. They sat down quietly in a circle. There were about ten of them. Somebody sitting near me coughed and said quietly, 'Well; let's begin with prayer.'

He led us in a simple prayer. He prayed for other prisoners and for prison officers by name. He prayed that God's power would be present in that prison and touch the lives of all inside. As he prayed I wept. It wasn't so much what he said, it was the overwhelming sense of the presence of God in that small room. We were surrounded by the din of prison, but in that circle there was a peace and quietness which you could almost touch.

We were able to spend an hour with the group. I spoke for a short time, and so did Ross, and the men shared with us, talking about what the Lord had done for them in prison. Afterwards I was told something of the man who had prayed. He was inside for the most appalling crimes. The things he'd done terrified me. But he had become a Christian in prison.

414

I got into conversation with him, and I asked him a question I don't very often ask. 'How did you become a Christian?'

He told me the story of his conversion. He'd gone to a Prison Fellowship open meeting in the prison. It had sounded good for a laugh and he was bored.

'So I sat at the back. Then I saw a woman sitting at the front and I recognised her. I was a member of the IRA, and we'd shot her husband. She was a police widow, only twenty-eight, with two or three young kids.'

He swallowed, and went on, 'We were a mixed lot in that audience, a lot of us were in the IRA. And this woman – I couldn't believe it! She knew who we were, oh, she knew, and she stood up in front of us and she said, "I just want to say that if any of you have any relatives or friends who'd like to come out to visit you here, let me know and I'll be only too glad to arrange it."'

He looked at me squarely. 'It hit me hard, right deep inside me. How could she say that? Members of my organisation shot her husband dead, left her on her own with kids. And she could stand up and say something like that . . . '

He'd gone up to her at the end of the meeting and challenged her to explain why she had said what she'd said. So she shared the love of Jesus with him. She told him what he'd done in her life, how she had found the strength to forgive.

'That was how I became a Christian,' he told me quietly.

Back in England I told Trevor what had happened. 'I'm never going to make judgements again,' I said. And I really have tried not to. It's too easy to categorise, to assign blame according to easy formulae. God isn't like that. One of the most amazing prayer meetings I have been to in Northern Ireland was in a Catholic stronghold, and it consisted entirely of Catholic women. Before I went to Northern Ireland I'd assumed I would tend to sympathise with the

415

Protestant political position, but over there, I've shared platforms with Christians from both sides.

I spoke at several meetings with Liam McCloskey, who was one of the IRA hunger strikers. He was convicted of terrorist crimes, and he went on hunger strike as part of the IRA campaign for their prisoners to be given 'political prisoner' status. He almost died, he was blind from starvation, and it was only because he was under age that his mother was able to persuade the authorities to force-feed him. Liam became a Christian, and when he was on parole we both gave our testimonies at a number of churches.

It's a continuing sadness to me to see that bigotry and intolerance not only appear on both sides of the Northern Ireland divide, but also infect individual Christians. I will never forget one meeting during that visit, at which Liam and I had been giving our testimonies. It was a Protestant church, and afterwards I went downstairs to a room where tea was being served.

A small group had surrounded Liam and were arguing with him. I wandered across to eavesdrop. I could hardly believe what they were saying to him.

'How can you possibly call yourself a Christian,' one was saying forcefully, 'while you're still going to the Catholic Church?'

The shock was almost physical. I felt I'd been punched in the midriff. I'd had my eyes opened to the fact that to such people, Christianity and Catholicism are mutually incompatible. Of course there is intolerance on both sides, and I've met Catholic Christians who feel similarly about Protestants.

I don't believe that the differences between Protestants and Roman Catholics are trivial, nor that they are not evidence of different views of the Bible which must eventually be sorted out. Neither do I believe that the long history of troubles in the tragic communities of Northern

416

Ireland have no basis in fact or that there are not real problems to be dealt with if the province is to have political peace again. What I do believe is that the Holy Spirit is moving through Northern Ireland. He is transforming individual lives and whole communities. He is kindling love in peoples' hearts where once only hatred burned. In peoples' homes, in the streets, in the prison cells, the Spirit's work is bearing fruit. Men and women are becoming Christians. They don't sort out all their problems immediately. Sometimes God heals wounds and wrong attitudes over a period of time. But the change that takes place in the heart is immediate, and what these new, born-again brothers and sisters need is the love and the support of local Christians. That is what Prison Christian Fellowship, along with many other Christian groups in the province, seeks to offer. We have been so blessed in seeing what God has done.

The other major event of October was the publication of *Freed for Life*. Our months of snatched days working on the book had born fruit. The publishers, Marshalls, held a press launch in the Church of St. Bride's in Fleet Street. It was a lovely occasion, when Ross, John, Sylvia Mary and several of my colleagues from Prison Fellowship were present. David and Tricia came up from Hampshire and afterwards Marshalls took us for a celebratory dinner.

The press were very kind to the book in their reviews. Plans were well advanced for an American edition by Tyndale House Publishers, and in Britain it sold so well that it had entered the Christian best-seller lists by Christmas.

18 Blessings

Your life has been adventurous, rewarding and a blessing – what more could you ask?

Letter from Margaret Cole, July 1983.

I realised that I was falling in love with Trevor. In so many ways he supported me and fulfilled me. He was homely, but not in a boring way. He was quite separate from the work I was doing, and some people were concerned about that; but for me he was ideal. He was interested in my work, and he stimulated me to think about it in fresh ways, but while other men I'd known would have been irritatingly in awe of the fact that I worked with the wife of a Member of Parliament and a member of Richard Nixon's presidential team, Trevor tolerantly let me get on with it and didn't go on and on about my colleagues.

I once persuaded him to accompany me to a radio station where I was to give a broadcast talk. While I sat in the studio in front of the microphone and talked, he watched open-mouthed. Afterwards he shook his head incredulously.

'You were amazing!' he said.

I smiled graciously. He grinned back. 'You just talked and talked and talked – I've never seen you like that. You were unstoppable. Just like Esther Rantzen . . .'

418

In so many ways he was right for me, and I believed I was right for him.

My workload increased dramatically after the publication of *Freed for Life*. Invitations to speak came flooding in. I discovered openings I had never heard of before – a Christian women's luncheon club, for example, which had local branches in towns all over the country. The book sold in large numbers in the prisons, and I often found that when I went to speak to a group for the first time, *Freed for Life* had gone before and paved the way.

In the London office, Christine's workload increased in step with mine, as she dealt with the mounting piles of invitations. We prayed very hard about which we should accept and which we would have to decline.

In May 1983 I went to America again, for a speaking tour to promote *Freed for Life* and to do deputation work for Prison Christian Fellowship, sharing with American audiences what God was doing in England. Before I left I prayed earnestly about my relationship with Trevor. I prayed, and others did too, that if it was right for us to become further involved, the Lord would make it very clear to me. I asked the Lord to reveal his will to us both while I was in America.

It was an exhilarating month, with many speaking engagements and the chance to renew old friendships and make new ones. Since my previous visit, the offices of Prison Christian Fellowship and Prison Fellowship International had separated for reasons of space. The International office was now in a house, occupying the downstairs rooms. The upper storey was used as a hospitality house for international visitors. Ferne Sanford was living there as a hostess, and she looked after me for the whole of my tour.

We took up our friendship where we'd left it since my last visit, and a couple of visits Ferne had made to England since then. We had a marvellous time. I don't have many close friends because of the life I've been leading; but Ferne is one of them, even though we don't see each other very often. She is a very special person in my life.

I missed Trevor dreadfully, and while I enjoyed the trip enormously (I visited Canada for two days at the very end and met Prison Fellowship groups there), I looked forward to getting back to England.

When I returned we set aside time to be together. We talked for hours. Trevor told me that while I had been away he had experienced a deepening of his faith. When he talked about it I realised that the Lord had given Trevor a very special time while I was away, and now had given me the sign I had asked for. From that time our relationship was different, deeper and more committed. Trevor suggested we go and look for an engagement ring. I said 'Yes!' immediately, and we set August 6, 1983 as the wedding date.

It was hard to get back into gear, after the American trip and our engagement. July, however, was a very special month. The first International Prison Fellowship conference took place in Belfast, Northern Ireland. Fifteen chartered countries were represented, and it was thrilling to hear the delegates speak about the situation in their national prisons. Many were similar to Lard Yao or worse.

So it came to our wedding day, when I walked up the aisle on my Uncle George's arm. Trevor's grandfather had died suddenly, and we decided not to have a honeymoon, but we had a perfect day and a lovely time in our new home. We had a small wedding, but were delighted that Ross and Sylvia Mary were able to come up and represent Prison Christian Fellowship. It was the first time that Ross had met my aunts, and he really enjoyed talking with them. Ferne Sandford was there. She had attended the Belfast conference and was able to stay on for the wedding. Many letters from friends all over the world arrived, with lovely messages. We were blissfully happy, and I had a long break of several weeks, so we were able to spend lots of time with each other.

When I returned to work, I was hectically busy. I entered upon a crowded timetable that often meant that I saw Trevor only briefly at weekends. In many ways it was a strain for both of us, but he was understanding and supportive. We went to church together when we could, and when we were alone the time I had with Trevor was all the more precious.

It could not go on in that way, of course. Part of it was due to the holiday backlog, but part was due to the success of the book. People said to me, 'Isn't it a problem that you're so well known and Trevor isn't?'

My reply was always the same. 'Of course not, because when we're together, I'm not well-known!'

After some months, we were delighted to discover that I was expecting a baby, and this hastened the plans of Prison Christian Fellowship to control my timetable and decline more invitations. Now that I had a date on which I was to go on maternity leave, we planned my timetable like a military operation. Invitations that allowed a logical trip without detours or horrendous connections were accepted; many more we regretfully had to decline, because the travelling involved wouldn't have been fair to the baby or its mother! Christine shielded me from as many distractions as possible, and arranged my bookings so that I had as much time as possible with Trevor. I really appreciated very much the concern that the Fellowship showed me at that time, and the efforts that were undertaken to ensure my wellbeing and that of our baby.

Ben was born in summer 1984. He is beautiful. Among the letters of congratulation we have received have been hundreds from prisoners.

Earlier in the year Edward England, David and I had been discussing the possibility of a sequel to *Freed for Life*. We'd been working on it as and when time permitted. When David rang to congratulate us on Ben's birth, he added a final comment.

'I've got a title for the sequel, by the way. How about *Freed for Ever*?'

19 Full Circle

Ain't it funny how you get to be
The last thing you ever dreamed you'd be . . .

'The preacher's song', by David Rees.[1]

Sometimes people ask me in what ways I think I have grown as a Christian since I was released from prison.

One very important realisation has been that Christianity isn't a rigid mould into which people fit. You don't have to do a particular job or be a particular person before God will accept you. He accepts us because of what Jesus has done, not because of what we have done. As I have come to realise that, it has helped me to relate to prisoners more on the basis of the unity that Christians have with each other in Christ, than on whether they say the 'right' things or have a view of God identical to mine.

Another important step in my Christian life was realising that my story is not just a story about Rita Nightingale who was in prison and who was set free by a miraculous pardon. It is a message for everybody. As I had to come to terms with being an ordinary person, attending a local church, helping to nurse my Mum in her sickness, I saw the same

---

1. Words and music by David Rees, from The Mighty Flyers, *Low Flying Angels* (Word UK, 1974).

423

God who had come to me in prison going out to all sorts of people, to where they were, answering their needs. So when I stand on a platform and tell what God has done in my life I am telling what God can do in anybody's life.

I have come to see the Christian life as a series of steps, in which it is all too possible to step back as well as forward. When I began to work with prisoners I was distressed to see how many who profess conversion do fall back when they are released, or even when they are still in prison. I used to feel a great burden for such people, and I would pray, *Lord, why is it that so many go back?* I used to be angry at the church because it wasn't there, helping to keep these people close to the Lord; but since then I have realised how hard it is for many churchgoers to relate to prisoners, either in prison or when they are released. How easy it is, when introduced to somebody who you know to have been in prison, to stand back, and to allow that involuntary expression to cross your face which tells the ex-prisoner, *I have decided that you are different from ordinary people* . . . It is to help people overcome such prejudices that Prison Christian Fellowship exists.

I have learned not to be too swift to say of somebody who has gone back to prison, 'Ah! His conversion wasn't real . . . She was only playing at being a Christian . . . His faith was psychological . . . She wanted sympathy . . .' Many whom I have known as radiant Christians in prison have been back inside months after their release, convicted of some crime that we had thought they had given up for ever. But God doesn't write us off. He teaches us through the bad times as well as the good. And which of us knows the pressures that an alchoholic, a compulsive gambler, a violent man, a quick-tempered woman have to bear? Only the Lord knows how strongly or otherwise we would come through stress and tensions if we had such handicaps. Ministering to prisoners, I have learned a little about being slow to judge others.

424

And each day I have learned more about the goodness of God. Looking back on it all—on my life before I was sent to prison, my experiences in Lard Yao, and from my release to the present moment—I am constantly amazed at his goodness.

Sometimes I am in the middle of some mundane piece of housework, and I stop and think: *Lord, you are so wonderful!* When I say that, I'm not thinking of material things, even though he has given me all I need and more. I'm thinking rather of the love that surrounds me. I think of Trevor's love, and Ben's, and that of the people all around me who love me. It strikes me as freshly as ever, how God has brought me from prison and my life before. And I give thanks.

Often I find myself smiling. The life I lead now would have appeared to me, when I was eighteen, as the one situation I didn't want. I had no idea what I expected from life then, but I knew for sure that I didn't want marriage, home and children. It was boring, it was what everyone else had, and I didn't want it. Even without the 'religious bit' I would have hated the idea of becoming what I now am.

And yet God has led me in a huge circle. I live in a house in Rishton, nor far from Blackburn. My husband is not only a local Blackburn man, but somebody I was at school with. Since Ben was born I have had to reorganise my diary, and now I spend much of my time at home with my family. What God has for us in the future I do not know, and I'm happy to wait until he shows us. In the meantime, life is so rich and busy that I have no time to do anything but live one day at a time.

God has taught me that it doesn't matter where you are or what you are, as long as you are in the place where he wants you. He loves us so much that he has a plan for each of us which, if we trust him, will give us the richest, most wonderful life that it is possible to live.

In the glamorous nightclubs of Hong Kong, I discovered that you can be miserable even when you have all the material things you ever wanted.

In the prison cells of Lard Yao, God showed me that you do not need liberty in order to have real freedom. In prisons in England I have seen Christians who are finding exactly the same thing. A prisoner wrote me recently and said, 'God has not taken away the walls – but he has certainly taken away the roof.'

He has taught me that he is above all a God of love, for whom no walls of pride or selfishness, nor of prison stone, are a barrier.

When I was a teenager I would have considered Christianity to be a system of restrictions. But the Lord Jesus has given me freedom. He has not only freed me from Lard Yao, he has freed me from myself. He has made me into a new person, still with much to learn and much to discover.

In his love, I am free – for ever.

Postscript

We are still having good Bible Study groups. The Thai group has really grown. They are still meeting in the library with about 78 in attendance.

Letter from Gladys Martin in Bangkok, June 1983.

I continue to get news of Lard Yao, from Linda and Mary and others, like Lucille and the Martins, with whom I keep up a regular correspondence.

They say that the prison has changed dramatically from what it was like when I was there. I was part of a very small group of foreign prisoners. Now there are at least forty foreign women, half of whom are serving ten, fifteen or twenty year sentences. The prison kitchen, where I spent many happy hours with Hannah baking food for the shop, has now been transformed into a highly efficient food factory with a gleaming new oven. It turns out innumerable loaves of bread and fancy cakes every week. There isn't leisure now for the privileged foreign prisoners who work there to take a late breakfast in the interlude between bakings.

While Jenny was still inside I sent her a parcel with some things she'd asked for – skirts, T-shirts, cosmetics, things

427

like that – and in her letter back she told me that I wouldn't recognise the place. Uniforms are now compulsory; you wear a particular colour to indicate what crime you have been sentenced for.

Jack and Gladys' work in Lard Yao has been growing steadily. The Thai group has seen a large increase in numbers, and some of the foreign prisoners have become Christians.

Lucille is in poor health, but is able to keep going. Characteristically, she is busier now than she ever was. Margaret Cole too refuses to allow advancing years to slow her down. 'I'm a very busy 77-year old who hasn't yet realised that the years have made her old' – last summer, she wrote to me and told me that she had spoken twenty-one times during June; she had found herself speaking at old peoples' convalescent homes and pitying the residents because they were so elderly – in fact, she was often the oldest person present!

Linda and Mary continue to wait for the machinery of international prisoner exchange to deal with their cases. They have had several disappointments, and have often asked for special prayer as they try to get on with day-to-day living in Lard Yao and try not to think too hard about going out.

I am still enjoying spending a great deal more time at home now that Trevor and I are parents. After the hectic last few weeks before I went on maternity leave from Prison Christian Fellowship, it is lovely to be with my family for most of the week. Ben is a happy, active little baby who is adapting well to accompanying me as I travel about. I have begun to accept some speaking invitations again, mainly those near to my home, but it is still too early to make decisions for the future.

Prison Christian Fellowship is changing, as all organisations do, and we are now seeing many instances of the Lord continuing to bring to fruition the things we were praying for in the lives of prisoners and churches only a few short years ago. In this book I have described the situation as it was then. For more information about the Fellowship's current programme and projects, write to:

> Prison Fellowship England and Wales
> PO Box 263
> London SW1.

Even after several years of working in prisons I still find it difficult to give an answer to the question that is often asked: 'What do you think about prisons as punishment?'

I have to admit that I believe that many people now in prison ought not to be there. I am sure that most of them need to be punished and many have done wicked things, but punishment by putting people behind bars is to me a terribly negative act. I like the American word 'penitentiary', which expresses the concept of prison as a place where offenders are put for penance – the punishment is the fact that you have been taken out of society and imprisoned (sadly, the reality in American prisons is often far from the ideal).

But today much of the punishment which offenders receive is punishment by the internal prison system, or by other prisoners, especially in the case of young offenders who fall into a pattern of life which too easily degrades and brutalises prisoners. I believe that prison is intended to make people good; but it all too often simply makes them bad. It might seem idealistic, but for the Christian such a view is intensely realistic. Jesus came to set the prisoners free, to make men fully human, and to put an end to sin and crime. He died to make us good. Many people have served prison sentences and in the process found that to be wonderfully true.